D0595773

F**K IT THERAPY

F**K IT THERAPY

THE PROFANE WAY TO PROFOUND HAPPINESS

JOHN C. PARKIN

HAY HOUSE

Australia • Canada • Hong Kong • India
South Africa • United Kingdom • United States

Tradepaper ISBN: 978-1-4019-4079-9

12 11 10 9 8 7 6 5 4
1st edition, November 2012

Printed in the United States of America

Dedicated to Mary Wright,
my beloved grandmother,
and last gran standing,
who died during the writing of this book.

CONTENTS

NAME: GARY SPRAKES
CRIME: TAKING LIFE
TOO SERIOUSLY

PART I
SEEING THE PRISON (UNDERSTANDING WHY WE NEED TO SAY F**K IT)

NAME: SARAH MAYER
CRIME: NOT FOLLOWING
HER DREAMS

PART II
IMAGINING WHAT'S OUTSIDE THE PRISON (IMAGINING A F**K IT LIFE)

NAME: FRANCO FRANKS
CRIME: BELIEVING
HE'S NOT GOOD
ENOUGH

PART III
MAPPING THE WALLS (MAPPING YOUR 'ITS')

NAME: SUE TAYLOR
CRIME: NEEDING
TO BE GOOD AT
EVERYTHING

PART IV
BREAKING THROUGH THE WALLS (F**KING THE 'ITS')

PART V
A GUIDE TO THE BREAKOUT TOOLS
(HOW F**K IT WORKS)

PART VI
WALKING THROUGH WALLS
(REACHING THE F**K IT STATE)

NAME: OSWALDO ORLANDO
CRIME: LISTENING
TOO MUCH TO OTHERS'
OPINIONS

PART VII
GETTING SHOT AT AND SURVIVING IT (SAYING F**K IT TO WHAT OTHERS THINK)

NAME: FINN FINLAY
CRIME: PUTTING HIS
CAREER ABOVE ALL
HE LOVED

PART VIII
LIFE ON THE OUTSIDE – BEING FREE (LIVING THE F**K IT LIFE)

BREAKING FREE, BEING FREE, STAYING FREE, UNDERSTANDING 'FREE'

APPENDICES

F**k It (fuk-eet): to let go by realizing that causes of worry, distress, and pain don't matter so much in the grand scheme of things.

therapy (pfe-rippi): a process that creates healing in an individual, whether at a mind, body, or soul level; literally 'to make whole again.'

unimaginative (un-imaj-in-atif): lacking imagination, creativity.

writers (ry-tus): artists who express themselves through the creation of blocks of text or books: and who often start their books with quotes from dictionaries (see 'unimaginative').

desist (dee-zist): if you're a budding writer, don't ever do this. I have because a) I teach F**k It and rules are made to be broken; and b) I've subverted this boring convention and thus made it (marginally) more interesting.

enjoy (en-djoi): now sit back and enjoy a book that will entertain as it heals as it changes as it inspires. No writing for you to do now. No work. Just sitting back and letting the words and therapy do their magic.

PLEASE COMPLETE THE SECURITY INFORMATION ON THIS PAGE.

Please enter the text as it appears on the screen into the text box provided, click the 'Continue' button.

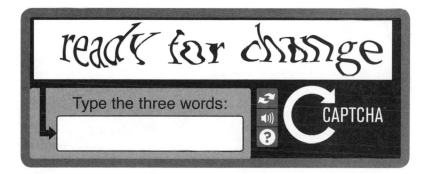

YOU DO NOT HAVE PERMISSION TO ACCESS THIS BOOK IF YOU ARE USING AN AUTOMATED PROGRAM.

FOREWORD

F**k 'IT.'

At one of my recent workshops, I opened the first day by saying that I was not going to give the participants anything…

And left it, like that.

And that led to this conversation, which started:

'What, you're not going to give us what we came for?'

'So what did you come for?'

'Well, I'm not saying I had expectations, but I wanted to experience something.'

'Isn't this something?'

'No, this is nothing.'

'So nothing is happening here?'

'Yes, something is happening, but it's not IT!'

And so, we began to discuss what 'IT' is.

How much time do we spend looking for IT, and generally thinking that 'this' is not IT?

How much pain does that give us?

And what is IT anyway?

Who knows, because we never get to IT.

IT is always somewhere else; IT is always something else…

Perhaps, someone else has got IT, but not us.

IT is something that we might just get to, if we try just a bit harder, if we become better, if we understand more or learn something else or, in the ultimate result of our searching, we get enlightened. Fancy that. Enlightenment (apparently) happens to a bunch of people in the whole world, and thousands of people think that they need it to be okay…

I mean, tell me, have any of you got IT?

When, after lunch we got back together as a group, I asked everyone:

'So, if IT is nowhere else, and is nothing else, and is no one else, what is this?' while pointing at us and the room.

And half the group shouted out, laughing: 'IT!'

Simple. This is IT. Me writing this. You reading this. Is IT. You getting up and pouring a glass of water is IT. Getting up in the morning is IT, going to the bathroom is IT, having breakfast ('Why have we run out of bread again?') is IT.

IT is so simple that we can't see it.

No need to look elsewhere, you are sitting on IT (particularly when you go to the bathroom), you lucky being.

This book explores how we can F**k certain 'Its' in order to uncover the great IT of happiness. But the true secret of F**k It Therapy is to see that IT is already here, and IT never even went away in the first place.

Gaia

WE
WROTE
THIS
FROM
PRISON

We've been planning this book for a long time. But it was only a couple of weeks ago that a metaphor emerged that suddenly allowed everything to fall into place, and work. The metaphor was of a 'prison': that most of us are, in one way or another, in a kind of prison (and clearly some of us are literally in prison. If you're reading this in prison, 'Hi, I hope you enjoy the read, that it passes the time in a moderately entertaining manner, and that it even helps').

Yes, most of us are in a kind of prison, and F**k It can help us get out of that prison. (Sorry, a message to you again, in your real prison. I'm referring to getting out of your 'metaphorical prison' here, not your literal one, as the advice on actually escaping from prison isn't one of this book's strongest points. Though, we do talk about tunneling out with a plastic fork at one point. So keep your eye out for plastic forks.)

Yes, the metaphor of a prison came to us a couple of weeks ago.

And, now, here we are, writing this from prison. You see, it started snowing a few days ago. And it was very pretty. And we were very happy. And on the second day of snow, the school closed, so our boys stayed at home and were very happy, too. But it continued to snow, even after it had snowed a lot. Then, after it had snowed even more, it snowed some more. Until it got to the point, when we knew we were snowed-in. And not in an 'ooh, how nice, we're snowed-in' kind of way, but in a 'help, our Jeep, even with chains on, can't get up the track!' sort of way. (We live on an isolated hill near Urbino in Italy, half a mile from the nearest road.) But you know if you put on some big boots and snow gear then you can walk out. No sir. This is big, deep snow. Snow that comes halfway up our front door, so actually getting out of the house is difficult. Snow that has drifted in the wind and is lying halfway up the house. Snow that's still bloody* falling. And, short of a helicopter, we're told it would take the rescue services about a day to reach us. But they aren't coming, because there are people in need they must get to first. So, we're here for some time, we think. We're stuck.

Most of us are in a kind of prison, and F**k It can help us get out of that prison. We are in a prison – not a prison of walls topped with barbed wire and the occasional watchtower with searchlights and men with machine guns, but in a prison of a sea of white crystals, lapping against our doors and windows. This is more Alcatraz than Wandsworth[†], the deep still snow replacing the swirling choppy waters of the Bay of San Francisco.

Most of us are in a kind of prison, and F**k It can help us get out of that prison.

We are, for the first time since we came here seven years ago, literally trapped. Not literally in prison, clearly, but 'like' being in prison. It means we're experiencing a 'simile' for our chosen 'metaphor.'

Shit, the lights went out then for five minutes, but have flickered back on… luckily I'd just pressed 'save.'

So, this prison metaphor feels bang on[‡] for us (and this has been confirmed by our current experience of being imprisoned) to describe what F**k It Therapy can do.

Since we wrote the original *F**k It: The Ultimate Spiritual Way* seven years ago, a lot has happened. The book has done well (it's available now in 22 languages and has sold more than 250,000 copies), and – because of the awesome work of our publisher, Hay House – is growing and selling at an accelerating rate, and we've been able to teach this philosophy personally to thousands of people from all over the world. Seven years ago we knew very well that the F**k It philosophy was working for Brits, because that's where we lived and taught for years. We knew the particular difficulties Brits were facing that made saying 'F**k It' so effective. But what's amazed us since the publication of the book is we've found that it isn't just the Brits who are stressed-out and f**ked up… but everyone, from all over the world.

It isn't just Brits who have so much trouble letting go, it's other Europeans including the Italians (much to our surprise). It's not just the Brits who have trouble saying what they really mean; it's Americans, too (again, to our surprise). It's not just the Brits who are suppressed and uptight, but people from pleasant, civilized countries, like the Netherlands and Denmark. There are, believe it or not, Irish who have lost the ability to have fun, French who have lost their *joie de vivre*, Italians who can't express their emotions, stressed-out Australians (strewth!), self-doubting Californians, burned-out Russians… and the list goes

> **The F**k It Therapy process we've developed in our week-long retreats works for everyone.**

on. We've learned that – yes, of course, we all have our differences, and we always enjoy seeing those differences and playing with them – but what joins us is greater than what separates us. We've laughed more with Germans than any other nationality. We've cried more with Australians. We've opened up more with Russians.

The F**k It Therapy process we've developed in our week-long retreats works for everyone. And we've seen that all of us, all over the world, can, relatively simply, access amazing resources within ourselves, heal deep hurts, come out of our shells and shine again, feel life coursing through us once more and, with the help of F**k It, find freedom in our lives wherever we are and whatever we're doing. It's about seeing that we can be free. And it starts by seeing that, in certain ways, we have come to a point where we're either not free or don't feel free.

Sometimes we find ourselves in prisons that are obvious, painful, and oppressive: as if we've been locked in solitary confinement in a pitch black, damp, stinking pit. The prison has become almost unbearable. For others, the prison is less obvious, life seems okay, but there's just something that's not quite right, and usually requires starting to see where the prison walls are and breaking through them gently. For others, they think they're okay; everything is hunky-dory until a tiny little thing sets off something within them and they quickly fall apart. They've been in prison, but haven't wanted to see it, because the seeing of it would have been too painful. While others still believe they're fine; everything is wonderful, they're happy to be alive, and things couldn't be better. And, sometimes, they're right. If you're in that group, you'll find many things in this book to explain what you already feel and some ideas to keep you where you are. Think of it like an insurance policy, if you will.

But most of us are, in one way or another, in a prison of sorts. And that's normal. That's life… and it's sometimes death. But it's generally life. Finding freedom (and the consequent spreading of freedom) is all just another wonderful part of the game. And this particular way of finding freedom is called F**k It Therapy.

Until now, F**k It Therapy was only available from us, John and Gaia, in person at our F**k It Retreats. But now we've written it all down, so you can experience it wherever you are in the world, whatever you're going through. And that makes us right chuffed§, we can tell you.

We've worked with people in all these prison states, from all over the world. And we've learned that the F**k It ideas we use work for

WE WROTE THIS FROM PRISON

everyone. We've seen amazing, inspiring, breathtaking transformations – we've had e-mails from countless people whose lives have changed after experiencing the F**k It Therapy we teach.

Right, we need to go and get some more wood, because if that electricity goes out tonight we'll have to come down here and sleep next to the fire. Brrrrr.

---

* An informal expression of shock (or emphasis) in the UK. According to the OED (Oxford English Dictionary), 'bloody' is not blasphemous, as many people believe, but originated in the 17ᵗʰ century to describe 'young bloods,' otherwise known as those young sons of the English aristocracy, who had a penchant for getting drunk and being rowdy. And, actually, while we're here, just so you know, this book is written by me (British) for both my British compatriots and my American cousins (and, yes, I do have American cousins)… so we've helped our cousins along by adding such endnotes occasionally, and altering certain spellings, and apologies to my compatriots for those certain spellings (it wasn't just that I was writing late at nite).

† A category B prison (whatever that means) in southwest London.

‡ Exactly appropriate; also means to 'go on' at length.

§ Very, very pleased and happy – and a bit proud, too.

PART I

SEEING THE PRISON

UNDERSTANDING
WHY
WE
NEED
TO
SAY
F**K
IT

WHAT
IS
A
PRISON?

A PRISON HAS A POINT

The point of a prison is to protect society from its dangerous inmates, to rehabilitate, or simply to punish. These factors give a prison meaning in our society.

And the meaning you've found in your life and society may well have become your prison.

Meaning, at least the conscious search for it, doesn't seem to bother us as children. Things just somehow *are*. We don't need to find purpose in things, do things that are more purposeful, or find our purpose within the grand scheme of things when we're young. Thank goodness. Sure, kids ask 'why' and 'how' a lot.

'Why is the sky blue?'

'Ask your dad.'

'Why does the sun come up and go down.'

'Ask your dad.'

'Why does Tommy have more video games than we do?'

'Ask your dad.'

'How do babies get made?'

'Ask your mother.'

But they don't ask the kind of questions that we ask: 'Why am I here?' 'What exactly is the point of me doing this soul-destroying work day in, day out?' 'Does it really matter if I'm good or bad?' And so on. At some point, we stop asking questions about the world outside ourselves (such as the sun and the moon) and start asking questions about ourselves and our place in this world.

And faced with the occasional horrifying glimpse of the likely reality that we have no real point in this huge, uncaring universe: the flash of 'life' we experience (80 years in the context of the 500,000 years humans have existed, and the five billion years or so that the world has turned); as one person in seven billion, on a planet that is just a drop of water in the huge lake of our solar system, which is a lake equivalent to a drop of water in the ocean of the galaxy, which in itself is an ocean the size of a paddling pool on the back lawn of a house in a country that is the vast universal everything, of which our tiny planet called 'Earth' is just a part. And faced with only the tiniest of glimpses of that reality – which is only a tiny peek through a keyhole so full of dust that we don't really see what's in the actual room, because to see it fully and to realize it deeply would probably lead us to instantly smash our own heads in…

Yes, faced with just that tiny glimpse of realization of our utter futility, we panic. And the panic ebbs and flows, and we forget it's panic at all; but the panic continues for much of our lives. And the panic takes the form of a relentless search for meaning in the most ridiculously meaning-less ways. Like dogs on heat, trying to shag* the legs of human strangers, lampposts, fire hydrants, benches, and occasionally cats, we

3

try to shag meaning out of anything that will have us. We are on-heat meaning machines, desperately trying to find meaning: in the pointless work we do; the fruitless relationships we have; the interminable stuff we accumulate (which we carry slowly from store to dump); the gods we invent; the rules of conduct we imagine and enforce; characters we dream up for ourselves; stories we tell… And on and on until we die, when we go… nowhere, and certainly not to finally see the point, because it wasn't there in the first place.

Sorry. I had to get that out.

We are RIDICULOUS. Not just because in our lifelong-drawn-out panic there's actually no point to ANYTHING, so we try to find meaning in EVERYTHING – which is actually quite endearing. But because the very things we attach all that meaning to then turn around and cause us pain. Because none of the things last for that long. We get attached to them. They are taken away. We feel pain. That's the human condition.

In fact, let's create the full chain of events of the human condition: we get a glimpse that our life is utterly futile and wonder what the point is; we try to find meaning in things out there; we get attached to those things; the things are taken away; we feel pain; we wonder what the point is; then we try to find meaning in other things out there; we get attached to those things; the things are taken away; we feel pain; we wonder what the point is; then we try to find meaning in other things out there; we get attached to those things; the things are taken away; we feel pain; we wonder what the point is….This is the human loop. That's why I like to use loops in my music; it reminds me of the joke that is our human loop. The loop is wired into our DNA, which is, you know, very similar to the DNA of a banana. We are, effectively, bananas.

The point?

What, you still want a frickin' point?

Well, at this moment we're sitting here smiling, so we'll back off from the nihilistic blathering. We'll even offer different ideas about what it's all about. But it's worth seeing that the search for meaning, which most of us are on, is a pretty potty[†] affair. It's worth seeing that many of us are actually trapped in a prison of our making; we have become attached to things that now restrict our freedom.

And to take us from the biggest possible picture back down to the prosaic detail of the everyday – hopefully without suffering from nausea, or the bends, or getting burned on re-entry – the problem for most of us is that we worry about things that, with even a little bit of perspective, REALLY DON'T MATTER and we spend so much time and energy worrying about those things that we don't have enough time or energy for the THINGS THAT OBVIOUSLY DO (if you're not getting big, nihilistic, and philosophical, that is, anyway). We worry about being late for a meeting, but don't see our kids off to school. We worry about the extra pounds

We need to say F**k It to those things that really don't matter so much.

we're carrying, but don't see the fellow human being on the street in desperate need. We worry about the lines appearing on our face, but we don't see the cracks appearing in the Earth pointing to global climate change. We search for gods and miss the miracle of life. We are burdened by the past, worry about the future, and we miss the present.

So, in this prison of meanings, we need to say F**k It to those things that really don't matter so much, and focus on those that do (or seem to anyway). This is about getting perspective, and it's a fundamental part of F**k It Therapy.

That's what a prison is. And that's why F**k It Therapy can help.

A PRISON HAS A STORY

Every prison has a story: a history, incidents that have occurred there, famous inmates, a dark past, and, sometimes, inspiring stories.

And we have a story. We have our history; all the things that have happened to us: hurt us, moved us, thrilled us, inspired us, depressed us, moved us forward, pushed us back, picked us up, and thrown us down. We have things we love to remember and other things we'd prefer to forget.

And we tell ourselves (and others, if they're prepared to listen) the story of who we are (which we believe is made up of our history and molded by all the things that have happened to us). We tell ourselves the story of our character: our good points and our bad points, our strengths and our weaknesses, what we're proud of and what we are ashamed of in ourselves.

And we tell ourselves the story of our growth and development from one thing to another. We tell ourselves about who we used to be, who we are now, and who we'd like to become. We sometimes see our story as an ascending journey from innocence to experience, from bad to good, from naiveté to experience, learning as we go, meandering along this journey of life, but getting somewhere that will reward the learning and be worth the pain. And, sometimes, we see it as a descending journey from playfulness to seriousness, squandering our talents, throwing away our dreams, going from health to sickness, getting older and weaker, never learning our lessons, losing what we had, and slowly, tiringly, meandering into our sad, lonely ending on this miserable planet.

*F**k It Therapy shows us how to say F**k It to the story and get in touch with life.*

And we tell ourselves a story about life and the world around us: that it's a wondrous, miraculous, ever-changing, dynamic, inspiring, mysterious place. Or it's a tragic, misery-ridden, sinful, hopeless, unfair, doomed place. Or it's boring. Or it's not like it used to be. Or it's going to hell in a handcart. Or it's a mix. Or it's supporting me. Or it's against me. Or it's indifferent to me. Or it reflects me.

We tell ourselves stories about ourselves and the world we see around us. But they're just stories. And these stories – the good ones, the bad ones, and the indifferent ones – can all turn into prisons for us because... Stories don't necessarily reflect reality. Stories fix everything. And 'life' isn't fixable. It's always moving. And it resists the stories we try to tell about it. By the time we think we've grasped our life – or our story – it's gone, moved on, left town. And we're stuck in the prison of the story we created.

F**k It Therapy shows us how to say F**k It to the story and get in touch with life.

A PRISON HAS AN AIM

A prison has the aim of protecting the population from its prisoners (and sometimes protecting prisoners from the population), and rehabilitating prisoners so that they can return to society (usually).

We have aims, too. We aim to do a certain thing by a certain age: we aim to pass our exams, buy a house, meet someone gorgeous and settle down, enjoy our lives, win the Nobel prize, get well, lose weight, shag more people, shag fewer people...

We have aims. And, if we're organized and determined, we write them down, too. We even put deadlines on them. We work our way toward them. We overcome obstacles to achieve them. We suffer for our art, brave storms to get to land, bear our cross, climb mountains, and take the hits to achieve our aims.

But our aims can become our prisons. Life has a habit of not going the way we planned. Other people have the habit of not behaving the way we want them to behave. The economy has a habit of dipping at the wrong moment. And, because we've fixed this path for life in the form of 'aims,' we find ourselves in a prison of expectations thwarted by life doing the thing it does best: unpredictability.

Aims can be helpful, of course. Much can be achieved with aims, and much squandered without them. But if you get too attached to your aims, then they can become your prison. Hold your aims lightly. Say F**k It to the held-too-tightly aims. Let them go. And sit back and enjoy the ride more.

A PRISON OF THOUGHT

Everything starts with a thought. God may well have started on day one by creating Heaven and Earth, then switching the light on. But what the Bible misses out is that God would have started with a thought. Before He CREATED Heaven and Earth, He must have had the bright idea of getting down to some creative work. Before his six days of hard work started, He must have had his feet up contemplating what to have for tea‡, when he got his bright idea:

Say F**k It to the held-too-tightly aims. Let them go.

Brilliant. A planet and some space. I am brilliant. Absolutely bloomin' brilliant. Even if I say it Myself.

He sat back and realized His thought was Good. Then another thought struck Him, and He stroked His beard as the thought took form:

Even... if... I say it Myself' (even God uses capitals in His own sentences), *'Why the fluckety chuck§ don't I create other, er... beings, that can tell Me how brilliant I am, then I wouldn't have to just say so Myself?*

Nice one, God.

I will create them in My own image.

I foresee a problem there, God. You'll give Yourself competition.

Ah, but I don't want any competition as God and Supreme Being, do I?

More beard scratching.

I will set them a ridiculous test. I'll create a couple of these mini-Mes, then tell them there's... I don't know... um... a tree that makes them wise (so they'll think they can become as wise as Me, even though, and they don't know this, they already are). I'll lure them into this cunning trap via a walking snake thing. They'll, naturally, eat from this tree of knowledge and BANG, I cast them out forever more..

God slapped his leg in congratulation at such a flawless mini-God creation plan...

That way, they'll spend the rest of their existence worshiping Me, arguing over Me, and believing they're nothing like Me, when they actually are.

Back to that first thought. The difficult bit for God – and the Bible neglects to mention this – was the actual thought. Imagine what it was like summoning up the whole plan for the Earth and space and animals and humans and, like, EVERYTHING from, like, NOTHING. There was NOTHING before; just God sitting there, not in space, but in NOTHING. He had nothing to go on. He didn't have any magazines to flick through to get ideas, no books to read. He wasn't popping down the local salon (i.e., salon for ideas not for a beard trim) to chat with fellow deity intellectuals. He wasn't brainstorming. He wasn't standing on the shoulders of giants. He wasn't in competition with another god to see who could come up with the best creation scheme. It came from nothing. NOTHING.

After that, the whole creation thing was a piece of cake. Project-management and construction work, that's all. Sure, they did a good job. They even came in on time (six days) and on budget. But God was the ARCHITECT. He was the ideas Man... er... God... ideas God.

Everything starts with a thought. Everything you see around you started as a thought. Everything you do starts as a thought. You started as a thought. Even if you go into territory apparently unaffected by human thought (like areas of wilderness), we're trying to get involved there, too, with the effects of our manmade global warming. And if that doesn't get the Earth, then our manmade nuclear weapons will. Nice thought, Einstein.

Funny that, of all the clever clogs[ll] civilization has ever known, Einstein has become our token clever clogs – with his funny face and mad hair. Ah, what a genius. It's ironic that his discoveries could lead to our final destruction. Started by a thought (of God). Ended by a thought from the cleverest mother yet (Einstein), with probably the dumbest mother getting to press the button (imagine a grinning Dubya-like character).

Everything we do starts with a thought. We can create wonders with thoughts. We can invent amazing things. Our lives are made easier by the products of thoughts. We're healthier because of hardworking scientific thinkers. We idolize the inventors, the scientists, and the thinkers. We hang on to every word of the scientist just as we used to hang on to every word of the priest (clearly, many people still do, but science has been the new religion for many of us for some time). We educate our children's brains and encourage them to make their way in the world by using their heads. We rely on rational decisions to guide our lives.

What else is there, though? You have to ask that. There is the heart. And there's the gut, or instinct, and intuition. And there's other information, too (does inspiration come from the brain, from within the body, or outside)… What about 'spiritual information'?

When we rely just on thoughts, we create a prison for ourselves. We are still, in many respects, a Cartesian society. 'I think, therefore I am.' But what if we're not just our thoughts?

Saying F**k It to an entirely thought-based approach to life can open you to amazing things. It also means that when the thoughts get too much, you know that you're not *just* that. For example, in depression or after a trauma, our thoughts (self-doubt, over-analyzing, self-blame, etc.,) can drive us mad. Sometimes, literally.

One quick way to realize that you're not JUST your thoughts is to try your hand/brain at meditation. But when thoughts have become your prison, when they're getting you down, when they're leading you by the nose, you can realize that you're not just your thoughts... you can say F**k It to a thought-led life, without leading a thought-less life.

*Saying F**k It to an entirely thought-based approach to life can open you to amazing things.*

A PRISON OF EMOTION

When we asked just now: 'What else is there other than your thoughts?' Possibly, there was a momentary blank for many men reading this. But the answer would have come quicker to most women: the heart and our emotional life.

We split nicely down the usual gender mind/heart divide. Gaia is very heart-focused. I'm very in my head. She's love. I'm ideas and laughter. She's all warmth and intuition. I'm all dreams and reflection.

Most people who come to F**k It Retreats are stuck in their heads (i.e., in a prison of thought), so they often benefit hugely by working with their heart: opening up more, feeling their emotions more, and expressing more. Gaia then, in particular, is able to help them feel freer very quickly, while I relax them and make them laugh. Gaia then opens their hearts and the deep healing begins. We're not good cop, bad cop, we're head cop, heart cop.

So getting trapped in the prison of emotion is less common. But it's possible and we do see it. What is it? It's when your life is dictated entirely by emotions. It's when you feel everything deeply; you take everything personally. You probably cry a lot and sometimes for no reason. As an aside, this is something that I've only seen women do, and it baffles us blokes[¶]. Well, I'm no longer baffled. If Gaia cries and, when I ask her why, she says 'nothing,' she's not saying 'nothing' in a way that actually means 'yeah, of course,

Most people that come to F**k It Retreats are stuck in their heads.

it's something really BIG, otherwise why would I be crying, but I'm not going to tell you because, even if it's not about you this time, it usually is, and you'll keep asking me, which makes me feel wanted and cared for, so I'll give you one more "nothing" then, on the third request, I'll actually tell you, okay?'… Gaia is saying 'nothing' because she actually means nothing. Somehow, for no obvious reason, she sometimes just feels upset, so she cries. Well, she's now telling me that sometimes she doesn't even feel upset, she just feels like crying, so she does.

Women, please skip this paragraph. Message to men: is it just me or is that BONKERS? There are things we'll just never get, aren't there? Do you fancy a beer? I need to get out of this teary environment and head for a watering hole, pronto.

Hello again, women and men. We're back. Women, get a grip. 'Ouch, Gaia, that hurt.' No, emoting is good. We men bottle it up far too much. And so do some women. But don't splash the bottle all over the place indiscriminately. Use rational thought OCCASIONALLY. And learn how to use an Excel spreadsheet, too. They're great for developing that side of your brain. That's my advice, when you feel very emotional, even if you're not sure what about, open up a new Excel spreadsheet and have a play. You'll brighten up in a minute.

The point: it is possible to be too heart-focused. The brain and its rational thinking has its place. Use it occasionally. Otherwise you're trapped in the prison of the emotions. And that, like everything else, takes a nice F**k It to get out of.

A MATERIALISTIC PRISON

By 'materialistic' we don't mean those who like shopping, and for whom what they own is more important than anything else, though it's self-evidently a pretty barren and restrictive prison to live in.

No, materialism here is the idea that everything is matter or energy (in the traditional Newtonian idea of 'energy', not the Eastern one). We are separate, solid human beings working within Newtonian physical laws, on a planet that is (largely) explained by the sciences. And most people live their lives with this perception (even if they say that they 'believe' in God, their day-to-day interaction with reality is materialistic).

A materialist has explained practically all phenomena scientifically. We understand how just about everything works in a way we didn't 100 years ago. In a very obvious way, materialism replaced spiritualism for many people. In times past, everything was a vast mystery, from what we saw in the sky at night to why it rained, to how our bodies worked, to how life was created. Unable to explain these mysteries scientifically, as we can now, humans explained them spiritually. There were gods for the elements, gods for love and war. Then someone had the bright idea that there was just one God. Anyway, the gods or God helped explain everything, because we're not very comfortable with NOT KNOWING. We want to know. Even when we watch a 'mystery' on TV, we're only happy with not knowing for a while and want to know who did it before we go to bed.

So most people now know. We know most of what could have bothered us in terms of the big questions of how things around us work, thanks to science. And the rest has simply yet to be worked out by the scientists. And, man, do they work hard to figure it out – just look at CERN (European Organization for Nuclear Research). Though many people still use God to explain the things that we don't get. In fact, some people use God to contradict the bits that we do seem to get.

13

But let's assume that most people are, in a practical sense, materialists. They look to science for their answers. And the answers are usually good (even if they aren't as palatable as the spiritual answers). It's not that they're cold, dry rationalists, as a spiritual person might imagine. The beauty, diversity, and complexity of such phenomena can still overwhelm someone who has a materialistic explanation for the manifest phenomena that surround them. The materialist might understand the process of reproduction, fetus growth based on DNA blueprints, and birth. But does the explanation of the process kill wonder at the manifestation of these processes? For most people, no. Most people are no less astonished by birth, by the beauty and magnificence of nature now they understand the materialistic derivation of such phenomena than they were when it was all a mystery and they decided it was all the work of gods/God.

Gaia and I prefer to stay open. To stay in the question, rather than try to settle on an answer: to be okay with NOT KNOWING. It doesn't mean we're not curious. We're philosophers in that we love the unending questioning. But we don't settle on any answer, we keep asking questions. We stay curious. We enjoy the wonder and mystery of life unfolding before us in every moment.

We use the word 'sense' a lot. It tends to indicate that ours is a continuous questioning, that we haven't fixed on any answers, and that we're humble enough not even to use the word 'know.' We have worked with energy or qi for many years. Our sense is that this energy underlies everything, and it is the conduit for the astonishing non-materialistic phenomena, as well as the essence of the equally astonishing materialistic phenomena, that we observe.

Do you see how that word 'sense' helps? We don't say 'we know,' as either a materialist or a religious person would, and not with any false humility but because the assertion of such 'knowledge' fixes it. And if we know anything about energy and the phenomena it seems to manifest, it is that it's ever-changing, impossible to fix, and very difficult even to name. (The Taoists, for example, assert that if you can describe the *Tao* – the force that pervades everything/is everything/ creates everything – then you haven't got it). And, for the record, we aren't Taoists.

We aren't anything. We question and experience and live in wonder, and share what we sense with you.

So, yes, we have more sympathy with the materialist than the fundamentalist. But a rigorously materialistic approach to reality, without any questioning about non-materialistic (spiritual/energetic/ magic) explanations or phenomena can create a prison of experience. The limited range of explanations for the complex and diverse phenomena bombarding your senses traps you.

We say F**k It to fixing anything into set theories and explanations.

A SPIRITUAL PRISON

It's probably obvious to you why the fundamentalist approach to spirituality creates its own prison. It is also dangerous to others. I've never understood anyone who can say 'I'm right. You're wrong. And you're going to hell.' I do get that, if you really think you've found the answer to life, the universe, and everything, and you sincerely believe this message can help everyone, then you'd want to go around and talk about it. But don't tell everyone they're wrong. Don't deny others the right to believe stuff other than what you believe. And certainly don't kill anyone if they believe something else, or say anything about what you believe.

We say F**k It to fixing anything into set theories and explanations.

But that's all probably obvious to you.

And there probably aren't many fundamentalists reading this anyway.

But there are probably many of you who regard yourselves as 'spiritual' people. I love the diversity of spirituality in today's Western society.

There's a huge openness to spiritual ideas and an immense range of spiritual ideas on offer, and everything is easily accessible (it has not always been like that).

Many of us now have a 'pick 'n' mix' approach to spirituality. Now, 'pick 'n' mix' is when you serve yourself from a range of candies, such as jelly babies, chocolate buttons, cola bottles, flying saucers, chocolate-covered raisins, pineapple chunks, gobstoppers (jaw breakers), licorice torpedoes, cola cubes, white chocolate mice, etc. You peruse the large selection of delicious, E-numbered sugar concoctions in their plastic containers, your paper bag in hand, then use the plastic scoops to create your mix.

The spiritual candies we scoop into our spiritual bag aren't as delicious, but they're better for your figure. Here are just a few samples from the range: Reiki, astrology, Buddhism, Shamanism, NLP, EFT, crystal healing, distance healing, Taoism, Hinduism, angel therapy, hot stone therapy, yoga, Tai Chi, energy arts, dark arts, healing arts… and so on. Some we add to our bag, others we leave because we don't fancy them. There's little set 'dogma' for the 'New-Age' spiritual seeker to subscribe to – either we say that we are 'spiritual' or have a 'spiritual side,' or that we get in touch with our 'higher self' or 'soul.' They cover as much to do with the mind as the soul, as the genres leak into each other. And they include as much to do with the body as with the mind and the soul. Some integrate the three (that's often the point of 'holism,' another 'ism,' to recognize the interconnectedness of all these elements).

Take yoga, for example, which has a spiritual aim (to create 'union' between the material and the spiritual), and uses the physical *asanas* only as one means to achieve this union. Many people, however, practice yoga solely as a physical discipline, like a twenty-first-century aerobics class. Having run a yoga retreat for seven years, we know something about this. I read countless feedback sheets filled out by the metropolitan new yogis with sentiments such as: 'The yoga was way too spiritual,' 'The yoga was great, just less of the spiritual stuff next time, please.' 'Loved the yoga, great teacher, but enough with the spiritual messages.'

'Dear Priest, loved the service… the hymns were excellent, really enjoyed that kneeling position, and the bread and wine were delicious… but enough with that God thing, way too spiritual for this day and age.'

We have 'spiritual' ideas in our spiritual paper bag, too: we believe that everything has a reason; that everything's perfect; we try to live in the now; we talk a lot about 'trust;' we 'go with the flow;' we recognize that thoughts create reality; we know we can spiritually manifest anything in our lives; we think everything has an energy; we like other people's energy (or not); we try to accept things as they are; we love what is; we try not to judge; we're on our 'journey' (a spiritual one at that) and everything is part of that journey; we don't believe in traditional moral notions of right and wrong, but we believe in love; we believe in free love (nice), and we believe in peace; and we want to cleanse negative energy and spread peace…

We put actual stuff in our spiritual bags to help us on our spiritual journeys: Tarot cards, angel cards, crystals, essential oils, prayer flags, incense sticks, smudge sticks, talking sticks, drum sticks…

We eat well on our spiritual journey, too: meat-free, dairy-free, gluten-free, cruelty-free, pesticide-free, humor-free, and certainly never 'free.'

And, though Gaia and I find it funny, we also use and subscribe to a lot of that stuff, too. But always in a pick 'n' mix way. And what we pick 'n' mix changes. We never get stuck on anything. And we always take it all with a pinch of salt (which doesn't quite work with the 'confectionary' metaphor, as it would make all the candies taste DISGUSTING), because the pinch of salt makes it fun and fascinating.

So, where's the prison in this type of pick 'n' mix spirituality? Taking it too seriously; fixing on anything; believing any one thing is the ultimate answer (and even worse, if you then think that everything else is wrong). Also, it's easy to create new hierarchies of 'good' and 'bad.' We may no longer think sex before marriage is 'bad,' but we might see anger as bad, or materialism as bad, or selfishness as bad… or we might detect bad energy (in people and places), bad vibes. We are relentlessly dualistic beings, we always want to differentiate and separate things. We often separate out our 'spiritual side,' we separate

Say F**k It to fixing any ideas.

the good from the bad, we separate our ideas from other people's, and we separate ourselves from others. (Or, rather, perceiving and believing we're separate from others and worried that others are 'better' than we are, we find ways to feel we're better. That's religion, actually. It's also the source of much of our pain, our fighting, and our wars. Believing we're separate, worrying we're not good enough, we amplify our separation by distancing ourselves from others and even fighting them.)

Say F**k It to fixing any ideas. Hold it all lightly. And get a 'sense' of one possible 'spiritual' truth: that we're not separate at all, that we're all connected, maybe even all one. Our perception of separation is just an illusion – an illusion that creates all suffering. But don't make a jump and 'believe' that, because you might well be jumping into another prison.

My, we do like our prisons, don't we?

---

* Act of abandoned copulation.

† Eccentric and a bit crazy (in an endearing sort of way).

‡ Idiom, in certain parts of the UK, for dinner and not to be confused with afternoon tea, which involves small sandwiches, cake, and the odd pot of tea – nice.

§ Revelatory exclamation not found in any worldly lexicon.

‖ Usually derogatory: meaning a bit too brainy for his or her own (and usually others') good, and a bit of a smart-ass.

¶ Meaning 'men,' and implying 'proper' men at that, with 'proper' manly interests such as drinking beer, sports, and traits such as crotch scratching.

WHY
DO
PRISONS
EXIST?

A PRISON IS SAFE

Occasionally, our metaphor will be stretched a little too far, particularly when I say that a prison is safe. Because a regular prison probably isn't a particularly safe place to be, especially if you're a pretty boy with a cute ass... or a sex offender.

You've created a prison for yourself for many reasons, and one of them is likely to be that it feels safe. It feels safer, for example, to fix your opinions and beliefs than to stay not knowing... that's not a comfortable or easy place to be. A more simplistic, fundamentalist faith always feels safer than a liberal, open, questioning faith. It's safer to believe that there's a God up there looking out for you and there's an afterlife, even if those beliefs close you to a more sophisticated understanding of the likely nature of 'God' and the meaning of His words in the scriptures.

Not happy with the prison of religion you grew up with? Choose another one then. Like lovers on the rebound, many people leap into the nearest, coolest version of, effectively, the same thing. Or they turn what are interesting philosophies into religions.

Buddhism is a case in point. Buddha was not, is not, a god. He was a man who 'woke up' to the 'true reality' of life (I know, I don't particularly like putting inverted commas in there, but they help to show that I'm not saying he woke up to true reality… who knows, but he thought he had, and so do Buddhists). But many Buddhists have deified him. The whole point is that he was an 'ordinary' man. (Oh, there I go again… this time I had to do it because though he was a mortal, and not a god, he wasn't exactly Everyman, as he started off as a prince.) He was like us, so we, too, can wake up… if we could only find that Bodhi tree.

But this isn't just about spirituality and religion. When facing difficulty, we find refuge in places that can so easily become prisons for us later. Let's say that someone finds they have a serious illness – a treatable form of cancer, for example. They can find refuge in the sophisticated science of oncology – learning about their good chances of survival with various forms of treatment, and beginning a course of the right one. Or they might resist the idea of any form of treatment at all and find refuge in their belief that the body is its own most powerful healer and, using a variety of natural therapies, work on remaining positive and relaxed in the knowledge that healing will happen naturally. (Incidentally, that's not an unscientific option; the power of the mind in healing is widely demonstrated scientifically.) Or they might, while undergoing treatment, find refuge in God who has a Plan for them, and this is just part of that Plan – they trust in God, no matter where God leads them, and that trust is very comforting. Or find refuge in trying to help other people who have been diagnosed with the same cancer, creating a support group for fellow sufferers. Or find refuge in raising money for further research to improve survival rates. Or take the diagnosis as another example of their rotten luck in life, and that it always happens to them. Or investigate what 'lesson' the diagnosis has to teach them. They work with a counselor to uncover the true cause of their illness – the emotional seeds that have sprouted such a toxic plant – and believe that once those seeds have been discovered, and worked with, then the cancer will recede.

There are limitless models that we create or subscribe to when we're in need and are facing difficulty. All have their value and can help. But all can become our prisons later, because fixed models are inflexible and tend not to respond to differing circumstances.

Say F**k It to holding on to any model, especially if it simply feels 'safe.'

So play with the idea of saying F**k It to holding on to any model, especially if it simply feels 'safe' and instead look out for what feels, simply, 'true,' in each moment.

A PRISON IS NATURAL

It's very natural to want to fix everything, though. It's very natural to find the model that seems to work, then stick to it. We are creatures of habit.

The neural network in the brain works in exactly this way: when we respond to incoming stimuli in a certain way, that response or behavior is laid down in the form of a neural pathway. If, the next time we are faced with the same stimuli, we respond in the same way, then that neural pathway becomes stronger. Just as if you walk across a fresh cornfield, you make a path, and the following day you follow the same path, then that path becomes more permanent, so numerous neural pathways are formed in your brain. And, as these pathways become established, it means that you're very unlikely, faced with the same stimuli, to react in any other way than you are accustomed to. You are a creature of habit.

In fact, it's not just that we're reacting in the same way to similar stimuli. We are actually choosing the stimuli we take in to process based on our programs in the first place. In any given moment your brain is being bombarded with billions of bits of information. You can most easily picture this if you imagine walking down a busy high street with all its activity, movement, noise, smells, heat, or cold, etc. With your eyes and other senses fully functional, you absorb huge amounts of information. But you're conscious of only a tiny proportion of it, and the unconscious parts of your brain register most of it. But you're still constantly filtering the incoming information based on models of what you've experienced before. It's most likely that you actually wouldn't recognize something that wasn't within your current range of experience.

And part of the F**k It Therapy process includes a conscious effort to break habits.

This is a peculiar thought – and if it's very unfamiliar it might not even have a chance to register! It means we only recognize what we already know. To help explain this phenomenon, the example of the indigenous people, who hadn't seen ships before the first explorers arrived, is often used. It was reported (by Captain Cook, Magellan *et al*) that while the locals greeted the small landing boats, they couldn't see the ships moored offshore – even though they were looking out to sea. Ridiculous? Don't blame me. I didn't invent that example. I didn't do the research into the brain.

It is very natural to fix our models, firm up our network of neural pathways, create our habits, and let them become our prisons. And part of the F**k It Therapy process includes a conscious effort to break those habits. It's possible to rewire some of the brain's networks. It's also possible to rewire them with a more open response to stimuli by developing and practicing new habits of perception.

In fact, in the 'F**k It State,' as we call it, you're naturally more open to stimuli. And that's the trick – to use F**k It Therapy to help you into a naturally more open state because it helps you out of your naturally more limited state.

A PRISON HAS RULES AND REGULATIONS

In music and movies we glorify the rule breakers, the rebels, and the pioneers. Freedom is our fantasy: we break out of whatever chains bind us and head out for the open road. There are those, of course, who have never had this fantasy, who are happy to live the 9–5 working life with 2.2 kids in a neat suburban home with a standard family car, weekend trips, staycations, the saving for retirement, the lawn bowls, the retirement home, the mid-priced coffin. I repeat: they are happy to live that life. So leave them alone. Don't knock them.

But most of us have a fantasy about freedom. And that's why those movies and music work on us, but not because we're free and on the open road of life. Do you think the true rebels and pioneers are watching *Thelma and Louise* and listening to The Clash? No, they work on us because we're still in our chains. Do you know how many white-collar workers there are out there with big motorbikes? Do you know how many Audi drivers listen to Eminem? How many grandfathers are listening to punk? How many media people say 'cool'? How many of the dudes at school became financial advisers? Don't knock them. It's probably me. It's probably you. Wait until your kids are in their teens, then you'll get the list.

Why – with such a common, strong, fantasy – are we all still in chains? Because we like it at some level, of course. We like the rules and regulations of regular life. They make us feel safe. No matter how much we dream about breaking the rules, we secretly fear what life would be like without them. People talk about soldiers or prisoners who become 'institutionalized,' reliant on order and routine. It's easy to look at someone who exits the military or prison after a long time and see why it's difficult, and say 'ah, yes, they've become institutionalized.' Well, you don't think you have? You don't think you're as reliant on your institutions as they were on theirs? You believe that you're not reliant on your work status, your routine, your family, the support of your friends, the economic web that feeds you, entertains you, the infrastructures that sell to you, ferry you around, comfort you, and heal you when you're sick?

Just try taking out some of the elements of the rules and regulations that you work within occasionally. If you work in an office and dream of being your own boss, of having the freedom of working from home, then try it for a couple of weeks if you can. And get your wake-up call – meet the truth you unconsciously suspected all along – that it's not so easy. Not that finding a way to give up the nine–to–five and striking out on your own with a business you can run from the beach isn't a brilliant idea – we'll give you some tips later to do just that. But it's a peculiar fact, that the more you idealize your fantasy alternative life, the further away it is from you.

Say F**k It to unobtainable fantasies.

You stay in prison because you're secretly afraid of what it's like without those rules and regulations. We'll learn how to say F**k It to unobtainable fantasies, and how to work out what you want to do, and how you can go about doing it.

A PRISON CAN BE VERY COMFORTABLE

Imagine those Mafia bosses with their luxury cells, running their empires on smartphones from gold-rimmed toilet seats. Now drop that image. It's not realistic, and it contributes little to this next point.

The prison you make for yourself can be comfortable. Not just because it feels safe and it's a natural way to live, or because of all the rules and regulations of the particular institution you've chosen, but because there are huge resources invested in making it comfortable for you. Much of our society is set up to support the individual and the collective prisons of its population.

Take your work life, for example. Although I am writing this book in the middle of a recession, in the age of austerity, most people have become steadily wealthier over the past decades. We really have never had it so good. Yet most people still continue to work 40-plus hours every week, even though a fantasy for many people is to work fewer hours, get more leisure time, or retire early. Meanwhile, we've all been living moments away from an easy-to-fulfill fantasy. All we have to say is 'I don't need all this stuff, I don't need a bigger house, I'll forego the new car, and work less. I'll trade in my stuff for time.' Unlike, say, 50 years ago, it's been possible to buy leisure time (you see, that's what you're effectively doing, when you work less, earn less, and enjoy more leisure time). The increasing gap between what is required to live a comfortable life and what we all have means there has been an easy opportunity to downsize and enjoy more time. But how many people have actually done it? Relatively tiny numbers, if you assess how many *could* have done it. Fifteen years ago I was the first man in our forward-thinking advertising agency to go part-time. I used the time I bought each week to write. I was amazed by how many people would say, 'John, my you're lucky, how did you pull that off?'

'I asked,' I replied.

They'd look at me as if they understood what I was saying: that they too, could ask. But that they wouldn't, would they? There was always a pause, then: 'Ah, no, but I couldn't, could I, because…' And the same old list was reeled off. But they were affluent people. They were also entrepreneurial, imaginative, self-confident people. Yet, they were happier to rest in the assumption that they couldn't do it because they hadn't been given the opportunity, rather than the truth that they wouldn't ever do it because they'd made their decision to enjoy the trappings of work success over the freedom they professed to desire.

Why have so few of us taken up the possibility of downsizing and enjoying life more? Because we've become accustomed to a higher standard of living. But it's more than that. It hasn't been in anyone's interest to encourage you to downsize, work less, and sit around more. Just imagine the effect on the economy. The more we work, the higher the country's GDP, the more money is generated for the company, which buys services from other companies and pays us more money, which we spend on more things produced by other companies, who are buying goods and services from still other companies and paying their employees more money, etc., etc. The problem here is – if your population actually wants to be free and they've already got more than they need – how the heck do you get them always to want more? You have to tell them, somehow, the following things:

'You won't be happy until you have this (a better car) or this (the latest iThing) or have been to this (expensive) place.'

'You can't really be happy until you've fulfilled your potential (done better in your career, got to the top, etc.), got smarter (by reading more, self-educating, etc.), look your best (bought the diets, joined the health clubs, used the hair products, undergone surgery, had your teeth cosmetically enhanced, etc.).'

And don't just blame the advertisers. Sure, they pump 'must-have' steroids into the market, making you feel inadequate and desperate without the purchase, but they're just the middleman between the company and you. You want it. They provide it. We're to blame. The media is to blame. It's a sick, incestuous mess. Fame and wealth are now the strongest currencies in our culture. When I was a kid, we all dreamed about doing something amazing (I wanted to be a footballer*, then a rock star, and later a writer). I wanted to do those amazing things because I loved playing football, playing guitar, and later, writing. I didn't dream of the money I'd make or the fame I'd enjoy. Though it was, of course, assumed you'd be both rich and famous. But it wasn't the *aim*. Oliver James, in his book *Affluenza*, cites the study where children were asked what they wanted to be when they grew up: most said famous. The follow-up question asked: 'What do you want to be famous for?' Most kids didn't know, because simply being famous was their aim, not the thing that would make them famous.

> *Everything is set up around us to convince us that the prisons we've created for ourselves are the only way to live.*

We live in the Big-Brother age, when people become famous for a moment, not for doing anything amazing, but for sitting around in a house being watched by everyone else.

Everything is set up around us to convince us that living in the prisons we've created for ourselves is the only way to live. We're comfortable because, yes, it can be a materially comfortable life, but also because everybody is in the same boat. Or prison. Prison-boat. That's what we're in – a huge prison ship with fur-lined cells, gold-rimmed toilet seats, and corporate lackeys of any gender, age, and persuasion paid to give you blowjobs whenever you want, as long as you KEEP BUYING and never, ever, think of trying to jump ship.

F**k It, get your bathers on.

---

* Or soccer player, if you live in the USA. One thing most Italians and British men (and many women, too) have in common is their passion for the 'beautiful game,' by which I mean English football (affectionately known as 'footie' in the UK or soccer in the USA) and not to be confused, now or at any point in the book when I mention it (which I do sometimes) with American football.

27

WHEN ARE WE IN PRISON?

SEEING THROUGH THE WALLS

So you might say that you're not in prison, and you've never been in prison. Someone who knows you might disagree, and pinpoint the exact reason you've always been in prison, and maybe always will be. It's clearly not as easy to define as a bricks-and-mortar prison. But it also means that, once seen, the metaphorical prison is easier to escape than the real one. In fact, sometimes, simply seeing it is enough for the metaphorical walls to dissolve.

But, if a degree of consciousness is assumed, then we're probably in the land of definition disagreement. Or at least, you're happy with the apparent 'limits' that exist in your life. You may be conscious that your dialectic materialism has had its philosophical day, that it probably limits you, but you're happy with your life within those confines, so that's that.

Others see their confines and want out. Still others don't even know they're 'in.'

AFTER A WHILE, PRISONERS FORGET THEY'RE IN PRISON

Though you might think that walls and bars are daily reminders of being 'inside,' they become invisible after a while. Other prisoners surround a prisoner... not the free. Prison life, after a while, feels normal. So other issues replace the issue of 'I'm in prison and I'd like to get out.' If you live in Nondescript-and-a-Bit-Ugly town – every country has one or several, so you know where I'm talking about wherever you are (in the UK it's probably Dartford) – then you're surrounded every day by other people who live there, too. There are very few outsiders to tell you how awful the place is, or how lovely, say, another town is (in the UK that's probably Canterbury – a not-too-distant but more pleasant place). And even those who do visit, a) get out quickly and b) wouldn't tell you how awful it is because (particularly if they're British) they're too polite. After a while of living there, surrounded by other people who live there, you effectively forget you're in hell.

This is a good enough reason to travel far and regularly: to cleanse yourself of the hypnotic and deadening effect of the wrong kind of acceptance.

So for the prisoners who forget they're in prison (or for the citizen of Dartford who never travels), he or she's likely to remain in prison for a good/bad long time.

Why does it matter if they've forgotten? (You'll find out soon in *Why Would We Want to Get Out of Prison?*)

AFTER A WHILE, THE OUTSIDE BECOMES A FRIGHTENING PLACE

There's the scene in *The Shawshank Redemption* (see Appendix II: Our Top Five Prison Movies) when the old guy who's been in prison forever is finally released. In the 40-odd years he's been behind bars, the outside world has changed unrecognizably. He's shocked by every aspect of an alien modern world – from the honking cars to the harsh working world. Within days, he's hanged himself. (Sorry to give that away if you haven't already seen it, though it's not the actual ending. If you can't be bothered to watch the movie and want to know the ending, and you'd like to ruin it for friends and family who also haven't seen it but can be bothered to watch it, turn to Appendix IV aptly titled The Ending of *The Shawshank Redemption*.)

We are probably most free as children. Being free comes naturally. We don't have to make any effort to be free. We don't have to steel ourselves, or face our fears, in order to do something. We just do it. But as we grow up and build the walls around ourselves, and become

We are probably most free as children.

accustomed to being in our prisons, and surround ourselves with other prisoners, the very idea of being 'outside' can scare us. It's such a long time since we experienced true freedom that we don't know whether we could cope with it. It means that, even though we might occasionally venture out of our prisons (e.g., when we're visiting another country or place, or have a few glasses of wine), we very soon return to the safety of the high walls around us.

REPEAT OFFENDERS

This lack of familiarity with the outside, this underlying fear of the freedom we experienced perpetually when we were younger, means that – even for those of us who crave freedom and consciously try to break down the various walls of our prisons – we end up back in the safety of prison.

We're repeat offenders. And some people live their lives like this. They live through times when they're trapped, and feel trapped, but don't seem to be able to find a way out or a way through. Then they manage to escape and enjoy freedom, make huge changes in their lives, but then slowly slip back into patterns, relationships, jobs, or places that trap them again.

LIFE SENTENCE

Some people would argue that we're all lifers: that very few people have the good fortune in their lifetimes to experience true freedom, which is usually defined as an experience of 'enlightenment,' and usually signifies a recognition of reality as a kind of imprisoning dream. True reality (i.e., outside the prison) is another 'enlightened' form of consciousness.

We could argue (and will do so toward the end of this book) that the opposite is true: we're all free; it's just that we can't see it. Instead, we see we're 'trapped' and crave 'freedom.' In fact, the natural process seems to be something like this:

We start free, as children, but without realizing it, because we know nothing else.

We grow up and lose our freedom, without realizing it.

We're in prison, but don't realize it (and might not realize it for the whole of our lives, in which case we are unconscious lifers).

We realize we are in prison, and strive to break down the walls and, usually, with the help of some good F**k It Therapy, we succeed.

We experience freedom, then occasionally slip back into prison, but with consciousness and a good bit of F**k It, we're able to get out again.

We finally see that all states are fine, that being in prison is the same as being outside prison when we live in full consciousness.

But I've just told you the ending. The thing is, unlike the ending of *The Shawshank Redemption*, no matter how many times you read about it, you don't usually understand it until you've gone through all the above steps: so it's like me telling you the ending of *The Shawshank Redemption* (again, see Appendix IV), but you not being able to understand a word of it until you've watched the whole movie.

So, what's the point of mentioning it? F**k It, why not?

WHY WOULD WE WANT TO GET OUT OF PRISON?

A PRISON CAN BE DANGEROUS

Just as in real prisons, your metaphorical prisons can be dangerous places. If you left your dreams behind long ago and settled for (whatever the reason) a job you never wanted, a partner who was never your ideal, routines you would never have imagined... if you feel like you're living someone else's life, then it rots you. It's a dangerous place to be. You never feel completely yourself or at ease.

When we get stuck and imprisoned in a situation, a way of living, a thought process, or a religion that closes off part of us, then it can eventually make us ill. We'll learn later about how energy works, in life and the body. When we suppress part of ourselves, when we shut off a strong desire, when we consciously ignore a strong voice within ourselves, then we're effectively blocking our energy. And it's the blocking of energy in Traditional Chinese Medicine (TCM) that leads to illness. That's why, in the sessions we run on F**k It Retreats, when people finally really let go, release their frustrations and move their bodies freely, amazing healing happens. And not just physical healing: deep emotional healing, too.

Even though most of the people around you are in prison, even though every message in society is inviting you to remain in prison, don't be tempted to remain stuck, no matter how apparently safe it feels. If we suppress our strongest desires or ignore our deepest pain, these strong forces have a way of forcing their way out anyway. It's best to get out of that prison first and allow those forces to flow, before they force 'flow' on you.

It's possible to see this in many people who become seriously ill or suffer other traumas. Those that face their illness or trauma consciously invariably recognize the 'teacher' element of the illness or event. Such experiences tend to snap people out of the prisons they've created for themselves: they transform their lives overnight, they finally do what they've always wanted to do – they go travelling, they leave jobs and relationships that aren't working, they follow their dreams. Faced with huge challenges, they see that what they used to worry about doesn't actually matter so much. They are given the huge gift, even in the midst of painful experiences, of getting things in perspective. So why not get some perspective before some difficult life experience forces it on you? Why not get perspective before perspective gets you?

Why not get perspective before perspective gets you?

BECAUSE THERE IS AN OUTSIDE (WHICH HAS BEEN FORGOTTEN)

The moment you begin to become conscious of your prison, you start to see what life outside could be like.

And just knowing there *is* an outside creates the desire to experience it. That's why it's worth traveling away from home occasionally: otherwise you'd never know there was anything else.

As you realize there's an outside, you have memories of what it's like to be free and to dream. In fact, when people relax deeply on a F**k It Retreat, it often happens that they're reminded of happy childhood memories: because that might have been the last time they were truly free.

As you realize there's an outside, you begin to dream again. You see that's it possible to get out, be free, and have what you want in life. It's a remarkable feeling, which then starts to create the freedom that you'll soon experience. Yes, really, just by getting the lovely feeling of freedom, you begin to manifest actual freedom – just by imagining what it would be like to be free, even if it feels wildly unrealistic now – makes the chances of it happening so much higher.

Now, it's time to sit back, close your eyes, and dream, dream, dream about what the outside could be like. Remember, just doing so will start to manifest your dreams and your impending freedom.

PART II

IMAGINING WHAT'S OUTSIDE THE PRISON

**IMAGINING
A
F**K
IT
LIFE**

A
GLIMPSE
OF
THE
FUTURE

This part of the book is an invitation to pause: to have a go at imagining what a F**k It Life could look like for you before we take you on the journey of F**k It Therapy.

So you could see it as if you're getting a breath of air before climbing into our F**k It Therapy limo: taking the luxurious route to freedom.

And as you're standing by the limo, getting that air, we'll whisper little suggestions to you, then leave you alone for a bit to ponder. And do please ponder. Dream. Get a real sense of what freedom could mean for you, in your life, now. It will most likely make the subsequent journey in the F**k It Therapy limo even more fascinating and transformative.

While you ponder each question or suggestion, you could make notes if you fancy: you could use each one as an exercise to explore fully.

But that's up to you. You've bought a book with 'F**k It' in the title, so that, like everything else, is up to you. In fact, that in itself could be a powerful part of F**k It Therapy for you – realizing that it's all up to you.

WHAT DID YOU MOST LIKE DOING AS A KID?

IF YOU ACCEPTED THAT
LIFE IS A ROLLERCOASTER,
COULD YOU ENJOY THE
WHOLE RIDE?

If you were told you
had only a year
to live, how would you
spend it?

PICTURE SOMEONE YOU KNOW WHO IS VERY F**K IT: DRAW THIS PERSON AND NOTE HIS/HER QUALITIES.

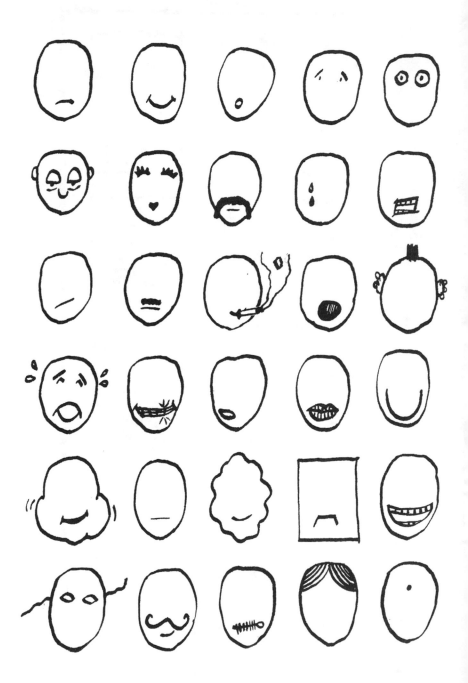

WHAT WOULD IT BE LIKE TO BE OKAY WITH ALL YOUR DIFFERENT SIDES (WHATEVER THEY ARE)?

What would
it feel like
to be free?

What are you
waiting for?

still okay

What would it be like to be okay even when things go wrong?

WHAT IS
THE WORST
THING
THAT
COULD
HAPPEN
IF YOU
STARTED
SAYING
F**K IT
BIG TIME?

PART III

MAPPING THE WALLS

MAPPING
YOUR
'ITS'

A
BLOCK:
THE
STORY

If you visited A Block, your first impression would be that it's noisy. Prisoners cry out at you from their cells, or talk gently to you about themselves, or whisper something across the gangway. Not like in *The Silence of the Lambs*. They're not threatening. They just want to be heard.

You see everyone on A Block has his or her very important story. And they want you to hear it. If you were to stay here for just a day, you'd hear many of them. Dr. Jay, for example. She was a Harvard-educated doctor. In her short but illustrious career, she worked at all the top hospitals as a consultant, and did pioneering research into the effect of the production of cortisol (the stress hormone) on the testes of bulls under pressure. She had celebrity patients, earned huge fees, and was big news in bull-testes research and the implications on male fertility. She will talk endlessly about what she did and whom she knew. What she won't tell you is how she got into this prison in the first place. But maybe she's forgotten. She seems to have forgotten any part of her story that doesn't match her high evaluation of herself.

Or there's Dave. Dave isn't so confident about himself, or so proud of his achievements. In fact, Dave is pretty down on life and being Dave. He'll tell you about all his bad luck. How he JUST missed getting into a good high school and got in with the wrong crowd. How it wasn't his idea to back his pickup truck into the local jewelers, so it wasn't exactly fair when he was the only one who got caught. He can't believe that he's confounded the doctors with early onset of Type 2 diabetes, which is only supposed to afflict those much older. He lost his hair in his 30s. He has bad genes when it comes to metabolism, otherwise how can you explain the extra 60 pounds he's carrying. And his bad luck continues to afflict him every day. He's the one who eats the dodgy* sausage in the canteen. He's the one who gets the worst shift in the laundry. He gets the last choice of books from the library. And only gets passed the porn when it's too worn out to make anything out. It's tough being Dave, as Dave will tell you, endlessly.

But maybe you'll get on with Jim, who is one of the older prisoners. He's in his 60s but bright as a button. He'll tell you stories about his youth in the '50s, when the world was a different place. There were morals then and people respected each other. Even the criminals had their code back then, and wouldn't step over a certain line. He makes you feel nostalgic for a time when the underworld was a better place – still under, but not so far under. He wishes people now could have a bit more respect, for him and for each other, but mainly for him. He seems decent enough, but even with Jim, you can't help feeling, well, BORED.

Everyone on A Block has their story, and they're really keen to tell it to you. Not surprising when you see what's written on the walls:

If you have a story to tell, tell it.

You are an important person.

Stand up for what you believe in.

Walls have ears, and we're ready to listen.

Every prisoner on A Block has a story, but now they're stuck in it, like an author who writes a great character in a thrilling novel, but becomes that character and gets trapped in the book. The stories they have created about themselves are sometimes proud and illustrious (like Dr. Jay) or hard-luck stories (like Dave), or stories with a moral edge (like Jim's), but they're all stories. The prisoners on A Block don't exist as real people living in the present, growing as human beings given the changing circumstances of life. No. They're stuck in a story about themselves: about how they'd like to be seen by others, or how they think life has treated them, or about how life should be. But theirs is a stagnant life. It doesn't change. Life is a stuck record; the tune might once have sounded pleasant, but with the needle stuck, it just jars. And everyone around them is left feeling bored.

I give you one day in A Block. You'll be climbing the walls with frustration and boredom. You'd want some action, some thrill, and a taste of the real… God, you'd even prefer the adrenalin of some fear to this hell of storyland.

If you'd prefer to get straight to Breaking Through the Wall of the Story, turn to page 84.

---

* Meaning of low or dubious quality and likely to cause harm.

B
BLOCK:
FEAR

Those who are sent to B Block probably imagine that it will be a larger version of Room 101 (Google it) – a place where his or her deepest fears are made real. If they fear snakes, then they will be forced to live in a cell full of snakes, like in an Indiana Jones movie, but without the flaming torch. Sleeping with snakes: just the thought would drive them mad (though typing that now, it's made me wonder what a movie with that title would look like).

If they fear flying, they'd be imprisoned in a flight simulator, only it would simulate the passenger's experience, not the pilot's. The prisoner would have to endure, for hours a day, the endless repetition of the emergency procedure, carried out by burly prison guards dressed as cabin crew. They would experience hours of the engines revving up ready to go: all the moments that render nervous passengers shaky with sickly anticipation. And then every day, the airplane would simulate a six-hour flight: like flying to New York from London every single day, but without the joys of New York at the end of the trip. And, sad to say it now, but the flight does actually go down in the Atlantic on its 623rd voyage. The airplane hits the water after a horrifying 35-minute battle to save everyone, despite two burning engines and losing the tail.

Others are most scared of finding themselves naked in a room of matronly but full-bodied beautiful Russian women without any hope of escape. Or so they said anyway.

But B Block isn't like that at all. On the face of it, it's not a scary place. On the contrary, it looks like a very safe place to live. Everything seems very orderly. The prisoners are well behaved and usually quiet, keeping themselves to themselves. The guards look cautious and uptight, but that's how guards should look, shouldn't they? They permanently wear helmets, and always have their guns within reach. But it doesn't seem like an unpleasant place to see out your sentence. There's no screaming, at least.

The walls, like everything else on B Block, are neat and well scrubbed. No one would dare graffiti anything here. Instead, the walls have their own (official) writing:

68 percent of prisoners die before they're released.

Prison food likely cause of high incidence of bowel cancer in prisoners.

454 prisoners injured in showers in 2012.

Traumatized guard loses it and pulverizes prisoner.

The many walls are covered in scary facts about daily life in prison. Not about disasters in far-off places, but the dangers that lurk everywhere – even dangers that can't be seen.

Superbugs out of control in prisons.

Even the dangers that you'd never usually think about.

Sleeping too much can lead to respiratory problems.

And dangers that simply confuse you.

Sleeping too little can lead to heart problems.

So, how much SHOULD I sleep? And that's one of the questions the prisoners endlessly debate – especially, late at night. It's a question that keeps them awake, thus directing them more at risk from heart disease than respiratory problems. Is eight hours too much or too little? What are the facts? Ah, but scientists disagree on the facts. In fact, one historian has just declared that, until 300 years ago, we all used to sleep in two parts: we'd go to bed and sleep for three to four hours, then get up for an hour, have a meal, or read a book, or visit friends, then go back to bed for another three to four hours. Perhaps we should try that?

Living on B Block is like living in a world where there is nothing else to read but the *Daily Mail**. In fact, the *Daily Mail* is the prisoners' newspaper of choice: it seems like the best place to get up-to-date information on all things to be scared of and all the terrible things that are happening in the world. And if there's one thing that can reassure a prisoner living in fear of terrible things happening, it's the knowledge that some REALLY terrible things are happening elsewhere in the world.

Not that anything can alleviate their suffering. They worry from the moment they wake up to the moment they go to sleep. And then suffer restless nights because their worries have penetrated their unconscious and take elaborate, dramatized manifestations in the form of end-of-the-world-scary nightmares. The prisoners talk endlessly about their fears: about their health, their safety in such a dangerous place, about the terrible things lying in wait in the canteen or the bathroom block or the exercise yard. They're constantly torn as to whether to do something that might seem dangerous:

Injuries involving weights up 33 percent.

Or whether not doing it is more dangerous:

Muscle waste in prisoners causes early-onset arthritis.

Their fears usually render them passive, tight, and suspicious. Even though the crime levels on B Block are remarkably low (though the writing on the walls would never say: IT'S ACTUALLY VERY SAFE HERE, because it wouldn't make a good headline), and the prisoners talk a lot with each other (and scared people talk an awful lot), but they always think the worst about what someone else could do to them or say about them. So no real friendships are developed; no confidences are exchanged. It's better to stay on a safe subject:

Danger, risk, and threat.

And it seems funny that, in their few quiet, solitary moments, the prisoners choose to read newspapers, watch TV news shows, or surf the net for more scare stories. It's almost as if they LIKE this fear stuff. And that's the sad fact. As B Block demonstrates, when people live in an environment of fear, they somehow start to crave it, to like it even. They want to know how much worse it could get. They want to know about the fine details of the dangers lurking everywhere around them.

On B Block, fear is the drug. And it's freely available. All the prisoners are addicted. And no one has even thought of the long-term effects of this form of drug abuse. No one has even considered that the biggest thing to fear could be… fear itself.

If you'd prefer to get straight to Breaking Through the Wall of the Story, turn to page 84.

---

* British newspaper renowned for its scaremongering headline stories – read and duly absorbed by around two million people in the UK each day.

C
BLOCK:
SERIOUSNESS

On every single wall of C Block is a large plasma screen. In the ceiling there are inset surround-sound speakers giving an excellent audio quality to the perpetual broadcast that prisoners in C Block experience night and day. Even the bars of the cells are made from transparent, toughened Perspex to allow the prisoners an unblocked and unremitting view of the screens.

The broadcasts consist of a man speaking to the prisoners – usually the same man but sometimes another who looks remarkably like the first man. The men have angular faces and waxed-back hair. They both have mustaches and talk in the same monotonous tone. Just like when your Uncle Ted has to go speak to a foreman, or the management, or has a chance meeting with a member of a higher social rank in the bank or post office.

The prisoners no longer watch. They know what's coming, after all. But they can't help but see. The only way not to see the images is to close their eyes. Sure, the screens don't just show the faces of the mustached men: the broadcasts occasionally cut to scenes to illustrate the point the broadcaster is making. But the prisoners have seen the scenes many times before.

It's not that those in charge of C Block don't try to vary the content of the broadcasts. They have a studio, and are constantly trying to create new messages and footage. But, given the 24/7-nature of the broadcasts, they can't help but include repeats. C Block is an ongoing government-backed experiment: to create a system for prisons all over the world. Government regulations, however, require that the system is tested for ten years, and the prisoners analyzed for their responses and behaviors before it's finally rolled out. We're in year seven now.

But it seems to be going well. The prisoners keep themselves to themselves (though it's hard to hold a conversation above the constant drone of the broadcast), carry out the necessary duties, and behave well. They are given a test every month: an interview to check for any changes in their responses to a variety of questions that test levels of honesty, consideration, and moral views... In fact, everything that a makes a good, responsible citizen. And there are significant improvements.

Let's listen to what's being broadcast at this very moment. We're cutting in mid-broadcast, but you'll pick it up soon enough, I'm sure:

... To be able to carry out your duties for the good of those around you.

Remember, as a good citizen, to take your responsibility to society seriously. A citizen isn't just responsible for themselves and their wellbeing. You must think about others and act accordingly. You must take your work seriously, because your work, as well as serving you in the form of a wage, serves the good of the country and the community – business benefits and all other citizens benefit in the form of taxes.

As a good citizen you must always set a good example to others: you must not swear, you must not drink alcohol or smoke cigarettes, you must not spit in public. As a good citizen you must take your duty to your family seriously: whether to your parents, spouse, or children. You must never do anything to jeopardize these relationships, and always act in the highest interests of others and not yourself. If the citizen has desires that may harm other citizens in any way, then these desires must be suppressed. It is the duty of the citizen to suppress all desires that might cause any harm or discomfort to anyone else in the community.

The good citizen will use all waking hours for work or for serving the family or community. There is no time for slacking or playing. There is no serious result from playing, including playing with children. Children can play with each other. Play corrupts society. It makes people lazy and disrespectful. In societies where play is prominent, the serious values and intentions of a community break down.

A serious citizen does not drink beer, spend hours outdoors playing sports, or cooking barbeques.

Take communication seriously. Say what you want to say carefully, succinctly, without expletives, or grammatical laziness.

Take your health seriously. Eat well. Exercise for health not for play. If you are sick, see a doctor and follow his or her advice to the letter. Take doctors seriously. Take any figure in authority seriously. Watch only informative programming on TV. Do not watch sitcoms, quiz shows, dramas, or fictional movies. Watch shows that will inform you of the serious events happening in the world, or educate you about something you are ignorant of. Always keep learning: take your education seriously...

If you like a good movie and a can of beer, let's hope you don't end up in C Block because, after months of perpetual broadcast, you probably won't feel like watching it ever again.

If you'd prefer to get straight to Breaking Through the Wall of the Story, turn to page 84.

D
BLOCK:
SELF-DOUBT

D Block is a model 'corrective facility.' The warden has taken his duty to 'correct' the ways of his wayward prisoners so seriously that he's turned correction into a fine art. There are cameras and microphones everywhere in D Block, so that guards can monitor the prisoners' behavior and then offer feedback on how to improve. They offer such feedback via the medium of the walls: they're able to transmit their comments about each prisoner to specific walls in the prison. So the walls surrounding the prisoners provide a continual feedback system for the required daily behavior.

Wayne has been in D Block for just two months. When he opens his eyes in the morning, he's able to read some feedback about his behavior the evening before on the wall.

Wayne, we suggest that you improve your reading material. All you ever read about is sports. If it's not baseball, it's golf. If it's not golf, it's tennis. How can you hope to educate yourself if you don't read something more challenging?

That morning Wayne goes to the D-Block library and takes out a couple of novels – crime novels about life in gangland. He immerses himself in the first one and has finished it by lunchtime. He likes this fiction and can't wait to start the next book. He's chuffed.

But while he's having lunch, a message flashes up on the wall:

Wayne, is that the best you can do? Reading about the disgusting criminal exploits of other people like you? We suggest you read something that might help lift you out of the stinking criminal mire you're currently in.

Wayne is deflated. He always tries to respond positively to the feedback he's given. After all, they're constantly reminded that:

Prisoners, we give you feedback for your benefit.

Or:

We're here to help you improve.

Wayne wants to improve. But it's hard being given such negative feedback all the time.

Jane is a model prisoner. She's in D Block for swindling hundreds of people out of millions with an elaborate investment scam. She walks with her head down and keeps to herself. She's just trying to get through her time inside without getting into any trouble. But she's started to dread seeing her name on the walls.

Jane, we saw you beat Paula at chess last night. Are you sure you played by the rules? Paula is a very good chess player. We will be examining the footage to make sure you didn't cheat.

The guards have a habit of subtly referring to the prisoners' convictions. They'd find fault in anything and somehow link it back to the original crime:

Jane, you didn't wipe down the sink after brushing your teeth this morning. Do you have no consideration for other prisoners?

One thing that has to be said for the guards is that they give all the prisoners equal treatment in their feedback comments. Here's a look at some of what's written on D Block's walls at this very moment:

Samantha, don't let us have to tell you again to put your tray back in the rack after meals.

Manuel, do you have a comprehension problem? Can you read? You need to speed up with those daily tasks. Old Cyril used to do the rounds quicker than you do.

Ben, you may think you're God's gift, but we know better. Now put away the hair gel and concentrate on doing something to help in this place.

Gillian, what do you think your cell is, your teenage bedroom? Keep it tidy.

Davina, a smile doesn't cost anything, you know. In fact, if you don't start smiling a bit more, we'll dock your allowance and then not smiling will start to cost you something.

Andrew, we found the porn.

If you'd prefer to get straight to Breaking Through the Wall of the Story, turn to page 84.

E BLOCK: LACK OF CONSCIOUSNESS

E Block is a mess. It's probably how you'd imagine a prison in a developing country to be: walls crumbling, damp everywhere, litter-strewn corridors, rusty bars, filthy bathrooms, a canteen that sends three prisoners to the sanatorium every week, a sanatorium that sends one prisoner to the morgue every month – a morgue that would make a more pleasant home for most sane people than E Block.

Not that E Block's prisoners would notice.

They don't even notice that many of the other prisoners aren't human. It started as an experiment 20 years ago – an experiment that worked… in certain respects, anyway. The warden noticed that prisoners on E Block seemed to be more malleable than the average prisoner in other blocks: they didn't think much about what they did or why they did it, they rarely caused trouble, and they never tried to escape. They seemed to be very influenced by what other prisoners did, just followed what others did, whatever they did. So the warden started simply: she filmed an actor dressed in prison garb, just sitting on a bench, reading quietly. The movie wasn't action-packed. And it wasn't long, just ten minutes. But a continuous loop of this footage was created and then projected onto a wall of the prison, life size, to create the (rather unrealistic) effect that a prisoner was sitting on a bench, reading quietly. But, as unrealistic as it was, the reading prisoner was imitated. Within days, dozens of E Block's prisoners were sitting on benches, reading quietly.

This encouraged the warden to create more little movies of prisoners doing innocuous activities, or conscientiously doing what was required as part of prison life. Over the years, the number of projections around the prison increased; the quality of the 'acting' improved; and the realism of the projections improved, too. The current warden was now experimenting with hologram projections of obedient prisoners. But this was just fine-tuning. Because the whole experiment was, on the whole, working. There were as many projected prisoners as there were real prisoners. And the real prisoners had lost the ability, if they ever even had it, to differentiate between the real and the projected fellow prisoners around them. The day-to-day life of E Block was a somewhat strange sight, with prisoners roughly mimicking the activities of the looped projections around them. Or were the projections now live footage of the prisoners? Split half and half, were the projections faded shadows of the live prisoners, or were the live prisoners 3-D shadows of the projections?

It was hard to tell. And certainly no one on E Block could 'tell,' or would even consider starting the process of telling.

E Block didn't produce interesting people: prisoners who reformed and went out into the world and made a difference. It produced obedient automata. And there wasn't enough evidence yet about what these automata would do when dislocated from their programming (the projections). There had been some nasty incidents – stabbings, slashings, and killings – when the projector system went down once. The prisoners lost it. But there are crimes in every prison. They are, after all, full of criminals.

But, overall, it works; E Block prisoners are generally an obedient lot. And E Block is very cheap to run – the cheapest in the whole prison. In fact, not one guard is employed on E Block, or one cleaner. The three projected cleaning prisoners are sufficient to ensure that the bare minimum of half-hearted cleaning is done by the actual prisoners. And that, for E Block, is enough.

If you'd prefer to get straight to Breaking Through the Wall of the Story, turn to page 84.

F
BLOCK:
PERFECTIONISM

The warden of F Block is himself a perfectionist. He's driven to create the very best prison block with the best statistics on prisoner behavior and rehabilitation. He is always watching the other blocks' figures and is very tough on his team of guards to make sure that F Block stays ahead. And F Block does perform very well. His idea has always been to instill the same desire for excellence in his team and his prisoners. He wants everyone to feel that they, too, can be the best, and take pride in doing a great job. He wrote all of the wall posts himself. And if one of them isn't motivating enough, it's soon replaced with something better. He didn't just want the posts written on the walls like other blocks either: he had signs made by a local signage company, so they look smart. He had a very clear idea of what he wanted for each of the lines; he even did the designs himself. If the signage company didn't create these 'signs' exactly to his brief, he sent them back. Inevitably, he argued with the owner of the signage company, who believed they'd fulfilled the brief adequately and was reluctant to throw away the sign and start again. But the warden insisted, and got his way eventually. He usually does. And they do now look rather neat on the prison walls:

Be the best you can be.

The good is the enemy of the best.

He particularly likes this one. And he actually imagines a 'good' army fighting the 'best' army. He enjoys watching the best army slaughtering the good army in his mind's eye.

Nobody remembers the runner-up.

Quitters never win and winners never quit.

Reach for the stars and you won't come up with a handful of mud.

He's even created a whole scene on the wall for this one: a star-speckled background to illustrate the idea.

So, it all seems to work: F Block is the top performer, its prisoners the model prisoners, its statistics exemplary.

But if you wander along the immaculate corridors of F Block, adorned by the sparkling, inspirational wall signs, you hear some rather unpleasant exchanges between the prisoners. Let's enter the kitchen, where the inmates are busy preparing lunch for F Block. Oh yes, in F Block, no catering staff are employed. Prisoners cook. Why? Well, prisoners took over years ago when they became unhappy with the quality of the food and decided they could do better themselves. And indeed they do. In fact, the food on F Block is famous in prisons the world over. The food has been featured in magazines and TV shows everywhere. Some of their best chefs have become celebrities and – once released – have gone on to become illustrious chefs. The most famous, Billy Gulliver, a very tall, tough Scot, established the hugely successful Michelin-starred restaurant in London (and now New York, too), called 'F Block' (the 'F' for 'food', you see).

So we're in the kitchen and the current chef is shouting at another prisoner: 'What the f**k are you doing there? Are you feeling ill or something? Because it looks like you've puked into the pan. I wouldn't give that to the warden's dog. I'd prefer the dog to lick my balls than have to give him a plate of that shit mix. Throw it away and start again. And if I don't taste something from you that makes me cry with joy before lunch, I'll get YOU to lick my f**king balls.'

Not pleasant to hear. Not pleasant to watch. And it must be hell to be on the receiving end of that tirade, even if no ball-licking is ever involved.

But when you sit down to lunch an hour later, any distaste at the scene you've experienced instantly evaporates. You have never tasted anything like it. You actually start to contemplate the crimes you could commit to get yourself into F Block. You'd even be happy with a life sentence.

If you'd prefer to get straight to Breaking Through the Wall of the Story, turn to page 84.

G
BLOCK:
LACK
OF
IMAGINATION

G Block is a quiet and relatively civilized place, as prisons go. If Prince Charles turned his ever-active mind to the architectural design of a prison, this is where he'd end up: classical and backward looking. It's pleasant enough, as prisons go: everything is orderly and neat. You know where you are in G block (not that you're likely to forget you're in prison). In fact, you can't fail to know where you are in G Block because there are little maps of the block everywhere for emergency procedures, just like they have in hotels and restaurants. In fact, these small maps are the only things on the walls. Unlike all the other blocks, there's no writing on the walls of G Block. When originally asked by the architects what they would like to write, the reply from the G Block prison team was –

'They're walls. Why would you want to write on them?'

They said it as if the architects were stupid. So the architects went away to write some more great headlines for the inmates of B Block, which was much easier and more fun anyway.

The prisoners in G Block do what's required as part of the prison routine: wash, eat, go into the yard for some exercise and fresh air, and watch some TV. Generally though, they just sit around, not saying much, looking into space. You know those people on the bus or the train who aren't doing anything – not reading, or playing with their phone, or chatting to someone, or looking out curiously at the passing world outside. They're just staring into space. But not in a Zen way, not in a 'I've normally got my head so crammed with stuff, with things to do, with ideas for what to do, that it's nice just to sit here and breathe, like a lovely little meditation on a bus.' No. There's nothing going on in their heads. And NOT in a good way. I mean in a nothing-going-on kind of way. It's not a welcome pause in the play or fast-forward button of a full life. It's like the movie hasn't started. In fact they can't even find the DVD, as there is no DVD because the movie hasn't even been made… or thought of. Maybe because the person who could have thought of that movie is this very person – full of potential, but with their lights switched off.

They're all like that in G Block. There's deadness here. It's not the peace and tranquility of a… er… peaceful and tranquil place. It's the peace and tranquility of a graveyard. And I don't go to graveyards for peace and tranquility. If I go, I go to visit dead people. Welcome to G Block that's full of dead people, but on some kind of miraculous life-support machine that makes them look and act alive. But they're not. Not really. They lack imagination. They don't have the imagination to see that there are other things they could be doing. They don't have the imagination to picture anything beyond what's in front of them, no matter how dire it is. Like frogs that boil to death as the water gets warmer and warmer, they don't even have the imagination to see there's the option of jumping out. So our prisoners in G Block have never even considered there's the possibility of escaping from this prison, and so none of them ever try. It makes life for the guards pretty easy and boring. They too, in fact, sit around looking into space.

STOP PRESS

Or at least stop the process of writing for one moment please, Parkin. I got up this morning to write the next chapter and read this in the Guardian newspaper, under the section 'Prisons.'

Inmate used plastic forks to dig through 5ft wall

A prisoner who dug through a 5ft- (1.5m-) thick wall using plastic forks was caught when brick dust was seen on the ground. Simeon Langford made tools by removing screws from his desk and taping them to plastic forks, then spent weeks chiseling the mortar from the wall of his cell in Exeter prison. He used papier-mâché to cover the hole. The escape attempt was foiled when an officer spotted a pile of debris beneath Langford's window. Langford was being held on remand after attacking three warders at another prison four days before he had been due to be released from an earlier sentence.

Now I haven't mentioned this yet. But it seems like a good time. There's a risk with using this prison metaphor that we fall back on the clichés of prison life we've taken from film and TV. My view of prison is probably part *The Shawshank Redemption*, part *Porridge**, part *Escape from Colditz*, part *Escape to Victory*. And then the numerous movies with some prison scenes (off the top of my head: *The Italian Job*, *The Silence of the Lambs*, *American History X*, etc.). The only prison I've stepped into is Alcatraz, and that closed down in 1963. None of them represent either a modern or accurate representation of what prison life is like in 2012. So if you're reading this in prison, or you know what prisons are REALLY like, please don't be put off by the inaccuracies and lazily ransacked clichés. We're not writing a book about prisons. We're writing a book about freedom. And this prison metaphor helps us to see how we can become free. In fact, our average reader might well relate more to our prison references than a more realistic representation of the true gritty reality of prison life – because our references are probably their references, too.

Now, when we were planning the chapters of *Breaking Through the Walls*, we originally came up with a list of ways to get out of prison such as 'tunneling,' 'escaping through the sewer,' etc. that we could use as analogies to describe therapeutic techniques to break through your walls. We had one escape 'using a kitchen knife.' It's in *The Shawshank Redemption*, isn't it, where Tim Robbins scrapes his way through the wall, then puts up poster to cover the hole. And that's what came to mind. He used a small hammer, which he kept in his hollowed-out Bible. But we thought a kitchen knife would work.

Of course, no self-respecting prison, when you think about it, would have metal kitchen knives. I was thinking that it's difficult to hurt yourself with a relatively blunt eating knife (we're not talking about vegetable chopping knives or carving knives here, of course). But it's probably very easy to hurt someone with even a blunt kitchen knife if you plunge it into their abdomen rather than just try to cut through a tough bit of meat. So, lose the metal kitchen knives. What *do* they use then for cutting meat? Plastic kitchen knives? Well, I'm not absolutely confident you can't do damage with the serrated plastic edge of one of those, either. Do they only supply plastic forks then? What do the prisoners then do with slices of meat or an undercooked carrot? Do the guards come around and cut the prisoners' meat into pieces for them, as you would for a child? When you do it for a child, the most comfortable way is to stand behind the child and put both your arms around them and then cut up their food? Can you imagine the guards doing that? It's just not going to happen, is it? Ah, maybe they only serve minced meat. Maybe they have someone checking all the vegetables to make sure they're not undercooked. Maybe a guard checks every food item with a plastic testing fork (he's called 'Head Forker') to ensure it's possible to be eaten comfortably with only a plastic fork. Or a spoon. They must have spoons, too. Otherwise, what would they do with soup? Yes, they must have spoons.

Which brings us back to Simeon Langford, our real prisoner in a modern prison with his plastic fork.

When I first read the article, I thought *hurrah*, like an excited boy in an Enid Blyton novel. (For anyone not British and of a certain age, Google it. The books are dark and edgy tales for children, and introduce the shadow side of life... the kind of thing Tim Burton would love to adapt into a film.) So I thought 'hurrah' because he was a real prisoner doing what I thought only the imaginative prisoners trapped in my head would do. *Here's a man tunneling out with a fork, not just any fork, a plastic fork,* I thought. Wonderful. It must have taken him months, covering the hole with papier-mâché. Ingenious. Though I still want to know more about this story. The information 'papier-mâché' isn't enough for me. Was the wall painted plaster or bare brickwork?

Either way, how did he make the papier-mâché match the hue and texture of the wall? Did he have paints, too? Who is this man? Is he a set designer who went off the rails? What was his crime? Did he tunnel into a bank vault with a plastic drill? Did he explode the safe door with firecrackers? Did he replace the stolen banknotes with Monopoly money so that no one would notice? Did he use a dodgem as a getaway vehicle? Did he go on the run dressed as Ronald McDonald (no one would think HE would rob a bank!)? Did he lie low by sitting in the one place no one would expect him to hide: in the police station waiting room?

Or did he have a fetish for forks (he found just the word so NAUGHTY), and lifted a handful of forks from every eatery he set foot in? Reported to the police on numerous occasions, he was given warnings (this in not a dangerous crime after all), but just couldn't resist, so was finally imprisoned because of his threat to the cutlery budget of small and struggling local restaurants.

I want to know more. So, if anyone knows more, or if you, Simeon Langford, are reading this, please get in touch. I don't know if it's altogether impossible. Simeon is there trying to turn over a new leaf in prison (or by the time he reads this, maybe, on the outside again), so getting a self-help book with a prison theme might really help.

Back to your exploits, Simeon. Brilliant work with all that digging. Brilliant work with that papier-mâché ruse. But then you went and pushed all the rubble out through the hole so that a guard noticed it under your window. Simeon:

I Have you not seen *Escape to Victory* and numerous other movies, where they take the dust and rubble, put it in their pockets, and release it slowly in the yard? No? Well, if you ever get sentenced again – and I hope that's not the case – spend a few days downloading prison movies. Get a pizza in. Enjoy using a metal knife for the last time in a while.

2 I know what you're saying now: 'How could you get that brick dust out anyway with a fork?' Simeon, Simeon. You needed a SPOON – a plastic SPOON. If you'd just thought to lift a plastic spoon as well as a plastic fork from the canteen, victory and freedom could have been yours for the taking.

But then, Simeon, as one reads more of this very short summary of your escapological antics, one does find the revelation of a fact that is beyond belief. May I remind you?

Langford was being held on remand after attacking three warders at another prison four days before he had been due to be released from an earlier sentence.

Four days? You couldn't wait four days to be released? Was that why you resolved to learn the art of patience? Did you think: *As a test of my newfound quality of patience, I will dig my way out of this Victorian prison-house using only... A PLASTIC FORK?*

Simeon, I hope you make it out next time (via the gate having served your sentence, rather than through the wall). And I hope you use your obvious abilities in constructive ways on the outside, and lead a fulfilling life. I'd even send you a book if I knew where to send it, and I'd sign it –

Fork It.

If you'd prefer to get straight to Breaking Through the Wall of the Story, turn to page 84.

* A '70s UK sitcom set in the fictional Slade Prison and second home to Fletch (played by Ronnie Barker), a kindly and lovable rogue; 'Doing porridge' is British slang for serving a prison term, and the phrase refers to the traditional breakfast served to prisoners.

We threw out two chapters here, because there wasn't room in the end.

But you can read them and other chapters that we had to throw out, and a whole load of interesting stuff that we can't think of now, but will have added by the time you get to read this book...

Here on our website:

www.thefuckitlife.com/extras

H
BLOCK:
BELIEVING
IT'S
REAL

H Block is filled with the materialists, rationalists, literalists, and the atheists along with all those who don't believe anything until a committee of experts and scientists has confirmed it's true. All other apparent evidence to the contrary is discounted as hokum. However, the hokum really enjoys poking fun at H Block by surrounding it and filling it with peculiar phenomena. H Block is where the fairies have their fun, where the angels get some time off from being good, where the wickedest ghosts haunt, and alien entities taunt, where the astonishing coincidences that happen to most people once in a blue moon happen during every cycle of the moon.

However, the H-blockers have a remarkable ability to ignore anything that doesn't cohere with their pre-existing model of how things are.

H Block is like a very sophisticated haunted-house attraction at an amusement park, but populated by graying rationalists who wander around insisting they know how everything is done. Their childhoods are long forgotten. There's no room for magic. And no room for any possibility other than how they think it is.

In one day, a ghost dressed as a guard walked through a prison wall. The prisoner convinced herself she'd imagined it. A fairy went for a swim in Harrison Fairweather's soup, looked him in the eye, and then spurted soup in his face. Fairweather went back to the serving hatch and insisted there was a fly in his soup. For one hour, the spirit of telepathy granted the highest-level telepathic powers to the prisoners, so that everyone knew what every one else was thinking, or knew what they were about to say before they said it. A lot of prisoners spent the hour saying, 'I knew you were going to say that.' But they didn't once suspect they'd been the recipients of a gift of phenomenal paranormal perception.

Later in the day, when one prisoner fell and cut his leg, one of the guards clicked his fingers and the wound instantly healed. The prisoner assumed that the frequent portions of boiled spinach explained the remarkable effect on his blood cells' clotting ability. Jimmy Wagfinger, who had been in a wheelchair since a motorcycle accident in his 20s, got up and danced a Highland jig* for a bet. But once the money was paid, he lost his incentive to dance, so sat down, never to get up again for the rest of his life. Those who saw it wondered whether he'd got hold of some potent drugs, then thought no more of it.

Close to dinnertime, it looked like a storm was on its way. Sure enough the heaviest, darkest storm engulfed H Block. It was ferocious but short. And when the sun came out, if anyone had cared to look out through the barred windows, they'd have seen the prison was now surrounded by an emerald sea, lapping at a beach of golden sand, which before was just the gravel yard. But no one cared to look out.

During the night, the ghosts of those lost on the *Titanic* made an official tour of the block as part of their world benevolence tour; griffins made a huge fire in the gym out of back issues of *Elves Weekly* and danced round it until dawn; God popped in for a flying visit and did a huge crap in the warden's private bathroom; and the prison's pet mouse spontaneously combusted. Luckily, all the sparks from the combustion became tiny baby mice, but with a superior DNA to their mother, which allowed them to squeeze through the eye of an ant sitting on top of a needle balanced on an aniseed ball.

And that was just one day (and night).

If you'd prefer to get straight to Breaking Through the Wall of the Story, turn to page 84.

If you'd prefer to get straight to Breaking Through the Wall of the Story, turn to page 84.

* A traditional dance in Scotland usually performed by burly men wearing kilts.

PART IV

BREAKING THROUGH THE WALLS

FKING
THE
'ITS'**

BREAKING
THROUGH
THE
WALL
OF
THE
STORY

We all have a story, of course we do. Some are good. Some are bad. Most are mixed. And if you're an A Blocker, you'll be stuck in yours.

One interesting element of having to talk to the media after the launch of F**k It was that I realized it was possible to tell your story in many different ways. As someone who doesn't often look back or talk about myself, it was weird to be constantly asked about my story (yes, people always wanted to know what my F**k It story was). The thing is, they wanted to hear my story in just two minutes or 200 words, before going on to the next feature or article, to the next story. And the media, and for the large part, other people, aren't interested in an ordinary story. They want sound bites, highlights, and newsworthy tidbits, stories condensed into headlines. And that's not to criticize the media or other people. We live in a market of information, bombarded with thousands of bits of information (stories), and it's only natural to want the most entertaining ones condensed into delicious, bite-size, memorable morsels.

So, I sliced up my past to see what made a nice story. I was the chronically sick man who said F**k It to fully healing and miraculously healed overnight.

True, but is it my whole story?

I was the man who hit a crisis in my life, physical and emotional, and ended up blubbing like a baby on a train, but realized in a flash of desperate realization that I no longer cared what anyone thought of me, and it changed my sense of self in relation to others forever.

True, but is it the whole story?

I was the son of Christian preacher parents, and I'd explored numerous Eastern spiritual traditions, and fused all the best stuff together into a philosophy based around the Western profanity F**k It.

True, but is it the whole story?

I was the advertising creative and writer who gave up a glamorous career to set up a retreat in Italy. And I was the owner of 'Europe's Best Retreat,' who gave it up to do what I loved best – teaching F**k It through books, gigs, and occasional retreats (in other venues).

True. True. True. True.

So why doesn't it feel like the whole story? Why doesn't any of it feel like the *real* story? Because the real story – the real-time, evolving story called LIFE – is not like that, just as a game of football isn't adequately represented by the 20 seconds of highlights on the sports slot of the late news program. The actual game might not be reflected in either the score or the highlights. One team might have dominated for most of the game – but not scored. The whole game could have been dominated by mediocre play, boring set moves, foul tactics, but the last five minutes saw two such beautiful goals from the most angelic, light-footed players that they will be replayed on TV screens, and iPads, and future pads into eternity. Did they represent the game? No, but they're good to watch.

I am not my story. Even though, the more I'm asked about my story, and the more I have to try to keep it consistent (even if it's boring for me sometimes), the more real it seems to become. I am not my story. And you are not your story. You are a living (usually – my readers do tend to be alive, although I heard recently from Gordon Smith, the medium and author, recently that I have quite a few fans in the spirit world, too), learning, changing, evolving, inconsistent, mixed-up, sometimes f**ked up human being.

Everything around us tends to demand that the story is consistent (just like the media wouldn't like it if I chose a separate 'slice' of my life every time they interviewed me). We want to be consistent. We're not like we were as kids, are we? We had no desire to be consistent then, or notion of what our character was, not when we were young kids anyway. But then people go and spoil it don't they? They tell you what you're like:

'Oooh, you're such a good boy/girl.'

'You are kind, thank you for being so thoughtful.'

Or:

'Do you have to be so selfish?'

'Why can't you just behave like everyone else?'

And you soon become the good, thoughtful boy/girl. Or the selfish, misbehaving freak boy/girl. What you actually are/were is a good/selfish/thoughtful/misbehaving/kind/freak/normal boy/girl.

We all are/were.

It's only this daft idea that we should have a consistent, entertaining story. We probably go through a patch when we try to resist being typecast for life. It usually happens as teenagers. But it's hard work. After a while most of us probably internalize the external desire for the consistent self, and settle into something okay, some median approximation of our many selves, like a tedious politician chosen to represent the many disparate elements of the constituency of Self.

If your story is one of your 'Its,' as it probably is, then F**k It.

Well, F**k It. If your story is one of your 'Its,' as it probably is, then F**k It.

Yes, you will always have a story. And sometimes you'll enjoy telling it. You'll even enjoy believing it. But don't ever forget that it's just a story. Don't ever forget that you're not your story. Story is ego. It's okay, but it can be boring. Life is also ID. No, not the fashion magazine. Google It. Google them both, 'ID magazine,' and 'ID Freud.' ID is the F**k It State.

Hey – and don't worry. You don't have to try very hard with a lot of this. Let it in one ear, and even if some of it goes go straight out the other side, enough of it will settle in the bit in-between to make a difference. A permanent difference.

Now, have I told you that when I was a young man I was nominated for a special prize for the...

Crowd shouts: 'Boring. Get off.'

And he got off. And all that was left on the stage was ID. No, not the magazine.

GAIA'S MAGIC WORDS
Give in to creepdom

At the moment I am totally in love with the song 'Creep' by Radiohead, and I often play it in our groups. (If you don't know it, we've put a link on our site so you can download it – www.thefuckitlife/extras.)

We all want to be 'special' (like the song says) in this wild world: we want to be perfect. But the reality is that we are incoherent; we are always less than we'd like to be; we don't make sense and we can't make sense of our lives; we can't quite ever prove to ourselves that we are good enough.

You see, we are creeps and weirdos.

The moment we realize that, we can give up trying to be normal.

The sooner we stop wanting that flawless body and that immaculate soul, the sooner we start having fun.

*The sooner we give in to our creepdom, the better. Because being a creep gives us all the freedom in the world to f**k up, get lost, look real, just be. And it's sexier than you think (in that uncompromising way).*

BREAKING
THROUGH
THE
WALL
OF
FEAR

If, as a prisoner of B Block, you peeled away the plaster of the walls of fear, beneath all those scary facts and warnings, lies one huge, scary fact: YOU AND THOSE YOU LOVE ARE GOING TO DIE.

Beneath everything you're scared of, everything I'm scared of, everything nearly every single human on this planet is scared of, is the simple fear of death and loss: the constant undercurrent of awareness that *this* is not forever. And what a bloody pain it is. Last night I watched an episode of *Family Guy* that was all about death. (Funny, given I knew I'd be writing this chapter this morning.) Peter Griffin's wife finds a lump in his 'breast' and they think immediately it could be cancer. He initially wants to ignore it, like we all would, but he goes to the doctor. Later, after he's been given the all clear, he's having dinner with his family; he's so happy to be alive and appreciates what he's taken for granted. But there's a knock at the door. You know it's coming, but Chris (his son) opens the door to Death, the grim reaper, come to take his father away. So Peter has to say goodbye to his family. He gets to tell them all he loves them.

His family gets to say goodbye to him. Of course, this is an animated comedy, so it's funny. But... But I felt very sad as he was saying goodbye. I was thinking: *this is remarkable, it's just a cartoon, I don't even know these characters, but I still feel deeply sad.* Of course, I was projecting the scene onto my life; what it would be like to have to say a final goodbye to Gaia and my boys. But that must have been happening more deeply, because what I was feeling in the moment was sadness for him, his wife, and his kids – him, a drawing!

I don't want to go. I don't ever want to go. I don't want to ever have to say goodbye to my family. I want life to last forever.

That's the truth. I want it to last forever. And anything that reminds me that it won't, hurts me. And so many things remind me and us that it's not going to last forever. In fact, almost everything reminds us that it's not going to last forever. And not just the scaremongering media. Even fall makes me feel slightly sad: it's the end of the long, joyous summer – no more lazy days on the beach, no more late evenings eating outside. The fall is the death of summer. Everything in nature retreats and begins to look as if it's dead (though often it isn't dead, it's usually sleeping).

And it's possible to feel that sadness, at loss and potential loss, almost everywhere you look. EVERYTHING MUST GO is the sign in the window of one of the stores on the road outside this hotel. And it's true: EVERYTHING must go, eventually. Not just the cheap bits of furniture in the store that's closing down, but the store's boss, and the building. And every brick of this street and city. Every single person, with their hopes and dreams, and all their family and friends will go. Every living thing, every inanimate thing, every creature, every spoon, every king, every worker, every football player, every watch, every phone, every thought, every memory, every love letter, every tear... must go.

I have a heavy and astonishing book on my desk at home called *Panoramas of Lost London.* And it's heavy and astonishing in myriad ways. It contains photographs of a 'lost' London between 1870 and 1945. Photographs of buildings that no longer exist; places that aren't even a memory for those who inhabit the same space 100 years later; people caught in one moment in their now-passed lives. This book fascinates me. The scenes and the people are familiar enough to relate to: after all, these are our great-grandparents' generation. It's not like looking, for example, at photographs of the Romans in Rome 2,000 years ago (though that would of course be astonishing and mind-blowing in itself, and would make an excellent though expensive photographic project). This is recent history. But it's also another world. The places have changed beyond recognition. The people are long gone. But not just that – their ways of living, the houses they lived in, the stores they shopped in, have long gone, too. It's that intersection of familiarity and lost-forever strangeness that makes the photographs fascinating, moving, and, yes, sad.

Everything must go. It's a fact. But it doesn't mean it's going to be easy to accept.

So is it true for you, when you look deeply into it, that most (if not all) of your fears are founded on your fear of loss, and ultimately of your and others' deaths? Think about it. What are you scared of? Are you scared of losing your job, of your house going up in flames, of becoming ill, of your kids getting killed on the roads, of your portfolio going down in value, of your parents dying, of your looks going, **Say F**k It and face your fears.** of global warming, of gaining weight, of crashing the car, of your hair falling out, of the meeting going badly, of time passing, of missing out, of not using your potential, of nuclear war, of meteorites hitting, of water running out, of your children growing up, of staying where you are, or leaving? What are you scared of? And, underneath, isn't it all about loss?

It strikes me that we have to face this loss thing head on one way or another. It's worth looking at what we're fearful about and understanding the source of that fear. It's worth confronting the fact, the inescapable and unavoidable fact (no matter how hard we try to escape it and avoid it) that Everything Must Go.

F**k It in this context isn't about saying F**k It to fear. That implies we ignore the fear that pulses beneath everything we do and just get on and do things. No, say F**k It and face your fears. And face the big fears underneath your fears.

And here are a few things that might help, as you take steps to confront your fears:

- We're all scared of something. And many of us are scared of quite a few things.

- Even the people who look tough are scared underneath. Read my tough guy mate, Peter M. Hammond's journey through cancer in *The Bad Times Bible* for an insight into how blind fear gets to us all.

- Whatever you're scared of, others are facing day-to-day realities that are much worse.

- It's okay and natural to feel scared, to feel sad, and to cry about it occasionally. I was reading recently about Charles Dickens. Contrary to our stereotypical image of the stiff-upper-lipped English man, apparently Dickens and his male friends would gather together to tell stories, and would weep over the sad parts. Of course, in those days, death was a more everyday experience than it is now (especially in infants). But it didn't harden people to pain, sadness, and fear. They were in touch with that pain and would weep together.

- Try to face the fact of your own death. Accept that it will happen. Try to live in acceptance of your inevitable death, but in a daily love and appreciation of life.

It's a sad cosmic joke that the more we love life, the more we get attached to it, and the more fear and sadness we feel about losing it. In fact, if we're overcome with fear and sadness, which grew out of love and enthusiasm for life and for living, it can lead to depression and less of a desire to live. Maybe that's natural. It's like the natural ebbing and flowing of life's energy: the natural carousel of tension and relaxation, the circular expansion and contraction of the universe. Maybe it's a self-balancing mechanism: we love life more until we love it so much that we can't bear the thought of losing it, until the fear becomes so great that we become depressed and less bothered about losing it, and lose the pain that it might be lost until we start to love life again, and we love life more until we love life so much that we can't bear the thought of losing it… and so on.

I said 'F**k It' to anxiety

*As a 24-year-old female who suffered with anxiety since the age of 16, I cannot express the relief I felt when reading the F**k It books.*

*I used to be a doormat for a number of people and had such crippling anxiety that 'It' prevented me from living my life normally. I remember when I first saw the book in the bookstore. I didn't buy it at first. I was drawn to it, as it stood out from other books in the Self-Help section. I went back the next day, as I honestly could not get the words 'F**k It' out of my head. I bought it and since then I haven't looked back.*

*I said 'F**k It' to the people in my life who decided they could walk over me and treat me like dirt. I said 'F**k It' to the voice inside my head that told me I couldn't do something because I wasn't good enough. I admit I'm not 100 percent cured and still get off-days when I just want to shut myself away. But the beauty is, that I can actually say 'F**k It' to that, too, and have a day where I end up having a threesome with Ben & Jerry, curled up on the sofa watching chat shows. I truly believe that I am finally experiencing and LIVING 'The F**K IT LIFE.'*

– Emma Stone, UK

*Just one of 100 F**k It stories in the new e-book I Said F**k It, available at www.thefuckitlife.com/extras.*

Say F**k It and face that fear. A little bit at a time. See if you can live with the two apparent opposites: love and innocent joy for the boundless gorgeousness of life, with a gentle awareness of its passing nature.

You probably know the story, told in many different ways of the king who wants one nugget of wisdom that can help him through all times, good and bad. His wisest counselors thought long and hard and they came up with this:

THIS TOO SHALL PASS.

Type it out. Print it large. Stick it on the wall. The words should be erected like 'HOLLYWOOD' over all our towns and cities.

In fact, I had the idea, a few years ago, of putting these words, created in metal, on the front wall of our retreat 'The Hill That Breathes.' I wanted people to remember that, as beautiful as the place and experience was, 'this,' too, would pass. Sure, I thought, it might take a long time to pass, but pass it surely would. Even I've been surprised by how quickly it passed, in the form it was at least.

That passed and this, too, shall pass.

BREAKING THROUGH THE WALL OF SERIOUSNESS

We all start off as kids. And kids don't take things that seriously: they play, they're spontaneous, they laugh a lot, they do as they fancy.

And we end up as adults. And adults usually take everything very seriously: they work hard, they worry a lot, they don't play very much, or laugh very much, and they – more often than not – do what they think is their duty, rather than what they fancy.

So, what happened?

We listened to the voices outside, is what happened. The perpetual broadcasting – which C-Blockers are subjected to – is what we get as we grow up. For a while we just have to listen to other kids and their silly broadcasts. But then adults get to insert their message more often. Schools are set up to bring adult messages to kids and thus help them make the transition from kids to adults. And look how successful schools are. They may struggle sometimes to get kids to read and write very well. They may struggle sometimes to persuade their pupils not to fight or carry knives. But what they're very, very good at is turning children from playful, spontaneous, care-free kids into serious-intentioned, care-ful adults.

That's how it is. And it all seems so natural. We train our kids to care: to care for the environment (well that can't be bad, can it?); to care for their family and friends (ditto); to care about doing well; to care about passing exams so they can go to college, get a nice job, to earn nice money, to buy a nice house, to have a nice family, to go on nice trips away, to get a better job, and earn more money, and buy a better house, and enjoy better trips away... And, along with all this, we ask them to care about their health – to eat right and exercise – be a good wife or husband, mother or father, daughter or son, and to be good in the kitchen, and around the house, etc., etc.

We're taught to care, because where would we be if we didn't care?

We're taught to care because adults care.

Why do adults care? Because they like all the stuff that surrounds them and don't want to lose it. And not just the stuff: every aspect of their lives. An adult very quickly gets attached to stuff he or she likes. As we become adults, it's as if we wear Velcro clothing – everything sticks to it. We appropriate everything we like, from stuff we want to the qualities we think work for us, to the idea of being a certain way, or a certain weight, or healthy. It's only natural, but we become deeply attached to everything as we get older. As much as we become attached to, say, our home and a certain standard of living, we become attached to ideas that life should be a certain way.

We're all attached, so we all care. Of course we care. If you don't want to lose something, you care. If you weren't bothered about losing it, or not even having it in the first place, you wouldn't care. And because you care, you're serious about it. If you didn't care, you wouldn't be so serious, would you?

So what on earth is the problem with caring – even if it makes you a little more serious?

The problem is that we care too much about too many things. And that's usually unsustainable – not in the sense of environmental sustainability; though, of course, our deep care for all that stuff is also environmentally unsustainable. In fact, it looks as if our global warming predicament is a bit of a catch-22 on these terms: environmentalists want us to care more all the time, to take things more seriously, yet if we cared less in general, and didn't take things so seriously, we'd probably work less, earn less, spend less, have less stuff, travel less, use less energy... all really naturally.

No, if we care so much about so much, then we're exposed when things change. And things always change. Shares can go down as well as up, of course. And life goes down as well as up. Health goes down as well as up. Relationships go down as well as up. House prices go down as well as up. Job prospects go down as well as up. Weight goes up as well as down. Boobs go down as well as up. Erections go down as well as up. Kids grow up. Global temperatures go up. Ice caps go down. Sea levels go up. The Eastern economy goes up, the Western economy goes down.

But don't get down.

Because, of course, there are things that you'll always care about, and take seriously (and you'll all choose different things).

But the problem is caring too much about too many things. That's why you're working too hard to keep the whole show on the road; that's why you're stressing so much about bits of the show breaking down; that's why you're getting sick of doing the first two things.

So here's a couple of exercises you can do to see what's really important for you.

1 Imagine you're 18 again. Write a letter to the older you (the you of now).

2 Imagine you're 85. Write a letter to the younger you (the you of now).

Go on, do it, you lazy arse. It works a treat*, believe me. In fact, I'll go out for dinner now, do the exercises again myself, and see what comes up. See you later.

John x

Okay, I'm back again.

Well, I don't know what you found out, of course, but the basic message to me was the usual one – jettison the stuff that's weighing me down, stop worrying about things that don't matter in the grand scheme of things... blah, blah, blah.

Think about what it would be like if you took your own advice: imagine what it would be like to care LESS about lots of things in your life (and watch the miracle happen as you're then able to spend more of your care energy on the things that really do matter).

F**k It. It doesn't matter so much.

This act is saying a big F**k It to lots of things in your life that you're currently worrying about.

For us, one of the core meanings of F**k It is this: it doesn't matter so much.

It's one of my favorite F**k It mantras, and I do say it again and again (as you would, with a mantra):

F**k It. It doesn't matter so much.

F**k It. It doesn't matter so much.

F**k It. It doesn't matter so much.

Sing it. Tattoo it on your belly, upside-down so you can read it when you look down.

It's magic I say... it's a magic mantra.

And you know what happens as this magic starts to work? You start taking things less seriously. In a big way. Not because you've had a drink or two, or watched a good comedy, but because you care less.

You're lighter, freer; you, my friend, are becoming a F**kiteer.

Sing that, too, if you fancy…

'I'm lighter, I'm freer, I'm finally becoming a F**kiteer.'

---

* Works brilliantly and is pleasantly surprising.

BREAKING THROUGH THE WALL OF SELF-DOUBT

Those people who give 'feedback' always say they have our interests at heart – especially bosses, teachers, parents. They do it to help us improve, because, otherwise we'd be lost and hopeless. And they remind us of that, too. They believe their place on this Earth is to help us see the light and find the better path and life awaiting us. If only we'd listen to them, take them seriously, see that they're just trying to help us, then we could benefit from their constructive wisdom.

But why does it feel so different? Why does it just feel like we're being nagged? Why do we feel that they're just using this 'I'm-saying-this-for-your-benefit' line to hide behind, when all they're doing is taking out all their insecurities and hang-ups on us? Why? Because they probably are.

The sad fact is that many of us have been (and sometimes still are) subjected to constant criticism, especially as children. Now, of course, parents and adults do need to teach children certain things about behavior. But we all know the difference between:

'Kylie, please wait for everyone else before you start eating.'

And…

'Kylie, why are you so selfish? I have to tell you every single day not to eat before the rest of us. Can't you see that I haven't even sat down yet? I slave away to put a meal on the table for you, and all you want to do is gulp it down and get back to your video games. Do you know how that makes me feel? You wait till you have kids, young lady, maybe then you'll understand.'

Children are free, spontaneous, innocent souls. And that can be beautiful and inspiring to behold. Unless, of course, you're a trapped, stressed, resentful, angry, unconscious adult. In which case that child offers a constant reminder of what you're not – of what you've lost and of what you'll never be again. And that just makes you even angrier, which is wrong and unfair. If you've had a shit life, why should they sit there feeling so free? Of course, you'd never think about that, or realize that. Otherwise, the pain might start to penetrate that frosted-up heart. No, you're doing this for their benefit. And we've seen you doing this for their benefit outside school, in the restaurant, in the grocery store:

'Kylie, would you stop messing around. Just keep up. I've got lots to do here. No, you can't have any Cheerios. Do you know how much they cost? You think money grows on trees? You wait till you have to earn some money around here, then you'll realize. You're just so selfish.'

That, and a similar range of comments, is what we hear every day, and heard as kids.

Now listen, I'm a parent, I know parenting is no piece of cake. It's close to impossible not to let your stuff get mixed up in the game occasionally. You lose your patience with your children more because something has upset you at work than because what your children have done justifies it. We've all done it. We all do it. We'll all continue to do it. But, please, stay conscious; know when it's you and when it's them. And go easy on the little ones.

And go easy on yourself – even when you're not going so easy on the little ones.

Go easy on yourself because no one else has been. So it's up to you. You see, all that criticism you've been subjected to, no matter what the motivation was, has had its effect. It always has its effect. Sure, some of the effects might apparently be positive. You might be a very polite, considerate person. But it also has many negative effects. Because what all those adults were saying (with your best interest at heart, of course) was 'You're wrong. You're doing wrong. You're not up to much. You're not good enough.'

That's the message we receive: YOU'RE NOT GOOD ENOUGH. And we receive it from people who are giants in our world: the parents and teachers who dominate our world, whom we often look up to, and sometimes love, too. But these giants are telling us, YOU'RE NOT GOOD ENOUGH, YOU'RE NOT GOOD ENOUGH. When we're told, 'Can you just try, for once, to keep your bloody room tidy please?' We hear, YOU'RE NOT GOOD ENOUGH. When we try our hardest at school and are told, 'Could do better, could try harder,' we receive, YOU'RE NOT GOOD ENOUGH.

And not just as kids. When we miss that job opportunity, when we get that work review, when we're dumped in a relationship, when we get to the meeting late and they look at us in that way, we receive, YOU'RE NOT GOOD ENOUGH.

So, slowly, but inevitably, we start to feel I'M NOT GOOD ENOUGH. Until we feel that, in almost every way, I'M NOT GOOD ENOUGH. And we doubt ourselves in everything we do. And become hard on ourselves. And push ourselves harder. But the voice is always there – 'I'M NOT GOOD ENOUGH.' And because we're now so deep in self-doubt (and the doubt is always 'AM I GOOD ENOUGH?'), we become hard on others, too. So we start to tell those around us, in one way or another, YOU'RE NOT GOOD ENOUGH. And the stinking cycle continues, knocking the self-esteem out of millions of people every day, as more and more people slip into chronic, and possibly permanent, self-doubt.

So, what to do?

Well, you have to start saying F**k It to those voices and that programming. Because it is a form of programming. You can see that with what was happening in D Block. If you're told perpetually that you're not doing well enough, then of course you start to believe that you're not doing well enough. In fact, what happens for most of us is that we internalize the external voices over time. So there's a good chance that the things you tell yourself all day long are actually other people's voices you've internalized. It's true, isn't it? If you listen hard enough to the nonsense that goes on in your brain every day, you can actually recognize the source of some of those voices. Oh, yes, that's my dad's voice all right, or that's my ma, or that's Aunt Mabel, or that's Mr. Pipkins.

Start to say F**k It to those negative voices and influences. Then the key to healing is in the very phrase 'self-doubt.' What's the opposite of doubt? Trust? So replace self-doubt with self-trust. Start to trust what you feel more. Start to trust that what you do IS good enough. Learn to tune into what's actually going on for you. Learn to tune in to what you actually want to do. Learn to tune in to what you actually think is the right thing to do in a situation.

> ## Say F**k It to those negative voices and influences.

And to do this tuning in, we need to say F**k It to those voices and messages from outside – and all the bits that have seeped into our brains.

For example:

You love music. And, 20 years ago, at school, you used to play the piano. And you've realized that you'd like to start playing again… because you used to love it.

Thing is, they didn't think you were up to much. The piano teacher seemed to prefer other pupils and always put you down. So you gave it up and never thought any more about it. Until now…

And, as you realize that you'd like to start playing again, you think, *Don't be silly, you were never any good at that, why would you want to do it now?*

So, here's the trick: recognize it's the voice of your piano teacher, internalized. Say F**k It to that voice. And listen to (TRUST) that other voice within you that says 'I'd love to play the piano again, I used to really love it.' With consciousness, you can differentiate between these voices. With trust, you can start to break through the thick old walls of self-doubt. And with a frequent F**k It to those voices, you can move rapidly from self-doubt into perpetual self-trust instead.

BREAKING THROUGH THE WALL OF LACK OF CONSCIOUSNESS

The unconscious prisoners in E Block never try to escape because they're not even aware they're in prison, just as they're not aware that many of the prisoners are mere projections. They don't examine anything. They are as uncurious about what's around them as they are about what's going on inside their heads. They blindly follow. They go through the motions. They're slaves to what they're told, just as they are slaves to what they feel. The odd E-Block prisoner occasionally goes bonkers because he or she has no idea what's going on inside. So the unconsciously suppressed rage occasionally bursts out. The unconscious E-Block prisoner is a human machine, susceptible to programming, but prone to malfunction because of its unsophisticated circuitry.

But it's no surprise that E-Blockers are as they are, and that many of us are like them. It takes a lot to be conscious, to be fully conscious. It's easier to follow instructions from parents, schools, society, and the media. It's easier to toe the line, follow the herd, keep your head down, and not think too much. It's easier to ignore any difficult feelings and switch on the TV instead. It's easier to keep your mouth shut than to tell the (often uncomfortable) truth. It's easier to subtly dissemble than to be straight and clear. It's easier to skirt around the issue than to tackle it head on. It's easier to stay in a job or a relationship you can't bear than face the harsh reality of an unfulfilling life, and the grim, cold possibility of finding an alternative. Better the devil you know. It's easier to stay in your warm comfort zone. It's easier to keep quiet than stand up and speak out. It's easier to put up and shut up. It's easier to follow than to lead.

After all, who do you think you are, thinking you know better, that you've got a right to tell me the 'truth'? Who are you to step out of line, to make a scene, to upset the apple cart? Things are fine as they are. Your kind isn't needed around here. We're happy, as we are, thank you very much.

It takes a lot to be conscious. Being conscious involves looking at yourself, who you are, what you are, what you do in the cold light of day – and facing the facts of what you see. Being conscious involves looking around at what's going on, at what people are doing – and facing the facts of what you see. Being conscious involves telling it how it is, when you think you know how it is. It means speaking your mind, no matter what the consequences. Being conscious involves a constant examination of what's going on – and being clear about it. It means facing the facts no matter how unpalatable those facts might seem.

And they often are unpalatable. Because the reason most of us go unconscious in the first place is because the facts of who we are, what we feel, and what's going on around us are too unpalatable to face head on.

So being conscious means facing things head on.

And that takes courage.

And it can feel a bit cold and tough, because it is sometimes cold and tough out there in the conscious world.

And here's how it softens, and becomes warmer…

When you do finally face the facts, however difficult that might seem, and you feel the pain of facing those facts, things do – eventually – become easier. You come to terms with things. You find your peace with things. You find your peace with yourself, however you are, whatever you do. You find your peace with the world around you, however it is, whatever it's doing. The facts, when initially confronted, are very difficult to look straight in the eyes. When you do look at them, it's uncomfortable; it can be painful. But after a while, you see the eyes softening and you soften, and you might even see love deep in those eyes that you were so afraid to look into. Because in everything we think we might find difficult, deep down, there is love. That's hard to imagine now. And it's hard to see at first.

But before you see love, when you start to become more conscious and face those facts, you start to feel freer. Yes, you think you've been feeling okay when you've shut your eyes to the facts, gone unconscious, and done whatever it's taken to block it out (suppressed, ignored, watched TV, eaten huge amounts of food, been polite, not mentioned anything, gotten drunk, taken drugs, stayed in line, kept your head down,

Say F**k It and make yours a conscious life.

etc., etc.,). The chocolate cake and the warm bath were lovely, weren't they? But the problem didn't go away, did it? In fact, it's not just that the un-faced problems and issues don't go away, they multiply, because they want your attention. And when you give them attention, that's when they soften, and you see the love.

Staying conscious takes guts. You have to say F**k It again and again. Because your instinct will be to ignore and go unconscious. Say 'F**k It, I will face the facts. Say 'F**k It, I will face the facts of myself and my life, and of life out there.' It takes a tough, clench-your-fists type of F**k It to do this. But it's worth it.

And F**k It has its two sides, of course. F**k It is always about drawing on the courage within you and really going for it, AND it's about giving up when it's too much. So, in your pursuit of greater consciousness, do fall back at times into the warmth of unconsciousness. There's nothing like chilling out, tuning out, blocking it out, sleeping it out when you've had your fill of facing the facts.

Just don't make a life out of it.

Say F**k It and make yours a conscious life.

BREAKING
THROUGH
THE
WALL
OF
PERFECTIONISM

You have in your hands the product of perfectionists (assuming at this moment that you're holding this book, of course. If you're reading this on an iThing, then you'll also have the product of one of the world's most famous perfectionists in your hands, of course. RIP. Though I can't imagine Mr. Jobs is resting, or in peace, up there. He's probably gotten to work on a whole host of stuff in Heaven. It's only a matter of time before someone in Brazil experiences a sign from God that is cooler, simpler, and more powerful than any previous sign from God. Everyone will flock to Brazil to experience one of God's new signs. But God isn't flooding the market with Signs. He likes to keep His flock wanting more Signs. And even those who've experienced this year's Signs, when He appears again with new and better Signs, they'll be happy to trade in their previous experience of His Signs on eBay in an attempt to experience one of the new Signs. But will anyone recognize the hand of Jobs in the Signs of the hand of God? Not at first. But after a few years, an article appears in a small provincial newspaper in a rural backwater in France – well, surely it must be a practical joke – but the carved wooden statue of Madonna in the local church changed subtly overnight... in her outstretched, upturned palm (clearly in supplication to the Lord) was a carved, wooden... apple.

We F-Blockers are perfectionists. We spent months just planning this book. We spent one month just getting the cover right. We worked 16-hour days writing it, drawing it, checking it, and adjusting it. We threw out many ideas. We threw out many chapters. We had many late nights and early mornings (it's currently 5:30 am). We wouldn't let anything in the book or about the book go out without us checking it, adjusting it, and approving it. And hopefully you're enjoying the fruits of that perfectionism. We hope it's better because of our unending pursuit to make this expression of F**k It Therapy the very best we could make it.

So, assuming that you're enjoying the book, and it's genuinely helpful and inspiring for you, why would you (if you, too, are a perfectionist), want to 'break through the walls of perfectionism?' Why would we want to break free of our perfectionism, when it seems to create such good results?

Well, working 16-hour days has its effects. I (and this is John, deliberately excluding Gaia, because it applies more to me than her) haven't seen my boys for a week. When I'm fully stretched writing at home, I can be grouchy, moody, distracted, and stroppy. I am not that pleasant to be around when I'm up against a deadline or want my way about something. And I usually do want my way. I think I know best how things should look, or sound, or be expressed, or presented. I think I know best about a lot of things. And that makes me a pain in the backside sometimes.

Of course, that's not all I am, and I'm not like that all of the time. But I can be like that, and I'm just exposing the worst of me so you really get the picture. That side of me justifies such behaviors by alluding to the people on this planet who do really great things and achieve great success in what they want to do. They're often not very pleasant people to be around, to work with, or for. I'm probably much nicer than they are actually (mainly because I've largely figured out the 'conscious' thing). But still, I can be darned unpleasant at times.

So all that is a reason to look at perfectionism and whether it's really a prison you could do with breaking out of.

One option, of course, is to say F**k It and give up your obsessive drive for excellence. Decide it's not worth the hassle, the pain, the arguments, the tiredness, the frustration, the people you upset. No matter how successful you are or how brilliant your designs, creations, and projects, it's just not worth it. Become friends with the enemy, 'good' and abandon the 'best.' Get away more. Spend more time with the kids. Delegate more. Drop your principles. Get out of the office. Join the mediocre club: it's full, but its members are much more relaxed.

This takes a big F**k It, but it's possible. You have to say F**k It to a lot of things that have become very natural to you. But the new stuff that suddenly fills your life has to be more important to you than the drive you're leaving behind.

I have tried this route. And it worked, to a degree. But it's not for me.

Next option: become very good at saying 'no.' Only commit to a very few things. That way, you get to do everything yourself, you get to work hard in bursts. You get to stay in control, have your way. You manage to create exactly what you want, to the level you want. This means saying F**k It to many opportunities. Because you're a perfectionist, you're probably very good at what you do, so you get lots of offers to do more.

The whole F**k It thing has done very well, and is getting bigger all the time. And this success means we've had lots of offers to do great things. We've had invitations to do workshops and retreats all over the world; we've had offers to write articles and books, etc., etc. We've learned to say 'no' – no matter how tempting the offer – if we know it'll be too much for us. We've learned that this tiny word, 'no,' is a very powerful tool for making one's perfectionism manageable. Three great words, then: 'F**k It. No.' Okay, with four, you're really cruising: 'F**k It. No, thanks.'

And it's not just the offers we get from other people. We have so many ideas about new things we could do. So we have to say 'no' a lot to ourselves and to each other, too. We only say 'yes' to ideas that really excite us. The ones we think would also really excite everyone else – which is why we made 'F**k It Chocolate' happen. I love chocolate. And I have to say F**k It when I eat chocolate. So, to create a bar of delicious organic chocolate with 'F**k It, Eat Chocolate' on the label thrills me.[†]

That's one option – and the one we usually go for. It still requires bursts of hard work, and the occasional stint of relentless effort (such as writing this book), but that's the balance... it's worth it because of the satisfaction we get from the product and its effect on other people... the hundreds of emails we receive saying 'thanks' remind us that, yes, it's worth it.

Next option: find very (very) good people to help you. Find the very best in their field. Be willing to pay more for people who will give you more. Learn how to delegate, nurture, mentor, and teach other people to do what you do. Invest time in finding the best people to help you, and invest time in helping them develop in their role. You're probably after perfectionists.

Find people who are better than you at some of the things you do. That, itself, takes some guts. Perfectionists want to be the best. So it is, in a peculiar way, more comfortable to be surrounded by people who aren't so great at their jobs: it confirms your view that you're the best, and 'if you want a thing done well, do it yourself.' Your ego is boosted, but so are your stress levels. Better to find people who are better than you.

We're lucky to work with amazing people, and people who are better than we are at certain things. To name just a few amazing people: Hay House, our publishers; Rachel and Saul at F**k It HQ, who support us in everything we do; Marc Wisbey, who looks after all things web for us. Kate at Kdot Online for getting us talked about; Sue Okell for getting the F**k It Therapy online course out there*; Andrea for his design genius. Simone for his musical genius; and everyone else who helps us in one way or another.

We now go for the last two options mentioned above, and it feels like a good balance. And if things ever get out of balance, we just F**k It to get the balance back. That's the point of F**k It actually – whichever side you end up on, when things feel out of balance, F**k It gets the balance back.

When things feel out of balance, F**k It gets the balance back.

---

* Find a link to the F**k It Therapy online course at www.thefuckitlife.com/extras.

† And F**k It Chocolate can thrill you too. It's available in the F**k It Shop at www.thefuckitlife.com

BREAKING THROUGH THE WALL OF LACK OF IMAGINATION

Now, I intentionally, and rather joyfully, went off on one* when I was writing about Simeon and his plastic fork when I was writing about G Block. Because if I let my imagination run away with me, it really does. It runs away with me to magical kingdoms where fairies work in nail bars and bankers have to clean one public toilet for every one percent of bonus they earn. Upon hearing news of this banker 'tax,' shares in high-quality cleaning fluid company 'FLUSHED' went through the roof.

I generally don't go off on one. When I'm writing, I like to stick to the point. Sure, I'll make the point in as entertaining a way as possible. But still, I prefer to stick to the point.

In life, too, I like to live my life as entertainingly as possible, but I still tend to stick to the point (the point being usually something like: get up; get the boys washed, fed, and off to school; deal with emails; deal with business; eat something; exercise a bit; do some more emails and a bit of Facebook; eat something else; hang out with family; watch something diverting; and go to bed. Overall point? To support my family, to enjoy it, and to get liberating messages out there occasionally through words and music.)

But sometimes I have to go off on one.

I especially have to go off on one if I somehow feel trapped again (by any of our prison qualities, such as 'believing it's real,' for example), or have wandered off my point (by, for example, doing stuff that I don't really want to do).

And if you're in prison somehow, however you're trapped, 'going off on one' could be just the thing you need to do because being trapped is almost always accompanied by the lack of imagination to get out, as we saw in G Block.

If I had a piece of milk chocolate with little toffee pieces for every time someone has said to me: 'I'm really unhappy in my job, but I've got no idea what else to do,' I'd be a very happy man.

No, let me correct that, sorry:

If I had a piece of milk chocolate with little toffee pieces, and could eat them all without putting on any weight or getting an uncomfortable sugar high or a headache or anything, for every time someone has said to me: 'I'm really unhappy in my job, but I've got no idea what else to do,' I'd be a very happy man.

Please people, say F**k It, and USE YOUR IMAGINATION. Have a glass of wine or a beer if you need to. Have a candlelit bath, if that's your thing. Men, wear women's underwear if that's what relaxes you. Women, watch a movie about war if that's what relaxes you. But find some time and some space to use your imagination.

And, with your trapped thing in mind, start dreaming. It doesn't have to be good; it doesn't have to be doable or realistic at this point. This is your time to dream. Don't fix your dreams just yet; that'll be a job for later (in the book). For now, just dream away.

Go on. Have a go now, because I'm about to give you some pointers to help you if you're struggling. So, if you think you're big enough to do this without any pointers, toddle off now and get going, big boy/girl.

Pointers. Okay, let's find some pointers to make the points... dum dee dum, here we go...

Let's say we're talking about what you do for a living, as we often are...

- Where do you get your kicks in life? Make a list of everything that gives you a kick. Spend days doing this if you want. Most of us don't stop to consider where we get our joy in life. To do so means that you're more likely to increase the joyful bits and reduce the dodgy bits if you can.

- Next, where did you used to get your kicks in life? (This question is based on the observation that life has a sneaky way of eating away at the things that we love doing and replacing them with things that we do out of duty or necessity instead.)

- Next, where could you imagine you could get kicks that you've never experienced before and don't presently indulge in. For example, I've never kitesurfed, but I imagine that I'd like it very much, so that goes down on my list. The same goes for buying 1,000 clothes pegs (my favorite household item, incidentally, and if you ever want to buy me a gift, you can't go far wrong than with a set of bespoke wooden clothes pegs – maybe you could paint them yourself) and turning these 1,000 pegs into a modern sculpture of an open, cupped hand (and what this would say to the observer would be 'we are clothes pegs, we spend our lives holding others and, well, we'd like to be held ourselves, maybe in the warmth of an soft and open human palm, for example'). It would be very moving.

- So you have your lists of all that does, has, and could give you your kicks, Mr. Pips. So how the flockety crotch do you make a living out of it, Mr. Pitt? Glug the wine, feel the pull of the silk panties, enjoy the exploding of a grenade because now's your chance to... officially... GO OFF ON ONE.

Oh bloody hell. I know you'll soon start telling me that you can't make a living out of THAT.

Well, keep going for now. Don't worry about that.

I recall a F**k It Day we ran in London last year when we asked people to do this exercise. And that inevitable question came up: 'But I couldn't make a living from THAT, could I?' Actually, though it ends in a question mark, it was more of a statement than a question. You understand? There's a subtle difference in inflection on that 'could I' that turns it from a humble, inquiring question into a rather aggressive statement of fact, and a fact of a blindingly obvious nature.

So I, in my enthusiasm, foolishly threw down a challenge to the crowd of 80… a challenge that probably overestimated my on-the-spot-entrepreneurial genius. I said:

'I bet I can find a way to make money from anything that you suggest.'

Now, what I had on my side was that they were all thinking about things they LOVED doing. It wasn't that they were just sitting there thinking, 'Let me find something that you so obviously can't make money out of that John will look like an idiot in front of 80 people.'

Nobody, for example, said:

'John, I've never done this, but it's what I'd really, really love to do.'

'Yes…' I'd have said, with not a little trepidation.

'John, I'd like to knock one out†, on stage at Wembley‡, in front of 100,000 people to the beat of 'Bohemian Rhapsody' by Queen. In fact I'd insist that the real queen was in the audience. She could have a royal box if she wanted. But for the whole of my 'show,' her reactions would be relayed live via one of the huge screens that flanked the stage, while the other screen would show my… er… show.'

Why he bottled out on that relatively innocuous word given the content of his suggestion will baffle me to my dying day.

If they had, would I have been able to respond with a moneymaking scheme to make his Wembley fantasy possible? Maybe not, but I can already see several ways how just the idea could make him some money. For example, he would have had some rights on the use of his idea in this, our book... so I would have had to pay him something in order to use his suggestion to make my point.

Which was...

Yes, this is what someone asked. In fact, that someone was the wonderful Gemma Birss, who is a journalist at *Prediction* magazine.

'I'd like to meditate all day, every day. How on earth can I make money from that?'

And that was a good start for me. Because, by a quite remarkable coincidence, I'd had an idea a few weeks previously for a huge project involving hiring meditators to go into 'problem' urban areas of the UK, to rent an apartment in the area, and sit meditating all day, every day. You see, it's been demonstrated that if a certain proportion of the population are meditating, then crime levels drop. So that was my thought. The project has a great name, which I won't tell you because it hasn't happened yet (though it might never happen, like many things that pop up in my head).

Everything starts with a thought. Even human life (I must F**k It).

But I had a very quick and true answer for Gemma: 'I know how.'

The truth is, in a world where you can buy just about anything or any service over the web, and thus reach huge audiences or niche audiences in far-off places very easily, it's possible to make money from almost anything.

But the point here isn't about making truckloads of cash – though that might be the 'kick' you're after, I suppose. The point is to do what you love and make a living from it.

For now, whatever prison you're trapped in: relax, and go off on one... use your imagination to dream your way out, to dream of other possibilities and other worlds...

Everything starts with a thought, everything. Think about it, even human life (I must F**k It).

---

* To digress and often at some length and fervently, but as Laurence Sterne wrote 'Digressions, incontestably, are the sunshine.'

† Also described as 'spank the monkey,' 'throttle the snake,' 'shake hands with a close friend,' etc., – but, perhaps, more universally known as 'to masturbate.'

‡ Wembley is the ultimate dream sporting and music venue for any Brit wanting to showcase their skills in front of a big crowd. Look it up on Google – it's a lovely place.

BREAKING THROUGH THE WALL OF BELIEVING IT'S REAL

You might not be so lucky as to experience such a range of extraordinary phenomena as those on H Block during that day. Not that they appreciated it, of course. They have the universe of magic putting on a show for them every single day and they don't notice a thing.

But are you so different? Maybe the universe is putting on a magic show just for you, every single day of your blessed life, and you – like the H-blockers – haven't noticed a thing.

Is it all as 'real' as you think it is? Are the solid things as solid as you think they are? Are you as separate from other people as you think you are? Is 'cause' always followed by 'effect'? Are coincidences just that, or is there a link you don't understand? Is all organic matter dictated just by the scientific laws that we know already, or is there something else to it all, an 'energy'?

It's possible to challenge any assumption we have about what we are and our place in the universe. And, of course, people have been challenging their assumptions since assumptions were first had.

Everything we think of as solid, is nothing of the sort: it's all energy in one form or another (according to physicists, as well as gurus and qigong masters). So, in theory, we could all walk through walls, just like in *The Matrix*. Uh?

You think you're separate from everyone else? Haven't you experienced the strange coincidences when you were thinking of someone and they called you? Or when you knew what someone was going to say before they said it (it happens to our twin boys all the time… maybe because twins are more tuned into this ability, but it's remarkable to see this phenomenon playing out in front of your eyes every single day of your life). What connects us? Thoughts? Energy?

In 1983, Braud and Schlitz, researchers into consciousness, conducted an experiment into whether one's intention could influence another person's state. A nervous person would sit in one room and someone in another room would use intention to calm them down. By measuring the electrodermal activity (EDA) of the nervous person, the researchers could then tell if the calming intentions were having an effect. And they were – a huge effect. In fact, the third parties were having a calming effect on the nervous people that was almost as great as when the nervous people used relaxation techniques themselves. So someone having good thoughts about you is almost as beneficial as you having good thoughts about yourself. How is this possible? Uh?

Read Lynne McTaggart's excellent book *The Field*.

You think your physical state is separate from your thoughts? A study was done in 2004 in which 15 volunteers were asked to flex and contract one of their little fingers for 15 minutes every day for 12 weeks. And another group of 15 volunteers were asked to just imagine doing the same thing, for the same amount of time.

The strength of the fingers of all the volunteers was tested before and after the 'training.' Those who actually moved their fingers increased their strength by 53 percent. And those who just imagined moving their fingers increased their strength by an astonishing 35 percent.

This means that, instead of going to the gym, you could lie at home on the couch, just thinking about doing the exercises at the gym and the results wouldn't be far off. (I'd like to see the first Mr. Universe who never lifted a dumbbell, but just thought about it.)

Dr. David Hamilton tells that story in his excellent book, *How Your Mind Can Heal Your Body* and, rather entertainingly, in his regular talks.

You think that when you sit still and quietly, the only benefit is for you? Think again. In 1972, an experiment was done in the US that confirmed the so-called 'Maharishi Effect,' after Maharishi Mahesh Yogi, who stated that if one percent of the population meditated regularly, there would be a reduction in crime and violence. So in this experiment, carried out across 24 towns with populations of 10,000 or more, there were indeed meaningful changes in crime levels when as few as one percent of the population participated (using transcendental meditation).

Gregg Braden details the above experiment in his excellent book, *The Divine Matrix*.

You believe that what you're seeing is 'reality': that it's a fixed, objective thing? Watch the movie *What the Bleep Do We Know!?* and learn about the baffling and magical world of quantum physics, when what you see is only fixed as 'what you see' when you actually see it, fixing itself from the limitless possibilities of reality only when viewed.

You believe that even your view of reality, once fixed, is an accurate version of what's 'out there?' It's not really. Look at color, for example. Your eyes and brain work very hard to create the visual picture in your brain that you think of as reality. What's 'actually' out there? The answer is an ocean of electro-magnetic radiation with a vast range of wavelengths, most of which are invisible to you. And the 'stuff' that you think is emitting such wavelengths is in itself mainly empty space anyway. What's out there? Nothing much. The vivid colors of the 37 ice creams I find in our local *gelateria* are not actually properties of the ice cream: they're properties of my 'model' of the ice creams, a model created by my brain, in my brain.

Uh? Read *The Ego Tunnel (the Science of the Mind and the Myth of the Self)* by Thomas Metzinger. It's brilliant. But you might end up saying 'Uh?' even more than while reading this chapter.

Read all or any of the books I've mentioned and concluded that we're now discovering amazing things about life, the universe, and everything? Think again. Masters, gurus, mystics, seers, shamans of all races, spiritualities, and philosophies have perceived such phenomena for thousands of years.

You think you know anything? F**k It. Think again.

F**k the theories; the fixed positions. F**k the religions that believe they, and only they, have the answer. F**k the dogmatists, the rationalists, and the materialists. They deal with dead ideas.

If you want to find a position, go join the Agnostics Club. An agnostic is cool. An agnostic is not uncurious or indecisive. An agnostic looks at the infinite mystery of life and the universe in wonder. He or she enjoys wondering, too, how it all works but recognizes something in a perception of utter humility – *I'm never going to know for sure, and I'm cool with that.*

F**k It will allow you access to some wondrous magic. Magic may well flood into your life as you start to practice F**k It in one way or another. But you want me to

*Magic may well flood into your life as you start to practice F**k It in one way or another.*

give you the definitive explanation for how it all works? You want a map of the paradigm? Think again. For now, let's stick with the map of this prison and how to get you the f**k out of it.

And what an appropriate time to talk about the *Breakout Tools* and helping you to *Walk Through Walls.*

PART V

A GUIDE TO THE BREAKOUT TOOLS

HOW
F**K
IT
WORKS

F**K
IT.
LET
IT
GO

(Music to play while reading this chapter: ambient, trip-hop, chill-out, though not 'Chill Out Classics.')

You may have already noticed from the way we've been talking about F**k It, that it goes in one of two directions. Letting go, slowing down, giving up, is the first – and the most easily understood. In fact, most people assume F**k It is *just* about this. And it is actually the predominant quality of F**k It required in society today.

Look at anyone around you. Look in the mirror. And tell me what you see.

You probably see someone who is working too hard, who has little time for the things that really matter, who's tired, often stressed, worrying about things that might never happen, striving to do better, to be better, always trying to get to next thing, the next level, that will hopefully end in their/your happiness.

So F**k It works very powerfully when you realize that most of those things you're worrying about aren't so important after all; that it's possible to give up on stuff that's causing you pain, to do less, relax more, and go with the flow of life instead of trying to make everything happen and work all the time.

For them/you, it can help to think about the idea of 'taking your hands off the steering wheel.' And it's never been a better time to tell you why. Most of us believe that, unless we grip the steering wheel of life and steer in various directions in order to get to where we want to be, nothing will happen (or, even worse, we'll crash). And the gripping of the steering wheel, the constant steering, and trying to work out which way to steer, can be very tiring – exhausting, in fact.

But what would happen if you took your hands off the wheel?

You'd crash, of course. Really? Well, maybe your passenger would intervene and help. Or maybe the car would steer itself. What? Yes. It's possible. In fact, I read just yesterday that self-driving cars have just become legal in Nevada in the USA.

Isn't that wonderful? When I talked about 'taking your hands off the steering wheel' in my first book, seven years ago, I had to use the analogy of being on a car ride for children at an amusement park. I remembered that when I was a small boy I believed I was actually driving, but slowly (and very disappointingly) realized that I wasn't, and that the car was on a track, and would effectively steer itself. I made the point that, though it was disappointing to me then, it would probably be a great relief for most adults, who are tired of driving, to take their hands off the steering wheel, and let the car steer itself.

And now it *is* possible. Google, in fact, cracked it first. And it's Google's cars that will be the first to self-drive (well, with people in them, of course, checking that the software doesn't fail or that decide they want to try to fly).

So, in the car of life that you've been driving – the one you thought you were in control of, and had to steer successfully to get anywhere – well, there's a chance that, if you did take your hands off the steering wheel, it would drive itself. Life's a Google Car.

Come on Google, let's brand this one: 'Google Life – relax, we'll do the driving.'

But, yikes, how does that work? Surely, it would all go to pot if I simply stopped 'steering.' Well, try it. Take your hands off the wheel just for a little while and see what happens. If you're trying hard to make something (anything) work, see what it's like to ease off and not strive so much, to sit back and see what happens.

You may well be in for one helluva journey.

So this is how F**k It works for most of us: we're trying too hard, striving too much, over-controlling, over-worrying, over-working, over-thinking, and over-cooking everything.

It's time to take the F**k It chill pill, and slow it all down, give up a few things, do less, try less, control less (if at all), under-perform, trust it will work out, go with the flow, think less, and generally enjoy your life more.

It's time to take the F**k It chill pill.

But that's only one direction: the one most people need to take.

Most people understand it. But some people say:

'Yes, that's all very well. But if I did all that, I'd get nothing done. I'd end up lying in bed then getting up and sitting on the sofa watching TV all the time, eating pizza, getting fat, lose my job, have no friends… It would be a disaster.'

And I reply:

'Try it.'

If they did (which they won't), but if they did, they would soon get bored of lying in bed, or watching TV, or vacationing, or doing nothing. And that's when the next F**k It direction would kick in. Read on…

F**K
IT.
GO
FOR
IT

(Music to play while reading this chapter: thrash metal, urban electronica, dubstep, hip-hop.)

You're sitting on your sofa, eating Häagen-Dazs all day, getting fat. You don't know what to do with your life. And you can't be arsed*. You like to sleep. You like to smoke weed. You watch the TV for 12 hours non-stop. You go to sleep with the TV on. You have no idea what job you'd like to do. So you drift from dead-end job to dead-end job.

That's not you, is it? No. Well, not most of you, anyway. I know, because we get lots of e-mails. And they're usually from stress monkeys who've become chilled chimps with the help of F**k It. We don't get many e-mails saying:

Yo J&G,

Just dropping you this missive(ile?) to say THANKS, dudes. I was like really down, totally out of it, high on smack most of the time, down on Dazs the rest of the time. But your F**k It message really pulled me up, man. I wouldn't be where I am now without you.

Where am I? McKinsey's no less. Suited, booted, and loaded[t]. Top dog in 'change management' and there's no change in my six-digit pay packet, just notes, and big ones.

Cheers,

Alex Jermin-Smithe

Maybe this is you.

You've somehow drifted into a life that isn't yours. You had plenty of dreams, so how did you end up in this job, with that man/woman, living in this town? It doesn't make any sense. Where did it all go wrong? Is it because you were scared of failing, that you didn't go for it? Is it because it felt like the best option at the time – everyone else took that route, so you did, too? But now, you don't know what to do, where to go. You've no idea what you should be doing; you just know this is not *it*. You hope to God this is not *it*, anyway.

This direction of F**k It is for those of us who've gotten stuck in a rut, lost our way, forgotten our dreams, settled for the safe route, listened too much to what others wanted for us, rather than what we ourselves really wanted.

This direction doesn't allow us to slow down, let go, relax, and give up.

This is not a rehearsal, get the f**k on with it.

This direction kicks us in the arse and says 'Go on, life is short, get moving, follow your dreams, this is not a rehearsal, get the f**k on with it.'

It takes courage. It takes grit. It takes a good deal of energy, and sometimes a burst of adrenalin. But sometimes there's nothing else to do but to take the plunge, to say:

'F**k It, I will go for it.'

It sometimes looks like this: jumping from the nine-to-five ship and setting up your own business; selling your own business and becoming a cobbler in a tiny village on the coast; signing on to an online dating agency and finding the man/woman/sheep of your dreams (note to self: investigate sheep dating agency possibility, GSOH – Good Sense of Humor – becomes GSOW – Good Sense of Wooliness); dumping your boring partner; telling your bullying boss to go F**k himself; finally writing that novel; finally making that trip; finally taking those (language, piano, tantra) lessons, etc., etc.

GAIA'S MAGIC WORDS
Passion

If you love something, please go and do it.

If you hate something in your life, please go and change it.

If you love yoga and want to become a yoga teacher, and do yoga all day long, do it. Train, teach, and find other people who love it.

If you hate your job and you truly can't stand another day of it, go change it.

If you want a relationship, be honest with yourself, and go find one.

If you are not happy with your lot, throw your life upside-down and do everything differently.

If you want to meditate all day long, do it.

If you love sex, have as much as you can get.

If you want to set up a business and become super-successful and super-rich, then go do it.

If you do it because you need to demonstrate to yourself that you are good enough and that your life has meaning, still do it. I will certainly not be able to stop you; those are the most motivating forces in life.

But please remember that, whatever you go for, if you are lucky enough you may eventually realize that it means f**k all if you are good enough or not, and that life doesn't need meaning to happen.

In that realization, a partner, a career, yoga, meditation, or sex make no difference at all.

So you may as well follow your passion and do what you fancy, rather than trying to do the right thing.

If you become a porn star, please let me know.

---

* Severely lacking in motivation to get off your backside and do – well – whatever it is you need to do.

† Smartly dressed and affluent.

F**K IT. THE TWO-IN-ONE HANDY LIFE TOOL

And so this one beautiful phrase has two opposing applications:

1 To help you let go and slow down.

2 To help you go for it and get moving.

So F**k It helps you to find balance in your life, whichever direction you're coming from.

Going too fast? Say F**k It to all that, and slow down, man.

Going too slow? Say F**k It and grab life by the balls, missus.

In *Alice in Wonderland,* Alice realizes she's too big to get through the door, so she finds a handy bottle of something that says, 'Drink Me.' She shrinks but becomes too small, so she eats a bit of cake that says 'Eat Me' and grows again.

F**k It is the drink and the cake all in one. It helps you shrink when you need to shrink. And it helps you grow when you need to grow.

The trick is find the right size or, for you, 'balance.' So, no worries, because you have your handy two-in-one F**k It life tool.

That's what F**k It does — it balances your life.

And that's what F**k It does — it balances your life. It allows you a quick and powerful way to either slow down or speed up.

So, how come F**k It has this magic ability of being able to help you let go AND go for it? How can it be the drink AND the cake? The answer lies in the magical mystery world of the F**k It State: a balanced, neutral, blissful state to which every mention of the magic words 'F**k It' allude.

So, it's time to enter the magical kingdom and explore that state.

PART VI

WALKING THROUGH WALLS

REACHING
THE
F**K
IT
STATE

USING MAGIC TO WALK THROUGH WALLS

There is a state we reach when we're very relaxed that's literally different from our normal state: the brain is even at a different frequency.

This state is very F**k It: i.e., the qualities of the state are akin to those you'd identify in someone who was acting in a F**k It way. So in this state, as well as being relaxed, you typically wouldn't care so much about things, you'd feel more playful, less inhibited, more creative, more open, etc. This is why we call it the 'F**k It State.'

It seems to be that by identifying the qualities of this F**k It State, and introducing them into your daily life, you can tap into this state more easily and more frequently. And when you do, some very interesting things start to happen in your life. For the purposes of this section, we'll call these interesting things 'magic.' Magic happens.

And this magic means that sometimes you don't have to laboriously break through the walls of the prison, but can simply walk through them. So accessing the F**k It State using these qualities creates magic, which means you effortlessly break free of the prison you're in. And that's a nice way to do it.

It's also a glimpse of why the expression 'F**k It' works so well: just by saying it, we're reminded of that more playful, care-free state (a child-like state, if you will), and we all want to be back there.

By playing with these qualities and techniques, you'll find that you can return at will, with a click of your fingers, and the utterance of the two words 'F**k It.'

FIRST, A QUIZ

Everyone likes a quiz. This quiz tests how often you're in the F**k It State. There's no prize. Just the understanding of how much walking-through-walls practice you have to do.

> *Accessing the F**k It State using these qualities creates magic, which means you effortlessly break free of the prison you're in.*

And just to relax you, pre-quiz, I'll tell you about a quiz I took part in recently.

I was watching an educational show on daytime TV yesterday, which included a quiz section. Now the quiz challenged me, made me dig deep, got me stretching in my mind gym, and hopefully delayed the onset of Alzheimer's by a couple of days.

The prize was tempting: £30,000. They even preceded the quiz by several vox pops of people on the streets of London being asked what they'd do with £30K. Their answers were shocking: 'I'd invite hot celebrity X out for a drink.' (Uh? You think because you're willing to blow mega-money on a 'drink' that she'd say yes? Loser! She'd run away faster than if you asked her to share a banana milkshake at the local McDonald's.) Next up, vacant female pensioner: 'I'd buy a bungalow.' (Uh? I've just done a little research on exactly where you could buy a bungalow for that money in the UK, and it looks like she's moving either to a cliff-edge property that's likely to fall into the sea within five years, or into the most dangerous part of inner-city Glasgow, where she'll soon be wanting to jump off a cliff.)

And those were the clips they chose… what did they throw out? 'I'd build a nuclear warhead and threaten Vladimir Putin with it so he'd have to give me, like, more money… and a Russian wife.'

I knew then that I had a good chance if I was going to be pitting my wits against these cretins.

And so, the questions commenced. Roll the drum. Fingers on buzzers. John, rev the motor of the turbo-charged engine of your encyclopedic brain…

'Which musical instrument…' (aha, a question about the heritage of Stradivarius, a tricky question about the tuning pitch of a French horn)…

'Which musical instrument in the following list has strings?' (Uh? I sense a trick):

A The trumpet

B The flute

C The violin

I panicked. It HAS to be a trick. They're trying to catch me out. But no, even my cunning mind couldn't see any possibility for a trick within those three possibilities. Perhaps I had overestimated the intelligence of even my cretin-like competition.

What now? Just call this number with your answer, calls cost £10 a minute from landlines, but could be much more on a cell phone, or much less on a plastic cup attached to piece of string.

And like a kid being told about Santa, I grew up. It wasn't a 'quiz.' It was a simple, random lotto and all they wanted was my money. They might as well have said:

'Is there anyone out there who can say the word "win"? If you can say the word "win," you could win the jackpot.'

Oooh, ooh, yes, I can say the word 'win.' Look, 'win,' 'win.' That's put me right ahead of all those on the estate* who can only say the word 'wanker†.'

So, on to your own F**k It Quiz…

The F**k It State Quiz

Considering how I am in this moment (check one answer for each statement),

1. I lead a life of purpose.
A. Not at all   B. A bit   C. Yes and no   D. Mostly   E. Completely

2. I don't feel attached to any particular outcome.
A. Not at all   B. A bit   C. Yes and no   D. Mostly   E. Completely

3. I focus only on my positive side and emotions, and don't dwell on anything else.
A. Not at all   B. A bit   C. Yes and no   D. Mostly   E. Completely

4. I know that life can be a serious thing and treat it accordingly.
A. Not at all   B. A bit   C. Yes and no   D. Mostly   E. Completely

5. I feel totally present to what's going on now.
A. Not at all   B. A bit   C. Yes and no   D. Mostly   E. Completely

6. I don't care about what's right or wrong.
A. Not at all   B. A bit   C. Yes and no   D. Mostly   E. Completely

7. I am fully in touch with how I feel, physically and emotionally.
A. Not at all   B. A bit   C. Yes and no   D. Mostly   E. Completely

8. I love life, and feel full of energy.
A. Not at all   B. A bit   C. Yes and no   D. Mostly   E. Completely

9. I feel stressed.
A. Not at all   B. A bit   C. Yes and no   D. Mostly   E. Completely

10. I worry a lot about how things will turn out.
A. Not at all   B. A bit   C. Yes and no   D. Mostly   E. Completely

It's worth doing the quiz at different times to see how your score changes. Now, turn to Appendix III on page 312 to work out your F**k It score.

We've also created an online version of this quiz, which calculates your score automatically, at www.thefuckitlife.com/extras.

---

* A densely populated area of housing.

† Worthless idiot (and doesn't necessarily refer to a person's habits of masturbation).

**OPEN
TO
IT**
■

OPEN TO THE POSSIBILITY OF MAGIC HAPPENING.

Just opening is magic in itself, and can allow much magic to happen.

But let's take a step back. As we've seen, for many reasons, most of which are understandable and natural, we close ourselves off from much of what's available in each moment. We develop opinions and stories and ideas and filters that narrow our range of perception and experience to a small slit of what it could be.

So open a little. Or a lot. But open. Open to the possibility that the world might not work the way you thought it worked. Open to the possibility that you're not entirely who you think you are. Open to ideas that you might disregard at first. Open to the possibility that you could be very different, that your life could be very different. Open to change. Open to movement. Open to newness.

Open.

To.

Magic.

Not witchy magic, but those things that might happen in ways that you really don't understand: Positive, fantastic things; great life-changing things; healing and happiness things; things that leave you standing still in awe saying, 'Wow, that's *magic*.'

RELAX
IT

Whenever we talk about relaxation and ease in groups, there are always people who articulate a thought that probably bothers us all: 'Sure, of course, it's lovely to be relaxed and at ease, but if we were like that all the time, how on earth would we ever get anything done?'

So, before we investigate the magic and power of relaxation, let's nip this one in the bud. To do this I ask everyone in the group to name various leaders in their fields. You have a go now: Who's a leader in the field of business? Who's one of the greatest football (soccer) players of all time? Who's the most successful actor on the planet at the moment? Who's the dominant politician of our times?

Try it in your life. Who's the richest person you know? Who's the most popular person you know? Who's the sexiest person you know? Are you coming to any conclusions yet?

I can't guess your answers to those latter questions. But I can tell you the most common answers to the first questions. The suggestion for a leader in the field of business was… Richard Branson, owner of Virgin. What's he like? Well, let's just say he doesn't come across as a stress-monkey to me.

The most common suggestion for… Oh crap, this is beginning to feel like that quiz show, what was it… *Family Fortunes*?*

'We asked 100 people for the most popular dog names. You suggest "Fido." Let's see.' Ping. 'Yes, "Fido" was the second most popular answer. Jimmy, you suggested "Mr. Dog"… let's see if "Mr. Dog" was one of the most popular responses from the 100 people we asked.' Ee-urgggghh. 'No, I'm sorry, Jimmy; "Mr. Dog" wasn't one of the most popular answers. Do you have a dog, Jimmy?'

'Yes.'

'What's it called, Jimmy?'

'Mr. Dog.'

'Okay, Jimmy.

The most common suggestion for the greatest footballer of all time was Pelé. What's he like? Have a look on YouTube at some classic Pelé clips. It's astonishing. The man is so AT EASE. It's like a walk in the park for him. It's like he's dancing. It just looks so easy. And so beautiful. You thought of George Best, though, didn't you? YouTube him, too. It's the same. Ah, Maradonna? YouTube him, too. The same. Just don't watch any of those goals he scored against England, please. Though the one where he dribbles around every single English player, then stops to do a moony[†] to the English crowd before tickling the ball past the goalkeeper is something to behold. Don't watch that. And don't watch the goal where the shorty uses his hand to knock the ball in then later claimed it was the 'hand of God.' Let's not go there.

The most common suggestion for an actor was the gorgeous George Clooney. What's he like? Well, you just know that in real life, he's going to be like many of the characters he plays in his movies: cool, relaxed, and imperturbable. If there's someone you want around in a crisis, it's George. He'll keep his head. He'll work it out.

Politician? Obama. When he was running for President, I was astonished to see how relaxed, calm, and unhurried he was in every situation, every interview. Just imagine the pressure he was under, the hours he was doing. And yet he stayed composed. Have you seen the film clip of him being interviewed on TV, and being bugged by a fly? Now, if you're cool – a professional – you could probably manage to continue without being distracted. But Obama took the decision, on live TV, to go for the fly. We've all done that in the privacy of our own homes: rolled up the newspaper and gone-a-fly-hunting. So you know how it would go for me and you if we made such a rash decision: we'd miss it the first time, then the second time, then start flailing wildly in the air as we got more frustrated, until we were running and dancing around the TV studio, wailing at the pesky, unkillable bug.

Not Obama. Obama is still. Obama moves. Obama catches fly between fingers. Obama is ninja president. On that evidence alone, McCain should have done the decent ninja thing and fallen on his sword. Everyone in the country should have stopped what they were doing, and begun simply chanting 'OBAMA, OBAMA' until the ruling elite had no choice but to make him, not just president, but King of the USA, too. All hail President King Ninja Obama.

Now, what were you saying about 'no one got anywhere in life by being relaxed and at ease'?

Okay, okay, so you want to be relaxed, too. How?

Relax, that's how. Really, just by having the desire to be more relaxed, then trying to relax will do the job in many ways.

The best way to learn how to relax is to exaggerate the feelings of tension and relaxation, and start to learn what really happens to you when you're relaxed. Once you've learned what the qualities of relaxation are for you, you can use those qualities as techniques to create relaxation. That is, after all, what most relaxation techniques are: we observe people when they're deeply relaxed, and note what happens to them in this state (to their breathing, for example), then, if we ask someone who's tense to use a breathing pattern similar to the one we observed in the deeply relaxed person, then that tense person becomes more relaxed. Simple.

So let's exaggerate those feelings first. And this in itself could become your daily (and very useful) practice. Start with your hand. Make a fist. Clench it really tightly for a few seconds. Then release and let your hand be completely soft and relaxed.

Notice what you feel: how your hand feels. Then go around your body doing the same thing: tense the muscles in your forearm, then relax… tense your biceps, then relax, etc.

Lie down somewhere dark and have a go. Or stay exactly where you are now and have a go. Tense that part, then relax. And, after you've gone through the whole body, or when you get bored, just lie or sit there and relax. What do you feel like when you're relaxed? Note the answers down if you want.

Your feelings, sensations, and experience of relaxation will be different in some ways to other people. And do get a sense of your own before you read the list that I'm about to give you. Otherwise you might start swiping sensations that aren't yours.

So this is the kind of thing that happens to people when they relax deeply:

- Their breathing changes and becomes slower and deeper.

- They feel softer, heavier, and sometimes warmer.

- Their thoughts start to drift, like when they're about to go to sleep.

- They might feel a tingling sensation in their body.

- They might see colors and visions.

- They become more attuned to sounds.

- They feel a sense of peace and tranquility.

- Worries seem to recede.

- They feel very present to what's going on.

Nice.

So what are the predominant things that you found and experienced? Because you can then use them as a technique for becoming relaxed whenever you so desire.

I, for example, become very tuned into sounds when I'm deeply relaxed: I hear every sound, I love every sound, every sound makes me feel comfortable and at home. So a technique for me, if I want to relax, is to stop and listen to the sounds around me. If I tune in now to the sounds I get: the tapping of the keys on the keyboard; the hum of the heating system; warming the towel rail that I'm leaning against; the noises of someone moving around in an adjacent room; the birds outside chirruping… deeper… the hum of this laptop; a distant whirring, maybe a farm vehicle; a very subtle clattering, maybe from some part of the heating system; the rumbling of my empty stomach. And, yes, I feel more relaxed now. Lovely.

In that way, you develop your own relaxation techniques.

BUT WHY RELAX?

Apart from the fact that it simply feels nicer to be relaxed than to be tense, why relax? Well, it's good for you for one. Western medicine recognizes that stress and tension are harmful to the body (when we're stressed, one of the things that happens in our bodies is that we release the hormones epinephrine (or adrenalin) and cortisol which, though occasionally useful in short bursts, are very harmful when released and circulated over extended periods of time). Though these mind–body effects are being elaborated by scientists all the time (and do read Dr. David Hamilton's *It's the Thought That Counts* and other books for the latest science in this area), we've sensed that stress, anxiety, and fear have an effect on the body ('bloody hell, you nearly gave me a heart attack'). A doctor (of medicine), Dr. Kenneth Heaton, recently identified passages in Shakespeare (writing 400 years ago) that pointed to his perception of the mind–body link. He found that symptoms with roots in the psyche, including vertigo, breathlessness, fatigue, faint feelings, and cold feelings are all common in Shakespeare's works and argues that modern doctors, who are 'reluctant to attribute physical symptoms to emotional disturbance, resulting in delayed diagnosis, over-investigation, and inappropriate treatment' should read more Shakespeare.

But it's in Eastern medicine where this mind–body (–spirit) link is central, and where relaxation is part of the recognized therapy for illness. In Traditional Chinese Medicine (TCM), for example, the flow of qi or energy in the body is the critical thing. At a simplistic level, it's observed that energy moves around the body, and through the organs in 'meridians' – the energetic equivalent of our blood circulatory system. If this energy flows through the meridians and organs in a balanced and harmonious way, then we are well. But when the energy becomes blocked or stagnant, illness can set in.

So how does the energy get blocked? By physical or emotional tension – and the two are intertwined. So if you're very angry, this disrupts the flow of energy in your body (in TCM it would be said that the liver is affected). It's clear to us all that if you become very angry there is both an emotional and a physical effect (you become red and overheated for example, you even 'see red'). The same is true of being very stressed: we see it has an emotional effect, but also that it has a very profound physical effect, too, as our whole body becomes more tense and rigid – yes, that's it, start rubbing your neck. In Eastern medicine, these tensions create the blocks that lead to illness.

So, to reverse the process toward illness we have to release the blocks, and to do so, we have to release the tension (emotional and physical) in the body (i.e., you have to relax). And just by relaxing deeply, you can allow the energy to flow more so that healing can and will happen.

It seems that, in our modern society at least, our tendency is toward over-working, over-stretching, and over-stressing. So, to maintain or recapture our full health, we need to work with relaxation. We need to recognize how important being relaxed is. And it's key, too, to enjoy being relaxed. The moment you realize that you'd like nothing else than to sit still for a few minutes and breathe deeply, or lie down and feel the energy flowing through your hands, then you know you're on the right track as far as relaxation goes.

Is there a catch? Well, there is actually. No matter how good you become at relaxing, no matter how effective and sophisticated your techniques are, you'll still struggle if you don't address the source of your stress and tension. You know in those cowboy movies when the cowboys look up from their camp toward the surrounding hills and see some Indians on horses appearing. Well, fine, with their guns and expertise, the cowboys will have no problem, they can just shoot the Indians as they ride toward them howling and wielding their machetes. But as they watch, more Indians appear. Then some more… and still more… until the horizon is full of furious Indians. And the cowboys know their guns are nothing in the face of these numbers. So they prepare for a massacre. If you don't sort out the source of stress, it just keeps popping up and appearing in different forms and in greater numbers. In the end, your great breathing techniques are nothing in the face of the incoming army of stress. And you get massacred.

F**k It, you see, is the ultimate relaxation technique.

That's why F**k It Therapy works so well. If we combine learning how to relax and making the movement from tension into relaxation a part of our lives, at the same time as saying F**k It to the key stressors in our lives, we have a winning formula. Sure, there will always be things that stress us out. I will argue later that we don't necessarily want to lose those either. The key, though, is disabling many of the things that needlessly stress us out (because they're actually not that important). That's why it's important to use F**k It to break through those walls of 'meaning' (when we're attached to too much), to say F**k It and be less serious, to say F**k It to the story we tell about ourselves and life out there.

F**k It, you see, is the ultimate relaxation technique, because it allows us to relax around the MEANING of things: 'F**k It, it's not THAT important.' Just saying 'F**k It' naturally relaxes us. Just saying 'F**k It' is likely to slow and deepen our breathing, make the body feel warmer and heavier, relax those tense muscles, and so on. Use F**k It and your specific, personalized relaxation techniques and you have a winning, magic formula.

You have, against the apparent enemy of stress, invented the equivalent of an atomic bomb.

GAIA'S MAGIC WORDS
Please pay (less) attention

A very cool Chinese Qigong master, Dr. Bisong Guo, said one day (with a lovely, strong Chinese accent):

'You see, only 20 percent of you needs to be present in any situation. The other 80 percent is not needed.'

I love this. In the present spiritual trend of full presence and total consciousness, she was suggesting to switch off 80 percent of you – not just relaxation, but 80 percent absence.

What did she mean? She meant that it might be possible to live successfully by only engaging 20 percent of our attention in what we are doing. The rest can remain free, not focused, not concentrating on what is going on. Doesn't that sound liberating?

But is this really possible? Can you actually be productive, hold down a job, be reliable, while engaging only 20 percent of your attention?

> *Can you talk to people without them feeling you're not that interested if you are there only 20 percent?*
>
> *Well, try it. No better way to find out.*
>
> *When John was still working as a creative in London, he used to do this in meetings (and I saw him do it many times). He used to sit there and relax, slightly defocused, interested enough, but with no specific interest, while the others were arguing back and forth about big and small things (mainly small). They would usually struggle to reach a solution that satisfied everyone. All the time, John relaxed and kind of meditated without saying much. After a while, usually toward the end of the meeting as people were still struggling along, he would get an idea about the situation and calmly share it.*
>
> *And everyone quieted down, listened, agreed he was a genius, and did what he suggested.*

---

* Based on the US game show *Family Feud* created by Mark Goodson and Bill Todman, which ran 1976–85.

† To show one's buttocks (known as your 'bottom' or 'bum' in the UK) in a public place and an all-round crowd-pleaser in the UK, particularly when the buttocks belong to a football player or other celebrity.

ENERGIZE
IT
▬

The energy thing I've just been talking about isn't much good as a theory. In fact, it's much worse as a theory than the other theories most of us live quite happily with every day. And most of what we 'know' about anything is a theory, if you think about it. A theory is an explanation of something that is correct until a better theory comes along to replace it. The current theory that most of us subscribe to is that we're solid, separate beings made up of bones, flesh, organs, and pumping blood, interacting with a mainly solid and separate reality, all pinned to the ground by a force called 'gravity,' on a planet called Earth that's spinning at about 1,000 mph (depending on where you're standing) on an orbit around a hot thing called the sun, in a universe that is just one of billions of universes, and probably connected to infinite parallel universes via worm holes. Okay, so I've wandered off at the end from what most of us subscribe to, but it's what many cosmologists and astrophysicists subscribe to. Despite all that: the picture we have of what we are; of what we are in relation to everything around us; what this planet and universe are… it's all a theory.

It's a theory to me (and probably you, too) that your bones are alive inside, that you have hormones pumping out from various points in your body controlling various functions, that you have a network of nerves sending information back to the brain. It's a theory, because

I personally have no evidence that any of this is true. I've only seen dead bones that look solid and inanimate to me. I've never seen, touched, or tasted a drop of hormone (not human to my knowledge, anyway, I suppose I'm tasting hormones all the time in the meat I eat). As for nerves, I've never seen a nerve. Who knows if that's why I 'feel' stuff. Ah, John, but that's simply because you're ignorant in those areas. If you'd had medical training you would 'know' these things to be true. Sure, I may well have apparent evidence for my theories. But even then, they would still be theories until new evidence came along. It's just more difficult to be open to new evidence if your understanding of a theory is very solid.

For now, it's worth getting a little sense of the fact that you're living with many (for you, at least) unproven theories. And even those theories that you can prove personally ('I am solid and separate and what I'm holding in my hands here is solid and separate') are still only theories waiting for new evidence to come along.

But we accept most of the theories because illustrious (usually Western) scientists give them to us. And the idea of energy flowing around the body is not part of that illustrious body of Western science. So it's more difficult to accept this idea as a theory (until more Western scientists manage to get their brainy heads around it and then tell us how it works). But it's not just that. It's not just that the concept of energy is literally a foreign concept to those of us brought up in a post-Newtonian world of the physical sciences. The concept of energy is, by definition, difficult to grasp, because it is invisible, all-pervasive, and constantly changing.

> *The concept of energy is, by definition, difficult to grasp, because it is invisible, all-pervasive, and constantly changing.*

It's hard to pin down in many ways. And thus it defies most attempts to pin it down. Like God, really. And maybe it and Him are the same thing after all.

So let's jump out of the land of theory and concepts, and just *experience*.

I'll tell you my journey into the experience of energy. As a young man, having left university and working in my first job, I was not a well man. I had a number of allergies that manifested in a variety of symptoms. At times I was very sick and had trouble just getting everyday things done. I felt ill most of the time and was tired all the time. I recognized that stress was making me worse because when I was happy and relaxed, I was relatively better, and when I was unhappy and stressed, I was sicker.

Jump out of the land of theory and concepts and just experience.

So I set out to learn how to relax. I bought a relaxation tape: a double cassette set, in fact ('tape' and 'cassette' here refer to an antique audio playback system). And I would lie on the bed and press 'play.' And the exercise I was taken through was the one I took you through in *Relax It*: a 'progressive relaxation.'

(I know other relaxation exercises but, after more than 20 years of doing this stuff, including training as a hypnotherapist, there's nothing quite like exaggerating the difference between 'tension' and 'relaxation' to teach you how to relax.)

I would lie there then, being taken through the different parts of my body, tensing and then relaxing. After a while, my whole body would have been tensed and relaxed, and I would then feel totally relaxed. And it really worked for me. I did move from a general state of tension (mainly because of my illness) to a relaxed state. And I could then carry that relaxed state out into the world with me.

After a few days of doing this, I started to notice that the feeling of relaxation (after the exaggerated tension) had a particular, peculiar quality to it: it was, for want of a better word, a 'tingling' sensation. And the word 'tingling' doesn't do what I was feeling complete justice, but let's leave it at that for now. So, as I tensed, then relaxed, I'd know I was relaxed when I could feel that tingling.

After a couple more days, I didn't have to play the tape: I would lie down and, even without tensing a muscle now, I would imagine, progressively, each part of my body relaxing and starting to tingle. I would relax my hand and feel it tingling, then my arm, etc.

A couple of days later, I could just lie down and imagine 'scanning' my body, almost like a laser and, as I did so, this tingling sensation would appear. After just a few minutes, my whole body would be soft, deeply relaxed, and tingling.

After another few days I realized I didn't have to be lying down to do this. So I'd be sitting at work, or on a bus, or eating at home, and I'd do a quick 'scan' of my body, and begin to feel the tingling all over. I'm doing it now.

I loved the tingling feeling. The feeling amazed me. I couldn't believe I'd never consciously felt it before (it must have always been there, I'd just never noticed it). I would go back to trying to experience the feeling whenever I could. I loved the feeling AND I would feel better (i.e., my symptoms would diminish).

A couple of months later I was invited to a Tai Chi class. I went and was most surprised to hear someone talking about this qi or 'energy' thing that you could feel in your body as a kind of tingling sensation. I was amazed that there were exercises you could do (in Tai Chi and the related discipline Qigong) to help this energy spread and flow. And I've been fascinated by energy and all the associated arts ever since. I've practiced Tai Chi and Qigong (and other energy arts) over the years, but it never really departs, for me, from my initial experience and love of this feeling of energy in my body. I'm relaxing now, sitting here early in the morning in a hotel lobby in Milan, and I relax and I feel this energy everywhere. I LOVE it. I never seem to become tired of this particular lover, even though she's with me always. She's all over me, in a good sense, and I spend a lot of intimate time with her, but I never grow tired of her. I never feel I fully understand her, actually, and maybe that's part of it… if I ever

155

feel like I'm beginning to understand her, she shows me another side of herself that defies my original understanding.

So, would you like to experience some of this energy, too?

Yes, of course you would. We'll teach you some very simple and very powerful exercises. So powerful, in fact, that they still make up a significant part of my practice more than 20 years after I first learned them.

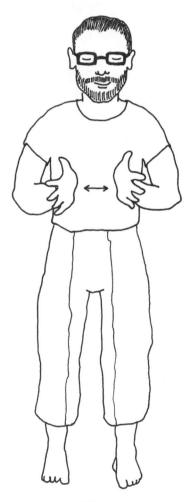

PLAYING MY ENERGY ACCORDION

1. SHAKING, STANDING, SENSING THE QI

So, working around the fact that you're reading a book (probably) rather than listening to this, I'll tell you what to do, then you can do it.

Stand and shake every part of your body. Shake for five minutes (sounds like a cocktail recipe). Then stand completely still (just like when the music stops in one of those childhood party games). As you stand completely still (after shaking) notice any sensations in your body. Put a name to those sensations. Stand for five minutes. Try to relax as you stand. Anytime tension comes up, relax. Move a little if you need to. Then bring your hands together so that your palms are facing each other, about one foot apart.

Pretend you're holding an accordion. You don't have to pretend you're French or anything, just pretend you're holding an accordion. Then start to play your imaginary accordion, very slowly, like a romantic French accordion player. Bring your hands together very slowly, until they are very close together (but don't let them touch, there's an accordion in between, after all), and then start to open them again. And continue this action, closing and opening your hands. Keep the rest of your body, especially your arms and shoulders, as relaxed as you can.

And notice what you feel. Put a name to those feelings and sensations if you can. If you're not feeling anything, fine. Try it again later. And after a few times, you certainly will start to feel something – unless you're dead. Zombies don't do this exercise so often. They tend to do the other exercise where they have their arms up in the air in front of them and walk forward very slowly. Now, I'm not going to tell you what you feel just yet, because that would spoil the surprise. So, please do this exercise, and experience it (whatever 'it' is) yourself.

2. SHAKING, STANDING

Once you've done Exercise 1 and felt something, you can move on to Exercise 2.

Shake for five minutes (and you can put on some music if you want; you can also do it for longer if you want). Then stand still again. This time, stand still in a very particular (and easy) way:

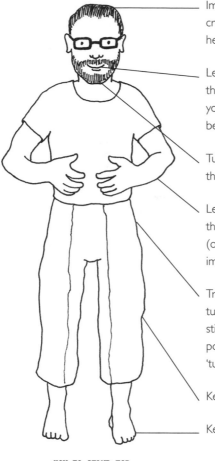

Imagine a cord is attached to the crown of your head and is lifting your head gently.

Let the tip of your tongue touch the roof of your mouth, just behind your teeth. Keep your knees slightly bent.

Tuck in your chin slightly to lengthen the back of your neck.

Let your arms dangle relaxed, and then let them hold an imaginary (or real, if you have one) huge belly: imagine holding a Buddha belly.

Try to keep your spine straight by tucking your coccyx in (to do this just stick your butt out, then do the op- posite, and you're there – it's called 'tucking your tail under').

Keep your knees slightly bent.

Keep your feet apart.

HOW TO STAND FOR
IMPROVED ENERGY FLOW

Weird? Well, there's not so much to it. But do try to follow all those points. After a little while of doing it, you'll remember all the points very easily. And each point helps the energy to flow more, so it's worth doing.

Once everything is in line, RELAX. At first, it might feel difficult to relax. Your legs might start to ache. Or the straight back won't feel natural. Or your buttocks will be clenched because of the tail-tucking-under thing. But soften and relax. That's actually the most important thing.

And stand. And notice how you're feeling. Again, put names to those feelings and sensations.

This is called 'Zhan Zhuang Qigong' or 'Standing Stake Qigong.' It is the foundation of all energy training. It is what the best (internal) martial arts masters do for hours on end to build up their (internal) power. It's as good after decades of practice as it is after a week of practice (nay, even better).

3. STANDING

Just to stand like this for ten minutes a day will change things for you. Just standing like this will significantly change your levels of relaxation (for the better). Just standing like this can heal you of illness or help prevent illnesses that would otherwise afflict you.

It's simple. But it's the most effective thing you can do. If your brain prefers the complicated stuff, that you have to go on courses and spend years learning, as it probably will, then go off and do those things. But don't forget this. In fact, if you want to go away and learn something complicated, go and sign up for a Tai Chi class. Tai Chi works a treat alongside this. And, after a while of doing Tai Chi (anywhere between 40 days and 40 years, in fact), you'll realize it's the same thing anyway.

If you instantly understand the power and sufficiency of this standing Qigong, or you just love it as it is, or you're just lazy-dog (lazy isn't a bad thing my friend), then do just this. I have spent years of my life, years of daily practice, just doing this. Nothing else. At other times, I've diligently practiced Tai Chi and Hsing I (Google It, it's also gorgeous).

HAND POSITIONS

If you want a little variation, here are some alternate hand positions:

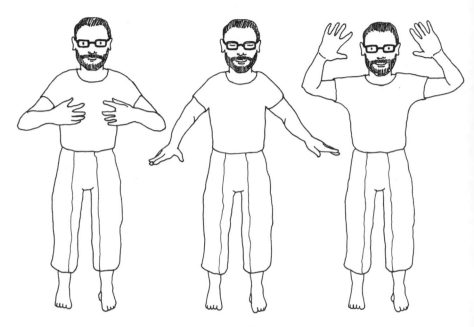

HAND POSITIONS: AIM TO HOLD EACH ONE FOR 10 MINUTES

But do go slowly. Only move to another hand position once you're able to stand for at least 10 minutes in your chosen position. And you might just want to stick with the original position. That's fine. That's more than fine, that's awesome. And that will do.

So what will happen for you if you practice this regularly? Well, as usual, I don't really want to tell you. It's great just to do it and see what unfolds for you naturally. But I know that some of you really, really, really want to know… and it might even motivate you to practice more. So…

This is a genuine magic art. Read any of the great books on Qigong and you can discover the magic that ensues from regular practice:

magic that has been talked about in relation to Qigong for thousands of years. Take your pick, really: spontaneous healing; the ability to heal others with touch; the ability to heal others with thoughts; psychic powers such as telepathy (hearing others' thoughts); prescience (predicting future events); distant viewing (being able to see things in other places without ever having been there), and so on.

This isn't the world of Harry Potter, it's better. There's no school, no classes. Just standing, relaxing, feeling, and letting the magic happen.

You might even learn how to walk through walls. Literally.

Having done energy work (and that's what 'Qigong' means, by the way: 'work' or 'practice' with 'energy') for more than 20 years, and having taught F**k It Therapy for more than seven years, I can say that Qigong is the most F**k It of all the arts (therapeutic, martial, magic, etc.,). It is, essentially, F**k It in form: when you let go and relax, things start to flow, and your life works (a treat).

*Qigong is the most F**k It of all the arts.*

It is Qigong that we teach (in depth) on our F**k It Retreats. So if you want to come to an amazing place (in a luxurious setting in Italy) and stand around with people experiencing the first shoots of magic in your life, come and join us.

GAIA'S MAGIC WORDS
Standing without standing

In our courses we teach this form of Qigong (the Chinese energy art), which is taught by very few people, simply because it has nothing to it. Most people prefer doing 'something,' so most Qigong teachers teach a more complicated form.

So, going back to nothing: There is something quite amazing about energy, which you can't trick – if you try too hard, it doesn't flow. The less you try, the more the qi flows. In this form of Qigong, you just do nothing and that's it.

Boring? Not at all. So much actually happens when you do nothing. But it all happens by itself.

You do nothing and then the energy gets the space and permission to take over, and it all kicks in. This is why it is called Spontaneous Qigong. It happens spontaneously, without any doing. So how do you teach this nothing?

As soon as you say something, people try to 'do it'...

For example, in the Spontaneous Qigong, one of the ways to set the qi moving is through simple standing. But just by telling people to stand, everyone's heads say: 'I will stand now.' And the whole body gets tight.

I find this amazing – it just shows me how even a simple instruction (such as standing or sitting) turns us into little soldiers. So how do you tell people to stand without them 'doing standing'?

What I do with the groups is this. First, I get them to lie down and relax, and only then do I get them to stand up – as if they were still lying down on a vertically placed bed. So in this way, we avoid the idea of standing up locking into our brains.

So then, when people lie down vertically, this concept of 'doing standing up' disappears, and they are able to do nothing. Their bodies and minds aren't locked. And then the spontaneous energy can move. When there is no doer, the qi does it.

Bodies start swaying and rocking – very soon all sorts of things start moving on their own, both internally and externally resulting in warmth, pulsation, tingling.

If people are happy to carry on doing nothing, the energy does things itself. All sorts of things can happen, such as arms rising by themselves, spontaneous walking, and internal adjustment in the body. This carries on as long as the person feels no need to take control again. Clearly an initial reaction to all these unexpected experiences can create judgment and surprise. But as people realize that this is simply the energy doing its job (they feel better afterward), they are progressively happier to get out of the way and let the experience unfold without judging what is happening.

Sometimes, in some people, you can see that the movement is totally ready to happen, but an unconscious idea of 'who they are and how they function' is holding the energy back.

Then, all I need to do is to point this out and give permission. A lovely guy in a group recently, after being given this 'permission,' started walking backward with his eyes closed just moved by the energy. And he could tell it wasn't him doing the walking. He found himself at the other end of the garden. Another guy got thrown on the floor by his qi, and some internal movement was rebalancing the right and left of his digestive system. All he did to kick this off was open up and not intervene (i.e., do nothing). The energy takes over.

So, simply, energy stops when you concentrate, when you judge what is happening, and when you want to understand too much.

Energy moves when you don't try hard, when you forget what you know, and when you hang out in the experience without judging too much what's going on.

Still wondering why you feel stuck so often?

NEUTRALIZE
IT
■

We do exercises on our F**k It Retreats that have to be seen and experienced to be believed. Imagine sitting on the floor with your legs stretched out in front of you, then three people lying across your legs – or as many people as you can have lying across them without the pain being too great. In fact, make that as many people lying across your legs that you know (by trying) that there's no possibility of you being able to move these people off your legs and getting up. If you can even move your legs a little, then we'd ask for one more person to lie across your legs. And you try again. So you're stuck. And it's not very pleasant, because those people are very heavy. And it's not very pleasant for them either. The person, or people, underneath really start to feel the weight of those above them. And your knees are jutting into their ribs. And you can feel their tension, as well as your own. But before we call the whole thing off, we ask you to try something.

To Neutralize It is to be entirely neutral around something and, maybe, everything. You have no judgment of it; you don't even have an opinion of it. You don't bring any experiences you've had in the past to this current situation (that involves this thing). You're not interested in what anyone else might think – of this thing or of you. You are completely fresh to the situation. It's as if you have been born in that moment, but born as a fully functioning (physically, at least) adult human being. Like a car in neutral (or park, if you drive an automatic).

You're not going anywhere, you're not looking forward or backward, and you're certainly not traveling forward or backward. You're just in neutral, ready. Ready, but not anticipating anything. Blank, if you want: a blank canvas; a fresh white page; a beach first thing in the morning, after the tide has washed over it, before people and dogs, joggers and beach-ballers trample the sand. That's you – fresh, open, not engaged, but fully present.

We ask you to get a taste of what it's like to be neutral. We give you some words and thoughts that might edge you toward that place or no-place. We suggest that it's possible to be unbothered by this situation. We ask you not to think about what's blocking you (the heavy people lying on your legs), or the pain, but to think about what you want to do (get up and out) yet without it being a big thing. In fact, not only is it not a big thing, it's the most natural thing in the world, as easy as getting up in the morning: just tossing off the covers and getting up. And if you relax, and don't think too much, you'll know when the moment is right to do that, and that moment is probably very soon, and you just have this impulse, it's not a big thing, to…

And with an ease that shocks everyone, especially those people lying on your legs, because they're thrown off, you're free in a second and stand up easily.

We do many of these exercises. And all of them teach us something very profound and (probably) counter-intuitive: that we can be stronger and achieve more if we're relaxed, at ease, and in this 'neutral' space. Not that, in reality, it's so easy to pin down (just like you, when you get it right): the moment you think you've cracked it (i.e., you've got yourself into a 'state' that you think works), it suddenly doesn't work. That's because this stuff (energy) doesn't like being pinned down (just like you).

Incidentally, if you want to try any of these exercises (they are very hard to teach in a book), do join one of our F**k It Retreats or events, or do something with Master Karl Grunick: he's the most powerful

Qi Master we've found on this planet; he does things you really won't believe; he's an awesome man who lives in neutral (though he'd never be so simplistic or boastful to say so). He teaches workshops around the world, including as part of our program of F**k It Retreats.

But this isn't, of course, about being able to throw people off your legs. It's not a practical everyday skill…

You wouldn't BELIEVE what happened to me today… I was in Starbucks, sitting on one of the leather sofas, minding my own business and Tweeting on my SmartThing, when this couple came over to me and just lay across my legs. Other people started looking – as you would. And as I started to struggle and protest and try to move my legs to get them off, and it was clear I could move my legs, another two people came over and lay across the original couple. Yes, REALLY. So I'm pinned to the sofa. And just as I'm thinking it can't get any worse, the somewhat porky guy that works there, yes, him, he comes and lies on the four of them. It was murder. And now the four of them are in pain and complaining (not that it was anything to do with me). They even had the cheek to say I had knobbly knees. And then, like a flash, I remembered this thing I read once in one of Parkin's F**k It books about going neutral. So I tried. Or rather, I not-tried. I turned the Frappe-Latte-Cino'd head of mine, in that moment, into a glass of crystal-clear water, and I just had the thought 'I will get up and go home.' And that's what I did. And here I am. And those four dodge-heads* are probably still sprawling on the false-aged floorboards of Starbucks where I left them.

*Imagine someone very F**k It. And you have someone who can neutralize things at will, like a Jedi warrior with another skill to add to their force-using skills.*

No, but Neutralizing It is, because you can neutralize everything, and it's magic.

Resistance is futile, he says swinging the bright bare bulb into your eyes. Resistance IS futile. Give into reality as it is, just as it is. Don't bother fighting it, resisting it, judging it, questioning it, trying to plan it or learning from it, seeing its higher plan or greater purpose. Get out of gear and slip into neutral.

Imagine someone very F**k It. And you have someone who can neutralize things at will, like a Jedi warrior with another skill to add to their force-using skills. In fact, Neutralizing It is the primary way to use 'the force.' Just don't go over to the dark side.

GAIA'S MAGIC WORDS
Tea with G. Pollini

If they made a movie about this, it would be a very boring one. But then they could pass it off as being arty and reminiscent of Andy Warhol.

A group of people sit around a low table, sipping tea from tiny cups. An Italian woman pours the Chinese tea (this is already a bit strange). Everyone's eyes are slightly glazed; smiles appear on faces, expressions get soft. Someone lies back and seems to fall into a half-sleep, 'til their cup is filled again, and they come back to life to empty it.

Occasionally someone says how time seems to have disappeared, how the tea is doing stuff to their heads, or that their hands are tingling; how they feel content and don't know why.

Then more tea is poured.

This is why I make this tea.

I think I have seen people getting this de-focused just at the beach. But perhaps only after a week, after they've finished all their books, done all the crosswords, and eaten all the ice creams. Then they give in to just being.

The tea only takes a few minutes to get there.

Brains go soft, minds get not bothered, bodies fill with energy, and then just being is the only option (really, after an hour or so, for some people speaking is a hassle).

This is how we spent most of our early childhood.

That was before all the prodding and pushing, teaching and guiding. After that, we agreed to spend the rest of our lives focusing, concentrating, solving, resolving.

When I finish with the tea, no one wants to move (what is there to do anyway?). Not even when there's another amazing Italian lunch awaiting us at the restaurant in the F**k It Retreats venue...

So in the absence of my magic tea (not 'magic' in the same way as magic mushrooms – this is just tea of the purest, loveliest form), just remember that next time you get defocused, you don't need to snap out of it in order to 'get on with it.' This is the most natural way to spend a fair amount of our time. And it's very lovely indeed.

* An original description, and possibly a term of endearment, not recognized by any worldly lexicon.

UNTHINK IT

If you've got kids, or are around kids a lot (as a teacher, for example), you'll recognize what I'm about to talk about. Our boys (now ten years old) often just sit and look into space. Sure, it's happening less than it used to. Especially now that they're into video games. The time that they would have spent staring into space is now spent staring into space invaders, or its modern equivalent anyway (that said, they do like the retro games on their Nintendo 3DS, so they have been playing such '80s classics). That's why we limit their time on such games to six minutes a day. No, it's more. But when they plead to go and play on the PlayStation, we say, 'If you can sit there and stare into space for 30 minutes like you used to, then you can play a bit of PS if you fancy.' But, of course, they couldn't do that. They could as much do that as lose the desire to spend every moment on a video game, because we would prefer it if they didn't.

I drive the boys to school frequently, and back again, too. Often they chat away to each other in the back. And sometimes there's just a lovely silence. I've learned to resist the temptation to strike up a conversation ('Right boys, what do you think about the new increase in the top rate of tax, then?'), and leave them in silence instead. I take a sneaky peak at them in the rearview mirror, and they're either just looking blankly out of the window, or at the back of the seats in front, or at their hands. They're not reading anything or doing anything, just staring blankly.

Once, they were doing this staring blankly thing for most of the journey home. I pulled up outside our house and turned off the engine. I sat there for a few moments, said nothing, and got out of the car. Nothing. I then walked to a place where I could see both of them, but without them seeing me (stalking your own kids, nice), and they continued just to stare blankly into space. I went into the house. A few minutes later, they came in, all chatty now.

Now, if we ever get to stare blankly as adults (and most of us don't), we call it 'meditation.' And that's if we're doing meditation 'well.' Most of us, when meditating, are sitting there thinking, *I must make sure I put out the food for the cats before I walk down to mail my letters, oh, I'm supposed not to be thinking here, give the old brain a break for once, ooooommmmmmmmm, blank, blank, blank, one... two... three... I hope I don't meet old Mr. Carson in the village today... I can't bear the way he looks at my shoes... I don't know what it is about my shoes, but he... oh, ooommmm,* etc.

But Unthink It is less about meditating to access a blank space (though this can help over time) and more about thinking less in general. I'll place myself in the stand as a prime example. I've always thought things through very carefully. I grew up understanding that the brain, and the ability to use it well and think things through, was our primary asset. As a teenager, one part of my brain wanted to be a lawyer (the other part wanted to be a rock star). I did well at school. My grandfather called me 'Brains 1' (and my sister was 'Brains 2'). I liked that. I liked to be top of the class (when I was). In a very insecure time (early teenage years), I found solace in the fact that I was clever, and, as I walked down the street, that I was probably cleverer than most of the people around me. Sounds awful, I know. But that was my response to feeling insecure (i.e., afraid I was inferior): I found a good reason for being superior. We've all done it in one way or another. And we all probably continue to do it in one way or another.

Thankfully, for me, I realized that there were plenty of very clever people out there in the world. In fact, in one subject or another, there would always be someone cleverer than me. But I could tell the clever thing wasn't working for me, anyway – not in the terms that I understood 'clever' to be then anyway, which was about working hard, learning lots of stuff, and spouting it out in the appropriate order. My imagination was too feisty and rebellious to be pushed into the corner by such hard work, so I rebelled against the hard work thing and made it my aim to do as little as possible to get through. And I did. It was only later that I learned the philosophical and energetic power of 'doing less to achieve more.' At times, I did more than just get through. Academics liked my madcap ideas about subjects that interested me. Yet the academic world wasn't for me.

But thinking everything through was. Even if I couldn't simply wander down rational lines of thought, I liked to think about every subject. I loved philosophy for its constant questioning. I loved great literature for its insights into human nature. That's what got me excited: working out how we all tick. So I'd try to understand everything, and usually that meant everything about people. I'd think through why people were acting the way they were; I'd think through why I was acting the way I was. I was very interested in psychology and psychotherapy. I loved to try to unpick my character, motivations, insecurities, and hang-ups.

It was, for me, all about thinking it through. And I suppose it still is in many ways. You're reading a book that is partially the result of a love of thinking things through. But to ONLY think things through and to ONLY approach things rationally, leaves us in a rather dry place. For example, I used to think it was great to work out my opinion on everything. So if, in a debate, I didn't have a pre-formed opinion already, I would quickly conjure up one so that I could argue from this or that angle. Listening to radio interviews with politicians, I would see if I could guess how they would respond to a question and then imagine arguing against them. Lame, I know.

Years of meditation, years of working with energy, and years of LIVING, however, have taught me that opinions aren't all they're cracked up to be. Having an opinion on something, anything, means we've fixed our position on that subject. This then leaves little room for changes in circumstances, changes in context, or changes in us. The true philosopher doesn't fix a position and then argue for it or from it. It's funny that the most common use of the word 'philosophy' is now when we say, 'Well, my philosophy is…' 'My philosophy is that you should always look before you leap.' We precede a statement of our fixed view with the suggestion that it's our 'philosophy.' Whereas philosophy is about simply questioning. I'm fascinated by how things work. But I don't (any longer) come in with a fixed idea of how I think they should work.

Imagine seeing everything afresh. Imagine having no opinions at all, just seeing things as they are, or investigating a question before you with absolutely no prejudices. The word 'prejudice' is important because that's what we're talking about, not just in the sense of bringing prejudice (i.e., prejudgement) to someone because of their gender, color of their skin, sexuality, or nationality, but also, just as most of us see how harmful it is to be prejudiced in that sense, to extend that principle out to everything in our lives. Realize that it can be unhelpful to prejudge ANYTHING. Come to every situation fresh.

> *Say F**k It to the stock answer, the thought-through response, the carefully constructed arguments.*

So if you laud the lord of thinking, if you relish your resource of opinion forming, how do you begin to Unthink things? Well, just by seeing that purely thinking everything through doesn't do it for you is a good start. Say F**k It to the stock answer, the thought-through response, the carefully constructed arguments… cut loose from your mooring of mentality and drift more freely. See what it's like to be fine not to have an opinion on something. Enjoy changing your mind on something. See the other side, but don't join the other side.

Combine Unthinking It with full consciousness, the impartial watching of phenomena, and you start to unleash some powerful magic. When you begin to think less, or at least be less fixed by previous thoughts, you create space: space for stuff that isn't just thought-based (like feelings); space for gentle dreaming (the staring into space stuff that kids do); space for other things to enter your life (you're now not just filtering all input based on pre-programmed criteria). You become floatier, softer, more in tune with yourself and others, more adaptive, more open to change, more willing to accept things as they are, people as they are, more tolerant, more flexible, more pleasant to be around.

That's got you thinking, hasn't it? Well, stop. Unthink It, and just relax.

GAIA'S MAGIC WORDS
Enlightened unconsciousness

I used to love digging: digging into experiences, digging out emotions, digging into dynamics. Any digging happening, I was there, not leaving anything unturned. Bring it all to consciousness, awareness, understanding. See it, say it, and name it. Whatever it took, I did it. All in the worthy name of truth (sometimes with not just a little cringing from John).

Now I don't. Now I hang around.

When something turns up, I hang around. It's not that I ignore it, or go unconscious, or run away, or that I got lazy (although I am really up for some laziness). Quite the opposite. I am there, but I just hang around with it, let it do its dance, let it play with me, and give it time.

It's simply that I'm not so impatient to get out of the unknowing.

I just don't have a strong need to work out what it is, and most of all I don't try to work out what to do.

So, I hang around.

Because you see, often when you reach for your beloved 'understanding tools' in a rush, you are bound to use them in the age-old way you've always used them. So you come to the same conclusions you always have. And possibly you are very bored with those.

So instead of that... just hang around with it.

Next time you ask yourself the same old question: 'What shall I do about this now?' you can just decide not to panic, and hang around with it for a while instead.

It's actually a rather lovely place to be (if you're interested in letting go of the addiction to controlling it all): you can remain soft-minded, enjoying a slightly hazy, detached feeling of not knowing yet what's going on and where precisely you're going. 'Can't be bothered to struggle' background energy sets in (not bad after an lifetime of struggling).

I call it 'Enlightened Unconsciousness.'

You are unconscious in the way you're not asking questions all the time and you're not bothered with working things out, but at the same time you're really alive, curious, and open.

And you know what, when you hang around like that for a while, without escaping, without pretending, but also without trying, life is given the chance to come up with something interesting.

When the time is right, you'll just be able to notice what emerges (from that nice soft space, by the way, so no need to rush). And, as you've just been spending time hanging around, you'll be fresh and full of energy to jump on that bus.

THANK IT

'For what we are about to receive, may the Lord make us truly grateful.'

That was said before all our family meals. It's puzzled me for a long time, that one. Why can't it be 'We are truly grateful, Lord, for what we are about to receive'? Why do we ask that the Lord 'make' us? Do we assume that we're miserable, ungrateful sinners, so would never be able to spontaneously thank the Lord for the bounty, the veritable ambrosial feast He's laid before us... so we have to beg Him to MAKE us grateful? Go on, God, I'll never be grateful of my own accord, I'll never be good of my own accord, so please MAKE ME. Go on, whip me, make me deeply, pathetically grateful, even if all that's on my plate is beans with two overdone pieces of toast (sorry, mum, that's not what you did really, you put in many long hours preparing fresh, balanced meals for us).

But, you know what? I get it now. Because 'grateful' is one thing that we're not very good at being. Whether life is good or bad, whether we're on an upper or a downer, we're very rarely 'grateful.'

However, this is good news because being grateful is an astonishing Magic Trick for enabling you to walk through walls. And if you're not using this trick regularly, which you're probably not, you're about to experience a heck of a lot of magic very quickly when you do.

So, what is gratitude all about? Well, it simply means being grateful, consciously grateful, for what we have. It means saying a definite 'thanks' or 'cheers' for many of the things that are going well in our lives (and even the things that don't appear to be going well, too, but more of that in a minute).

And we're not talking about manners here. I know you're all very well mannered out there. When someone gives you a gift, you say 'thank you' and (usually) are genuinely grateful. When the waiter brings you your food, you say 'thank you.' When the masseuse has finished you off, you say 'thank you.' You say thanks when a door is held open for you, or you wave thanks when another driver lets you out. Most of us are polite in our day-to-day relations. But that's not the gratitude we're talking about.

We're talking about a non-object-specific 'thanks' for everything in our lives. Sure you can talk about 'God' or any range of gods, angels, or spirits, or 'the universe' or 'Life.' But it's a general 'thanks.' And what are we saying thanks for? After all, have you seen what a miserable time I'm having of it at the moment? Chuck's been made redundant; we can hardly make the mortgage payments; Joline is acting up at school; the price of food is extortionate, not to mention the fuel; and this government is appalling, they've got no idea; and my mother-in-law just wants to stick her nose in; and my back is really playing up; and if I've told Jerry next door not to play his music late at night once, I've told him a thousand times; and people around here just aren't what they used to be; and it's all me, me, me nowadays, all money no manners. What was that you said about gratitude?

Well, there's always something to be grateful for.

Yes, always.

So, here's how you start building the magic of gratitude into your life: start building the magic of gratitude into your life, tee hee. Yes, set aside some time to write down all the things you're grateful for. You could decide to write 18 things every day that you're grateful for. If you can't be bothered to write it down (and please do if you can, because it does really help), then add some Gratitude Recitation to a daily activity. For example, when I run, I say thanks for something in the rhythm of my running.

Like this:

'I'm grateful for being able to run.

I'm grateful for this beautiful countryside.

I'm grateful for my pumping heart.

I'm grateful for my darling wife.

I'm grateful for my lungs.

I'm grateful for my beloved boys.

I'm grateful for my imagination.

I'm grateful for my balls.'

And so on. In my case, and so on, for 30 minutes every other day.

I wonder how much such 'Gratitude Running,' as I call it, is amplifying the benefits of my running alone (i.e., by being conscious of, and grateful for, and loving the various parts of my body, those parts of the body will be benefiting from those thoughts, as well as the exercise of running).

Decide to do such Gratitude Recitations while doing a daily activity... doing the dishes, or the ironing, or on your daily commute, or while scoffing down your breakfast, or having a shower, or having sex, or masturbating ('I'm grateful for my hand. I'm grateful for my...').

List the mundane as well as the spectacular: 'I'm grateful for running water. I'm grateful for my Ferrari.'

List what you wouldn't usually be grateful for: 'I'm grateful that I'm tired. I'm grateful I've been fired.' As even these recitations create something interesting in your life. Your brain will go, *Why the F**k are you grateful for being fired? What good has that done, now that you're sat at home, spending your time gardening, and sitting around, and reading again, and learning how to paint, and... oh!*

And watch the magic begin.

I'd prefer it if you went away and practiced some gratitude for a few days before reading the rest of this chapter. It won't ruin the magic, but it's nice to experience the magic before reading about how some of the magic is working.

One obvious psychological reason for the magic is that, by introducing gratitude into your life, you're taking your eyes off the negative things, the things to moan about, even for ten minutes a day. You're creating a new habit in your brain – you're seeing that, even if things look and seem crap in your life, there are blessings everywhere. And just like when you're thinking about buying an orange pickup, you suddenly see LOADS of orange pickups on the road, when you're thinking about the things you're grateful for, you suddenly see more and more things to be grateful for. In fact, the things to be grateful for crowd into your consciousness so much that the things to moan about hardly have any room to move, and they eventually get so uncomfortable that they bugger off* to clutter someone else's consciousness instead. That's the psychological magic. And it's no less magic because it's psychological. The brain is a magical thing.

> **By being grateful, we're effectively saying F**k It to all the things that we should be upset and moaning about.**

By being grateful, we're effectively saying F**k It to all the things that we should be upset and moaning about.

But gratitude is more than a psychological thing.

You know I mentioned the God, gods, universe, and Life thing? Well, it doesn't seem just to be your 'perception' of reality (i.e., psychology) that changes. It appears to be that you change reality, too. When we give thanks for stuff, we seem to be showered with more stuff to give thanks for. So it's not just that you start seeing more to be grateful for in your life ('oh, I hadn't really appreciated that just being able to walk or talk is in itself a wonderful thing'). But the things to be grateful for actually multiply. Is it that you're more positive, more open, and therefore attract more from other people? Yes, but it's more, too. And this is where you'll find the real magic (magic being magic it's hard to explain). But God seems to like it when you're grateful. Life seems to respond well in return when you go 'Cheers for sending that downpour, it really freshened things up,' by saying 'Okay, John, I'm enjoying your gratitude, so I'm going to grant you those wishes you had a little while back.' The universe just wants to be loved. The universe seems to say, 'You know, so many people just moan about what I give them, even when it's brilliant, that I just think 'F**k It, let me reward those who appreciate my work.'

I am grateful that I can write about things that mean a lot to me, and enrich my life in a way that people understand.

I am grateful that more of you have the opportunity to experience real magic by doing something so simple: just saying 'thanks.'

I am grateful for this wonderful place where I'm writing. I am grateful for this trusty laptop. I am grateful for the miracle of boiled water in the kettle over there. I am grateful for these legs that will get me over to that kettle. I am grateful for the wondrous taste of Earl Grey tea. I am grateful for the invention of sugar. I am grateful for the delicate china cup I am about to use.

I am grateful for everything I am. And I am grateful for everything you are.

For what you have just received, may the Lord make you truly grateful.

* A rather impolite and familiar way of saying it's time to leave one place for another.

MIND
IT

Mindfulness. More of you will know what mindfulness is than when I wrote the first F**k It book seven years ago. The art of mindfulness is a beautiful one. But it's not easy to write about – I tried for years.

And the best way I've come up with is through a character I've created: a character who finds beauty in the ordinary, who finds enlightenment in the everyday; a character called Bob the Buddha.

We're releasing a whole range of stuff around Bob the Buddha soon (or, if you're reading this after we've released it, that should read: And you can experience more of Bob the Buddha by going to www. bobthebuddha.com). But here's a glimpse into the wonderful world of Bob the Buddha.

Bob the Buddha

Bob shows the simple, mindful way to enlightenment

John C. Parkin

Bob Has Heard of the Buddha but Doesn't Know He Is One

Bob vaguely remembers learning about Buddha and Buddhism at school a long time ago. He remembers that the Buddha became enlightened when he was sitting under a tree.

Bob likes sitting under trees, too.

He remembers his teacher asked them to try some meditation by thinking about nothing. He remembers it being very difficult to think about nothing.

The truth is – and the best of the Buddhists would confirm this – that the Buddha was no god... and anyone can become enlightened and become a Buddha.

Though Bob doesn't know it, he's a Buddha (that's why I'm calling him 'Bob the Buddha,' but he doesn't know that either). And you can be, too. We're going to take a peek at Bob's life: what he gets up to, what he thinks about, and find out how utterly simple it is to 'wake up' (as Buddhists would call it), become enlightened, and be happy to put your name in the following gap: _____ the Buddha.

Something Bob Is Very Good at (but Wouldn't Know How to Name)

Bob is very good at bringing his attention to what he's doing.

He doesn't do it all the time. Like every other human being, he spends a good deal of time daydreaming, thinking about the past or the future, or worrying about whether something might or might not happen.

But, over the years, he's become more and more used to simply being present to what's going on. His experiences in sitting still for a while occasionally have taught him that he doesn't have to get so involved in what's going on, either around him or inside him.

Different people call this process of 'being present' different things. The Buddhists call it 'mindfulness.' This is clear: we instantly know what we mean when we say we're being mindful. But when we look into the word itself, it creates some difficulties (for me, at least). Our normal conscious state is to have our mind full of things, especially as adults. The process of 'mindfulness,' as intended by the Buddhists, is to clear the mind of the normal chatter by bringing your attention onto solely what is happening here, now. And by bringing your attention into the present, the mind often does clear, slow down, and become less 'full.' So, not really mindful at all.

Bob Likes to Do the Dishes

Though Bob now owns a dishwasher (a machine, not a person, that is), he stills enjoys doing the dishes.

Of all the good things you can say about a dishwasher (again, the machine, we're coming on to the person soon), it's not so good with a whole range of necessary kitchen implements: sharp knives (it blunts them), fine wineglasses (it scratches them), and large pots and pans (it has trouble accommodating them).

Bob enjoys everything about the process of doing the dishes. He organizes everything well, so that the pots are sitting there on the counter filled with warm soapy water loosening the grease while he gets on with other things. He likes to feel his hands in the hot water.

He wipes and scrubs and rinses. He doesn't think about other things, like what he's going to do when he finishes the 'job.' He concentrates on what he's doing: wiping, scrubbing, and rinsing. He enjoys the process of getting things clean.

Even though he knows that tomorrow they'll be dirty again, and need cleaning again, he enjoys this process. Maybe he enjoys it precisely because it is a circular process. Most people like to aim to achieve something, work hard doing it, and then appreciate when it is done and ready for them to reap the benefits. But housework is circular and continuous. You have to enjoy the process rather than simply the end product.

So, in the suds of the kitchen sink, Bob finds his life message, his Zen master. This Le Creuset Master doesn't allow Bob to think about the end product, only the process. If Bob's attention wanders, the Master whips him back to attention, in the form of the transitory nature of the final product (the short-lived clean pot).

And, though Bob doesn't know it, there's a long tradition in Buddhism of doing the dishes mindfully. The Buddha himself, it is said, had just finished a heavy bout of dish washing, before he sat under the Bodhi tree. And Buddhist scholars have strained over the question as to whether this chore was a necessary precursor to the whole waking-up thing.

What's good about doing the dishes as a mindful exercise is that you'd be hard-pushed to find a more mundane, menial, regular, relentless task in your life.

Because we so readily switch off in the face off this task (in the form of listening to the radio or daydreaming), it's the greatest opportunity to switch on, and thus wake up in the face of true reality.

In this one 'task' alone, you might well look down into the mucky water and see the reflection of the Buddha staring back at you.

Bob Likes It When It Really Rains

Bob's always likes it when it really rains. Some of his strongest childhood memories are of watching raindrops falling down panes of glass, or listening to the rain on the roof of the family caravan, or splashing around in puddles in his bright red Wellington boots.

Now, he enjoys darting into store doorways, pulling his collar close, suddenly sharing something with other people: a kind of Blitz spirit in the face of a harmless and regular meteorological phenomenon. And he loves it: the chance for a break from the routine and the schedule.

He likes driving, too, in the driving rain. Maybe, he wonders, driving rain was so-named simply because its such good fun to drive in. Bob drives slowly in rain – it's a great reason to exaggerate his usually careful, conscientious driving techniques.

Rain, especially big unavoidable rain, like many other things in his life, makes Bob feel cozy. Bob enjoys this cozy feeling. He gets it whenever he's really in touch with the suchness of life. Rain bounces him out of any thought patterns he's indulged in and reminds him of what's going on around him. And, when he makes that jump from the mind's constructions into the stuff of the material world around him, he feels good and cozy.

That's Bob the Buddha. I hope you enjoyed meeting him. And I hope he's helped convey the idea of 'mindfulness' and the magic that it can help create in your life.

Or, rather, for mindfulness is such an ordinary thing really, the way being mindful can allow you to see the beauty, the magic, the miracles, the divine, in the most ordinary things.

It's very, very simple really: the magic is there if only you care to look.

LOVE
IT

When you're relaxed, in neutral and simply being mindful to the present moment, you will, after some time, find that you start to love things – not 'things' in terms of the things you can buy in stores or online, nor things in terms of the things that you normally 'love', such as people and your parents and kids, but just things. Everything. No discrimination here. Once you're neutral around stuff, you seem to start loving the stuff (that's magic in itself), even the dodgy stuff – though that's clearly more difficult. But look at the times when you faced very difficult things, very difficult times. Now, this doesn't always happen, but it often does: when you emerge out of the other end of a difficult patch, you see what it has given you; you see that where you are now wouldn't have been possible without experiencing it; you see that, in a peculiar way, it was 'perfect.' Not always but often. You might put other words and explanations to it: you may conclude that 'everything happens for a reason,' it's 'part of God's plan,' that 'everything is perfect.' But it's just enough to see once we're in the better position of having come through something very difficult, that it had its purpose.

To Love It is to feel that, but in the present, not just in retrospect. 'Retrospect' is a lovely word, isn't it? To Love It is to Love It when you introspect (look at yourself), extrospect (look around you) when you nowaspect (look in the now). I like making up words very much.

I vow to write my next book only in made-up words. But words made up of other words that you vaguely recognize. Though I've just realized at least one genius got there first: 'Twas brillig and the slithy toves did gyre and gimble in the wabe'* (Google that, it'll be fun). Scrub that, I hereby vow to write my next book only in words that are not made up, and have been used before. I will focus instead in putting those unoriginal words together in a new and original order. People will be astonished by the heights of originality I scale in the way I put those entirely unoriginal words together.

I Love It a lot. I love reality just as it is, as it unfolds before me. And that feeling of Loving It is heightened when I'm relaxed: when I've said F**k It to the things that are bugging me, stressing me, upsetting me. Not that I don't love being bugged, stressed, and upset. It's just hard. I say F**k It. I Relax It. I Love It. Then when the bugging, stressing, and upsetting return, I'm more likely to be Loving It.

I say F**k It. I Relax It. I Love It.

Incidentally, speaking of things that bug me, is it just me, or does McDonald's tagline of 'I'm lovin' it' really bug you, too? You do have to wonder when a major corporation tries to put words in the mouths of the public. I suppose they can't legally force-feed us with their food, so they try the next best thing: force-feeding us with our response to their food.

I can't help but hear it being uttered through gritted teeth. Like a suit from McDonald's head office is holding a cattle stunner against your head, while another suit feeds you another Big Mac and asks, 'So how is it, Joooohhhhnnnn?' (They'd say 'John' like that, believe me.) And my eyes would dart toward the other suit with the cattle stunner pressing against my temple. And he would wink at me, and I'd say, through gritted teeth, 'I'm lovin' it.'

I hate the way they now put nutritional information everywhere on the basis that people probably won't really read the details – they'll just assume that if McDonald's can display the nutritional contents so prominently, then their food can't be THAT unhealthy.

I hate the way McDonald's lorries, in the UK at least, look like Ben & Jerry's ads these days. Suddenly McDonald's is sourcing everything from local farms, and loving the cows who are fed on lovingly watered grass, before they ask them how life is. 'Mooooo,' say the cows, 'We're lovin' it,' before they get hit with the stun gun anyway.

It's not just the cows that are being sacrificed for McDonald's bottom line. It's our judgment, too. We're zombies, walking slowly to the front of the line to order our meal deals:

'Please tell me stuff that makes me feel okay, in these health-conscious, locally sourced, environment-aware times, so I can eat the same old shit that I've been addicted to for years... I know it's basically the same nutritionally poor, but rich-in-fat-and-sugar concoction that it was when I was a kid, but I like it, and I just pray that you can make up any old nonsense to salve my conscience, okay?'

I'd prefer it if they were just straight with us: 'Sure we know most of this stuff is no good for you. But don't we make it tasty, eh? Especially after you've had a couple of beers or a shake that bursts your eardrums as you try to suck it up the straw. And have you seen the prices? You can't buy a salad leaf in a posh deli for the price of one of our hamburgers. Go on, treat yourself. You can have a salad tomorrow.'

In fact, I reckon just that line would transform McDonald's fortunes:

McDonald's. Salad's for tomorrow.

That's why I'm more likely to go into a 'Heart Attack Café' than a McDonald's. At least I know what I'm dealing with.

'I'm lovin' it.' I am, actually. I love seeing how things are. I love looking into the window of McDonald's and wondering. I don't go in. But I wonder. Then I wander some more. I love wandering and I love wondering. I love city places, and everything in the city places. I love the things people do in city places. And I love country places, and everything in the country places. I love the things animals and people do in country places. Places, people, animals, buildings, trees, generosity, and selfishness. It's all life.

And I, for one, Love It.

---

* From 'Jabberwocky' by Lewis Carroll (in case you're not Wi-Fi-ed up at the moment or can't be bothered to look it up).

BREATHE IT

Breathing has become an essential part of our F**k It Retreats in Italy. We don't let anyone join us unless they can breathe. So please don't even bother inquiring unless you're confident that you're breathing.

Okay, breathing. Isn't it great? Breathing in. Breathing out. Actually, Gaia's the expert on breathing (she's even got certificates), so let me hand over to her now.

Hi, Gaia here. Can I start by saying how lucky I am to have a husband like John. Wow! What a man he is! Boy, every day I just thank my lucky stars that I'm married to such a man.

Actually, that was still me.

Here's Gaia:

So, breathing: most holistic practices have some breathing component, and that says something about breathing. Basically, some really cool guys in India a few thousand years ago realized that your emotional patterns are connected to your breathing patterns: so when you feel peaceful, you breathe in a certain way, which is different from the way you breathe when you fill in a spreadsheet, which is different again from how you breathe when you're in love. And so they realized that if you do it the other way around – i.e., change the way you breathe – you can actually change the way you feel.

The other aspect of breathing is that it's the only automatic function of the body you can easily change at will. So you can ask anyone to breathe faster, or slower, or to hold their breath, and they're able to. (Ask them to do the same with their heart rate and see how they look at you.) So as we grow up, because breathing is connected to emotions and is easily controllable, we start creating breathing patterns connected to emotions, which eventually become fixed. As our great friend (and great breath master) Dan Brule points out: 'Your breathing patterns become like a fingerprint, unique to you.' So, by working with your breathing, you can work with your way of being, and you can shift patterns quickly and deeply. What I see in everyone is that the way a person breathes represents the way they live. Reading someone's breathing can tell you practically everything about him or her, and gives great potential for working with them.

Of course, the breathing we use and teach is in true F**k It style, and is inspired by a technique called Breathwork, which funnily enough isn't at all about work. What we do isn't a breathing exercise as such, it is a way to open fully and let go fully using breathing. (For this we have to give thanks to some magic experimental guys, including Stan Grof and Leonard Orr who, in the '60s, made this a therapy. And I need to give thanks to the great woman, Jane Okondo, who originally taught me.)

It's based on a surprisingly simple technique of inhaling fully on the in-breath and letting go fully on the out-breath, without holding on to pauses. Just try five of those breaths: deep full in-breath, short, relaxed letting go out-breath – no pauses. Simple stuff, it seems. But, as usual, in simplicity is depth, too. As most of us tend not to live fully (represented by the energy of the full in-breath), and are unable to let go (the totally relaxed letting go out-breath), this breathing immediately brings up most of the issues we want to unblock – and the possibility of moving beyond them. It is amazing to discover you can just breathe in the face of anything, instead of stopping and getting swamped by events, thoughts, and judgments. So breathing becomes a great way of saying F**k It: F**k It, just breathe.

Life comes up with its stuff, you breathe, you embrace, you keep breathing, you move on; it's just stuff. Then you touch on the miraculous simplicity of life. There's nothing fancy about miracles, they are all there is. But most of the time

*So breathing becomes a great way of saying F**k It: F**k It, just breathe.*

we can't see that, and we go on looking for miracles somewhere else while it's all happening under our noses. So, we get people to breathe and 'see.'

If you can't join us for some of our sessions, there is something you can do on an everyday basis: breathe. No, not just the in-and-out stuff. 'Choose' to breathe:

normal simple breaths but breathe. Whatever is going on, F**k It, you can breathe. When things hit you: breathe, and breathe more, till you aren't moving from fear, but from curiosity. When you're confused: breathe, and breathe more till you're happy to make time so you don't rush into a solution just for the sake of getting out of discomfort. When you need to do something big and new, breathe and breathe more, till you're fully present to the great thing you're doing, and actually excited more than scared. If you need to find out what you really feel about something, breathe and breathe more, your feelings will certainly show up (then all you need to do is not ignore them). And certainly, if you're having sex, breathe a lot.

FEEL IT

What's it like to really Feel It? Feel what, Parkin?

It. Whatever is there when you sit still for a while, or manage to relax, or simply bring your attention to what's going on in your body. It. It could be the pain you feel in your knees when you sit still for a moment, or the sense of sadness that's there when the noise of your life subsides; it could be the beating of your heart; it could be the memory of how you used to be when you still had dreams; it could be the shaky tension you feel in your whole body; it could be the blind fear you feel at the prospect of carrying on; it could be your deep, dark sense of loneliness; it could be your awful sense of regret; it could be your over-excited enthusiasm for living; it could be your sense that you don't really belong, or that you absolutely belong.

What's it like to Feel It? Not to ignore it or turn away and distract yourself from it.

It could be a sense of peace and oneness.

It could be a sense of desperation and separation.

It.

What's it like to Feel It? Not to ignore it or turn away and distract yourself from it; not to judge it; not to pretend it's not even there; not to wish it wasn't there; not to cover it in thoughts; not to want it to stay forever.

When you tune in, what do you feel? Qigong, meditation, mindfulness, and many other spiritual practices are about simply tuning in and noticing, without judging what's going on. We don't turn away; we look at whatever is there, being felt, straight in the eyes. And we feel it.

And, if we feel like it, we ask, 'What do I feel like doing (with that)?'

GAIA'S MAGIC WORDS
The poetry of rubbish*

When we feel rubbish, we seem to live that experience not as it is ('I'm feeling rubbish'), but as the absence of feeling nice ('Why don't I feel nice? I should feel nice!').

What would it be like to experience feeling rubbish as it is? What does it feel like? What is the experience like? What is feeling tired like? Or stressed? Or upset? How do your thoughts swirl, how does the heat move in you, what are the sounds of it? What happens in your body? What do you look like?

In the movie American Beauty, one character spends his time filming rubbish blowing around in the wind. And through the eyes of that guy, we suddenly see the poetry of (literal) rubbish.

When we stop seeing the idea of rubbish and we see what is actually there, then we see that the actual object is just so beautiful. That plastic bag is so beautiful, like the most poetic sculpture, so aimless, so un-made!

So what would it take for us to see the poetry of our rubbish?

---

* Brits often describe themselves as feeling 'rubbish' (known as 'garbage' in the US), which is a telling way to define your state of health – akin to the stuff you throw away.

EXPRESS IT

One of the most powerful practices during a F**k It Retreat is officially referred to as Free (or Spontaneous) Qigong. It's usually only taught after a lot of Qigong practice. We often teach it the first day. It's not dangerous, though it can look a bit potty from the outside. We introduce newbies to the wonderful healing art of Free Qigong by inviting them to ask, 'What do I feel like doing?' Though that's not a way I've ever seen it taught.

The first time I came across Free Qigong was in the mid-'90s. I enrolled in a Qigong course with a great Chinese master, Simon Lau, in South Kensington in London. He taught Qigong very methodically, very slowly: teaching over weeks the philosophy behind Qigong and how simply to stand and let the qi flow. He taught a basic form, too, but the emphasis was on standing (as described in *Energize It*, see pages 156–60). I was there for, I don't know, maybe six weeks. But I had to skip the class for several weeks because I was off on a shoot somewhere. When I returned, most of the people in the group seemed to have changed. We began the standing practice, just as I had learned and practiced while I was away. I had my eyes closed and was really enjoying the sensation of the qi flowing in my body. Then I heard banging coming from elsewhere in the room. I resisted the temptation to open my eyes and continued to stand. Then I heard other noises: someone was grunting, someone started to moan, there was a louder banging as if someone was stamping hard on the wooden floor. I resolutely kept my eyes shut, and tried to keep my attention within my practice. But it was hard. The noises got louder and more varied. Over the course of the next 30 minutes, I heard someone howling like a wolf, someone else moaning as if they'd had their pet kitten taken away from them, the sound of that pet kitten which had been taken away, and what sounded like someone beating their chest.

I never went back.

A few years later, I was doing a Qigong course with another powerful Chinese Qigong master, Dr. Bisong Guo. After a few weekends of practice, she too started to leave more space between the teaching and the formal set exercises. In one of those sessions, with nothing being said, nothing being done, just the space to sit or lie around and just be, I, again, was enjoying the peace and the feeling of qi flowing around my body.

Then, suddenly, there was a noise; the sound of a hand beating some part of the body... then a rhythmic guttural sound not unlike a Native American chanting by the fire. What a shock. Especially when I realized something.

It was me! Me doing the beating! Me doing the chanting thing! I hadn't thought about doing it. I hadn't wanted to do it. But it had just happened. Really naturally. And there was no stopping it. I seemed to be doing stuff and expressing stuff that I hadn't consciously thought needed doing or expressing.

And I loved it. Soon everyone was at it. Or most of us anyway. Others were asleep. Though I don't know how they slept through that racket. And the racket was just like the racket I'd heard a few years earlier, and had run a mile from. Only I was now helping to make it.

And I really got it this time. When you relax enough and tune in enough and settle enough, eventually the qi starts to move and, if you can fancy, you can follow that movement. Sometimes you feel like shaking, sometimes stretching, sometimes running around, sometimes shouting or howling, or sometimes sobbing. You don't decide to sob, the sobbing just happens. You don't decide to do the downward dog, the downward dog just happens. You open the door to it and that downward dog just bounces in to do its downward thing.

Free Qigong is VERY healing. You know it while it's happening, if you're aware of anything at all. When you let go and give in to whatever's going on there, you're unleashing whatever it is below (or above) all that's normally going on: whether it's the qi, or your instinct, or your higher self, or the Holy Spirit (those evangelical Christians get into some pretty freaky-looking stuff in the name of the Holy Spirit, including speaking *blaj l waj see dah flas lieu majjaww* tongues).

When you let go, you naturally begin to Express It. Whatever it is that needs to be expressed. Well, it's not even that *you* express it; the expressing just kind of happens.

If you watched one of those sessions from the outside, maybe on TV, the commentator would probably say, 'Please, don't try this at home.' On the contrary, my friend. Do try this at home. Here's how:

You could practice Qigong for a while, until you really begin to feel the qi and the flow of qi in different parts of your body. Then, if you stand or sit still and wait long enough, you will feel compelled to move in a certain (usually peculiar) way. **Do try this at home.**

Or, you could put some great music on and stand still for a little while. Relax your whole body. Breathe deeply. Close your eyes. Then start asking yourself, 'What do I feel like doing?' Whatever comes back, do it. It will probably be a stretch or a shake or a boogie. Follow that. And keep asking yourself, 'What do I feel like doing?' Follow it, wherever it takes you. You'll be amazed at where it does take you and how you feel afterward. As I said, Free Qigong is very healing.

And if you want to know how far it can take you. Listen to this. Gaia has done Qigong for years, like me. And Gaia is particularly intuitive, trusting, and spontaneous. Any of you who know her will regard that as an understatement. So Gaia was particularly into Qigong over the course of a couple of years. She'd do hours a day. She'd get up in the middle of the night to do it (the qi varies at different times of the day and night). And she'd do Free Qigong outside in the early morning. At the time we lived in a rented house on a hill. Around the house was a garden, and there were pretty steep drops on all sides. You probably wouldn't kill yourself if you fell down one, but it wouldn't be a pleasant journey. And the whole area was like that: little flat areas, some tracks and roads, and steep fields and drops.

Well, Gaia would close her eyes and start doing her Qigong, which would usually mean rolling around in the grass, or running around the garden at high speed – with her eyes closed. She came in one morning, as usual with bits of twig and grass in her hair. And she told me about that morning's 'practice' (clearly a ridiculous word for what she was doing). She had been running around the garden as usual, narrowly missing falling off the edges, and the qi had taken her off. She just wanted to run. So she ran… and ran… and kept running. No, not like Forrest Gump who ran for months. But she just ran, all the time with her eyes closed. Yes, indeed. And then she felt like stopping, so she did. And then she was guided to put her hand out, so she did. And, for the first time that morning, she opened her eyes. And there, in front of her, was a horse, sniffing her outstretched hand.

Now, don't do *that* at home.

But do have a go at this. We know many, many people who have made this a regular part of their practice/life.

And it's really about the most healing thing you could ever hope to do. Why? Well, it's probably the case that all the various forms of yoga, Qigong, and tribal dances were developed in just this way: by people like Gaia who were incredibly in tune with the qi or life force, and just moved as they were taken. They, or someone watching them, would then turn that into a set form for the rest of the world to have a go at. It seemed easier that way. So what we get in the various forms of yoga and Qigong are broad, therapeutic movement forms. It's like a form of physical exercise that manages to cover all the muscle groups – an off-the-peg suit, if you will.

However, if you really tune in, what you get is EXACTLY what you need and is right for you – a handmade suit, if you will. It might be that you're in perfect form apart from a slight blockage in your gall bladder meridian. Well, without you knowing, or ever having to know, anything about gall bladder meridians, or any other meridians, you find yourself doing a stretch and patting your legs, which (if you did know anything about the meridians) is the perfect way to sort out that blockage. It's like having the best Chinese doctor right inside you, or the best guru within you, or the best yoga teacher or energy healer. Whatever you fancy. When you tap into that qi, that vital life force, you're tapping into the best wisdom that money can't buy, without spending any money. Now that's magic.

TRUST
IT
■

When you practice any of the Magic techniques, it's worth trusting what comes up. You're playing with some powerful stuff (it's 'magic,' after all). Because you're tapping into your inner wisdom, or whatever it is, and it has immense value. So trust what comes up.

If you decide to simply sit still for ten minutes at the end of the day, and a peculiar image pops into your head: *I must eat radishes*, for example, trust that. Trust it because it's arisen in the powerful state that is stillness. Trust it because it is, in itself, random and peculiar (and difficult to explain and therefore drops into 'magic' territory). Trust it and follow the message… go and eat some radishes. Make radishes a part of your daily routine. Turn a radish into a necklace. Make radish your totem. Research radishes and see if they have any ancient meaning.

Hold on, let me do that now, because I wrote that down randomly, so it's worth me trusting that and knowing what it means…

Aha, there you go. Just looked it up, and it's about the lungs… clearing mucus, etc. And because I'm writing this as my favorite (not) blossom (acacia) appears pretty much everywhere I look, my lungs are a bit bunged up. So time to get some radishes in.

You see?

You just read my live experience of tuning in (when I write I'm generally relaxed and tuned in and free) and having a peculiar and apparently random piece of information appear (in my example for you of a peculiar and apparently random piece of information). Then I TRUSTED that piece of information and followed it up.

If I give something value and really Trust It, I do have to follow it up.

And the same goes for everything that 'arises' like this. You're relaxed and decide to go out for a walk on a whim (you used to only go for walks after dinner, now you're popping out for a wander at the drop of a hat). On your walk, while feeling so in tune and relaxed, you pass a billboard that is peeling off at a bus stop, so it's impossible to see what's being advertised. So you lift the hanging sheet to see that it's advertising a book you've never heard of. You make a note of the title. And you trust that this book might have something for you. When you get home, you look it up and order it. Cut to two years later. That book changed your life – it taught you how to make money from stamp collecting, which has always been your hobby. Now you buy and sell stamps online, and can even do it from your smart phone while you walk around.

> **When you're in an open, relaxed, mindful, neutral state, trust what arises. Trust It and you can't go far wrong.**

Of course, you can't trust everything, especially what you read on billboards. But when you're in an open, relaxed, mindful, neutral state, trust what arises. Trust It and you can't go far wrong.

I have a story about not trusting what was clearly arising for me, and I nearly went very wrong. Fasten your seatbelts.

This is a few years back. I was experimenting with what it's like to tune in, and trust, and then follow in A BIG WAY. So, I'd use all that I'm talking about here to really tune in to whatever messages I got.

Whatever arose, I would trust as very valuable, and follow.

And it takes some doing, as the messages that pop up are sometimes peculiar.

On this particular morning, I was traveling from London back home to Italy. I was flying from London's Stansted airport, and had worked back the timings so that I'd get the train from Liverpool Street station to the airport in good time, with a good hour's leeway. At Liverpool Street, there's one train every 15 minutes to the airport. So if you arrive and you've just missed a train, it's fine, because another one will be leaving soon.

I arrived a few minutes before the next 'Stansted Express' was due to leave. I made my way to the train. When I got to the platform and saw the guard and people boarding the train, I had a peculiar feeling. Something felt wrong – very wrong. I hesitated. Given that I was experimenting so consciously with tuning in and trusting, I tried to examine what was going on. Why did I feel like this? I'm not a nervous traveler; I don't normally feel like this. But, I argued with myself, it was illogical. What could go wrong on this short train journey? However, something felt terribly wrong. But the other part of me reasoned that if I didn't get on this train, and wait for the next train in 15 minutes, and there was something wrong with this train, then I'd be caught behind it anyway… I still wouldn't get to the airport on time.

So I went with my head rather than my gut feeling.

I sat down in a carriage and spread out a newspaper in front of me.

A short time into the journey, I thought I could smell the faint whiff of smoke. I carried on reading. Soon, there was the unmistakable smell of burning. I looked around and no one else on the packed train seemed to have noticed the smell. I started to worry a little. I got up to check how to get off the train if I needed to (in a hurry): I found out where the hammer was located, so that I could use it to smash a window and get out. I sat down again. But the smell continued to get stronger. I got up again and went to find a member of staff. Three carriages down I found a guard and told him I could smell burning in my carriage. He told me to go back to my seat and he'd investigate.

I went back to my carriage, but there was now smoke in the carriage, as if a couple of people were smoking. Still, no one else had noticed. The guard appeared, smelled the smoke, saw the smoke, and looked a little panicked, and then disappeared toward the front of the train. Two minutes later, the train stopped. The carriage was now filling up with smoke. The other passengers had finally noticed, and a couple of people even moved out of the carriage.

I found out 15 minutes later from the guard I'd notified about the smell that there was an actual fire under our carriage, but they'd put it out, and we'd now be making our way to the airport, though a little more slowly than usual.

As I was talking to him, a train passed on another track, going toward Stansted Airport. I realized in that moment that the train behind us didn't necessarily have to stay behind us because there was more than one track.

I also realized that, even though I had known there was something wrong with this train, I had not listened to my feeling… and there had been a fire on the train. No, not just on the train… UNDER MY CARRIAGE.

But I felt light and relaxed, like I got the joke. I admired the way the point was being made to me so specifically and so powerfully. I relaxed, too, in the knowledge that the train was now fine and would continue on its way to the airport, still getting me there on time because of the hour's leeway I'd left.

But we did go very slowly. And, after passing a station along the way, the train came to a halt again. After sitting there for ten minutes, the driver came onto the PA and said that we had run into a flood, so we'd have to return to the station and find another means of getting to the airport. Sorry.

Fire, now flood. This joke was getting funnier.

We got to the station, and I knew that inevitably I had to get onto a bus quickly in order to stand any chance of catching my plane. I was the first on the bus, which was very soon packed. I knew if we left shortly I could make it. But the driver announced in a wonderful friendly tone:

'Mornin', ladies and gents, we'll be on our way to the airport soon. Got to admit, though, that's it's my first day on this route, so hope you can help me out if I get a bit lost.'

He got lost, of course, badly lost. And none of us knew the roads round there.

Did this joke have an end, a punch line?

When we finally got off the bus, I knew that I'd missed my plane. Not because the plane had taken off, but because it was 35 minutes before it was due to take off and Ryanair is very strict about not letting people check in less than 40 minutes before take-off. So I went straight to the desk. There was a line, but I was the first in line from our train/bus. I also knew of two other possible flights that I could get to Italy that day, which would get me close enough to home.

I still felt relaxed. I felt it was an adventure. I was being taught a lesson. And I wasn't going to resent that lesson, I was going to enjoy it – even if it was darned inconvenient.

And when I got to the desk and asked about one of the alternative flights, I was told it was full. I asked about the other one (to Bologna), and it had just one space left. I booked it – and smiled.

It was an astonishing day for me. I did feel as if I was being taught a lesson of trust, but by a force that was benign. ('If you stay with this, John, and stay relaxed, and NOW trust me, I'll get you through it, but let me have my fun, won't you?')

This travel anxiety has only happened to me once since. I suddenly got anxious about driving on the country roads here in Italy. I even told Gaia that she should slow down, because you just don't know what other people are going to do (they tend to cut the corners). So I drove more slowly that morning. I wondered, too, if my fear could actually attract some trouble, but resolved not to be scared, just more cautious than usual.

Sure enough, on my return from dropping off the boys at school, on the last stretch before turning onto our track, I was driving (more slowly than usual) down the open road, and a car was waiting to pull out from a driveway. The driver was looking in my direction. But just as I was closing on her, she pulled out right in front of me. I braked. I swerved. I missed her by a few inches. If I'd been going faster I would have ploughed into her door.

Or would I have passed that driveway before she'd even gotten to it?

How the heck was that one working?

I didn't know, and I didn't think about it too much. What I knew is that I'd had that feeling again and I'd trusted it – and avoided an accident.

Did you know that there are usually fewer than average people on trains that crash? Sadly, there are still people on those trains, but there are fewer than there 'should' have been.

How the heck does that work?

Now, please don't suddenly stop getting on trains and planes because you feel slightly weird. This is a very rare and unmistakable, unusual feeling. If you're generally nervous about flying, for example, don't suddenly start to think that you're nervous because something is going to happen. Things usually *don't* happen. Planes are even safer than trains, and trains are very safe – even trains that burst into flames, and hit floods.

ATTRACT IT

A book could be written on this subject alone. In fact, many have. And very well they've done, too (*The Secret*, anything by Abraham-Hicks, etc.). The question is this: how do you attract the stuff you want? Well, even that is making an assumption – that you somehow believe you can 'attract' things to you. So let's rephrase the question in less presumptuous terms:

How do you get the stuff you want?

How do you get the stuff you want?

The magic answer (the 'secret') is this... drumroll, please...

You want it. I

But not too much.

Yes. Yes. I'm going to explain. Let's cover the ground either side of this proposition (for successful 'manifestation of whatever you want') first, though.

THE GROUND ON THE LEFT: NOT WANTING ANYTHING SPECIFIC

You can go through life not wanting anything specific at all. The people who do this are usually in two camps. One camp has a big + logo painted on the entrance. The other a big – logo.

The − lot (that's a negative symbol, by the way) drift through life without any idea of where they want to go. They usually feel that life is random, tough, and shitty. They act like victims on the receiving end of the terrible cards life has dealt them. They take no responsibility for anything that happens to them and spend their lives complaining about everybody and everything.

If you sat them down and gave them an easy-to-enact action plan for how to get out of the shitty situation, they'd start their response with 'But...' This camp is hard to escape. It's a prison camp. And everyone in this prison camp is kept in by habit, negativity, and the fact that everyone else around them thinks and talks the same way. If you find yourself straying inadvertently into this camp, and talking to one of the inmates, try to get away as soon as you can. If you have to sit and listen to them, close your ears and think about something else. They're unlikely to hear any sense. The only thing they'll respond to is if you say, 'Yes, it's terrible isn't it?'

The + lot (the positive camp) is a happy, laid-back place. This lot has realized that 'wanting' stuff is like being on a never-ending treadmill. You want something so bad. Then you get it. And it's okay for a moment. But then you want something else. Then you get it. And it's satisfying for a moment. Then you want something else. And so on, and so on.

This + lot have realized that you don't need to get anything else, or go anywhere else, to be happy. They're fine with who they are, they're fine with where they are, they're fine with what arises in their life in any moment. They have no particular plans. They certainly don't have any goals. If they feel like visiting another country, then, sure, they'll 'plan' a trip. But they don't plan to transform their life so they can have twice as much time away. They are spontaneous. They're very relaxed and nice to be around. And things seem to work for them.

So why isn't this chapter about them? Because not many people make it to this camp (and if you now make it your aim to get there, you've probably missed the point). This chapter is about them to this extent: the reason life tends to work for those in this camp, is that the law of attraction (which we're coming to) works in some very subtle ways. If you're happy with your lot and open, and feel good about most of what's going on for you, yet you have no fixed plans, then you're still likely to attract some amazing stuff into your life. In fact, you're likely to attract most of the amazing stuff that those using manifestation techniques want to attract. It's just that you're not using any techniques. You're just living, and it's working. Lucky you.

THE GROUND ON THE RIGHT: BEING VERY FOCUSED ABOUT WHAT YOU WANT

This is how most of us operate, because this is how we think we get the things we want. And getting what we want is pretty much what life is like for most of us. I'm not just talking about the material stuff, of course. Whether you want a Porsche, or to meet the perfect man or woman, or to get promoted, or to be happy in your skin, or to live in the countryside, or to have more friends, or to float your company for a billion dollars, or to find more peace in your life, or to start a family, or to make a difference, or to be able to access your higher self, or to meditate like a monk, or to have sex with more than 1,000 people before you're 40, or to complete your collection of Mickey Mouse teapots, or to free yourself from the confines of your ego, or to make a breakthrough in science and win the Nobel Prize, or to enjoy the heady scent of power, true power, or to become famous, or to get better, or to run a marathon, or to find enlightenment, yes, become enlightened, truly enlightened…

You want something.

And the way to get that something you want is, usually, to follow these four steps:

1 Be clear about what you want.

2 Work out a plan (with steps) to get it.

3 Persevere and work hard on those steps in order to get it.

4 Not give up.

And this IS an effective way to get what you want. Yes, I'll say that again: this is an effective way to get what you want. And this is how many people have gotten what they wanted. Maybe it's how most people have gotten what they wanted.

Period? No.

It has its price – in fact, prices. I'll number those, too:

1. NOT HAPPY

Are they happy when they get what they want? Often not. The very nature of the programming (which includes something like *I'll be happy when I get…*) means that, once the 'wants' are achieved, then they're replaced by other wants. Steps one to four are repeated forever. For the sophisticated seekers, it ends up with 'I want enlightenment.' Even Buddha wanted that. Conclusion: it's a bottomless pit of desire; the serially fulfilled wants never fully satiate the core desire (which is, usually, to feel good).

2. IT'S TIRING

Exhausting, in fact. Look around you and what you'll probably see is people literally exhausted by the process of following the above programming. It works on its own terms (you might get what you want), but it knackers* you out, and will probably make you ill.

3. IT EXCLUDES SPONTANEITY

If you're very focused and stick to your plan, follow your steps and persevere no matter what, you close yourself to the numerous opportunities and sights that exist around your plan. You'll know this to be true from every part of your life. For example, on a journey, say, in your car, when you're entirely focused on where you're going and what you'll do when you get there, you tend not to notice what's going on around you. You don't consider other routes that might be more picturesque or more pleasant or less busy. You don't notice the whole world of life out there through the window. You don't notice the old woman who's just eased herself onto a bench to enjoy a bar of chocolate; you don't notice the leaves held up above the street, momentarily motionless because of the meeting of two air streams; or the burned-out restaurant you used to go to with your wife before you were married; or the kid pulling on his mother's hand, wanting to go into the toy shop; or the poster pasted onto a boarded-up storefront advertising a meditation and mindfulness course. And that becomes your life. You don't notice what's really going on, because you have your eyes on something else. Well done, though, at least you're focused.

4. WANT VERSUS NEED

You might get what you want, but maybe not what you need. The two are often different. Watch any movie. Most movies are about a character who wants something very, very much and tries to get it. They are presented with challenges along the way, sometimes apparently insurmountable ones. But they usually prevail and (usually) get what they want. Along the way, however, usually by confronting what's referred to as their 'ghost' (something deep within them that they haven't been able to face previously), they realize what they 'need.' And it's often different from what they 'want.' So getting what they need usually becomes the point, and the satisfying aspect, of the movie. In the end, getting what they want becomes a sub-plot, less important to them and you than getting what they need. Therefore, if you can work out what you need, rather than what you want, you could save yourself a lot of time. Indeed, if you can work out what you really, ultimately 'want,' it starts to converge with what you need. With a bit of thought, you might realize that you simply want to feel good, now. And all your want-chasing is, underneath, motivated by that simple desire to feel good. If all you really want (and need) is to feel good, now, why not cut a long story short and decide you can feel good now, without anything else? I will, now. Ahhhh, that's better.

THE MIDDLE GROUND: ATTRACTING WHAT YOU WANT

I see now that this is literally the ground in the middle – and good ground it is to be on, too. So attraction does work:

It works for those who don't want anything in particular, but are feeling good in the now: they attract lovely stuff into their lives that continues to make them feel good. This is like the soft side of 'Life' (or the 'universe' or 'God' if you prefer, I'll use 'Life' this time): saying, 'Well, I love the fact that you're so laid-back and grateful just to be you and to be doing what you do, so I'm going to give you something really rather lovely… I know you don't need it to be happy, but I'm going to give it to you anyway; call it a "thanks-for-not-bothering-me" gift, if you will.'

And it works for those who are very focused. This is the more business-like side of Life. It's the subcontracted fulfillment house of Life saying, 'Yes, Yes, I know I promised that if you asked, then you'd receive, so we're working hard here on providing what you want… we're doing our best, you know, it's just that it might take a little time, please be patient, thank you.'

And if you combine elements of those two methods of successful attraction, you get something rather magic (which it's why it's in this magic section).

So, begin by learning from the first group: learn to be fine with who you are, where you are, and what Life is giving you on a moment-by-moment basis. (Turn to *Thank It* on pages 175–9 for how to do this.) Learn that you can feel good now, without going anywhere or doing anything, or improving anything about yourself.

Next, learn from the second group: if you keep something you want in mind, you're very likely to get it.

Then fuse the two together. You begin to lead a life in which you're fine with you, who you are, and where you are in life. But in this space of acceptance and gratitude, a desire arises for something else. And that desire for something else doesn't mean that what you are now is wrong. It's just a gentle desire. It's like walking in a park in a wooded area. You're enjoying being in this area, among the trees. But you then have a thought that you'd like to be next to the lake, watching the ducks and the swans. That thought doesn't make you dislike where you are, or unhappy with being among the trees, but you now start to walk gently toward where you think the lake is (you know there is one, you just can't completely recall the exact spot). You enjoy the walking. And when you reach the lake, you enjoy the experience. But while you're there watching the ducks, you realize you're hungry, and have a desire for Chinese food – crispy duck, in particular. And this desire doesn't make you dislike the experience of watching the ducks (though it's a little weird), but you now plan how to make your way to a Chinese restaurant. Later, on your way to your favorite Chinese restaurant, you bump into a good friend whom you haven't seen for a while. She's free and wonders if you want to eat together. You know she's allergic to MSG, and she suggests going to a great Italian restaurant she knows. So you agree. You let go of that thought for crispy duck easily. And you start looking forward to a *tagliatelle al ragu*, which, when you get to the restaurant, the waiter informs you they don't have on the menu. But they have *gnocci* with a duck sauce, which is strange and you go for it. You try some of your Italian on the waiter, and you get chatting. And a week later you're sitting in a Chinese restaurant with the sexy Italian waiter, eating a dish of crispy duck.

So you have a few apparently contradictory things going on here (which is what makes it an interesting art to practice):

1 Recognizing that you can be happy with what you have, but still 'wanting' something else, at the same time.

2 Being clear about what you want, but not being attached to it. This is the ability to hold something lightly: *Yes, it would be nice to have that, but my happiness doesn't depend on it* (and this is supported by point one, because you're happy anyway, so your happiness certainly doesn't depend on it).

3 Being clear about what you want, but not knowing how you're going to get it. If you can resist making your step-by-step plan and instead open to it happening in many different ways, then you open to Life helping you do it. It takes the strain off you (remember that exhaustion was a major problem for those who were focused on what they wanted). It means you can be more free and spontaneous. And it means you're likely to find amazing new things along the way that will probably fulfill what you 'need' as well as what you 'want.'

If you can figure that out, then you give Life a fine old time, too. Life is happy because you're happy, so the pressure's off (for you and Him/Her/It). Life is happy because the brief is clear, but the ways to achieve it are loose (this gives the fulfillment house much more flexibility and the opportunity to be CREATIVE – and they love being creative). Life is happy because if, for whatever reason, there's some kind of f**k up down at the fulfillment house (and mistakes do happen, that's Life), then you're not so attached, so it's fine.

Everyone wins. It's magic.

I said 'F**k It' – and bought a Porsche

I'm a consultant. I do well – well enough to pay the mortgage, lead a nice life, take the odd vacation, and run a sensible car. And it was on a F**k It Retreat in Italy, in fact, a couple of years ago, that I decided to say F**k It to the sensible car thing. I knew it would be a stretch on the bank account. But I also thought If not now, when? I'd always wanted to drive a Porsche, so I thought that I should take the plunge and try one out.

As we all shouted 'F**K IT' together at the end of the retreat, I wondered how long all our great F**k It intentions would last. I wondered how long mine would last. In truth, I expected that I'd still be driving my sensible car along sensible roads throughout that winter. But then I got home. I went into my house, put my bags down, and before I knew it I was in my local Porsche dealer...

Then I was driving my car. And that's what I've been doing ever since – not terribly sensible, but massively rewarding in a visceral, primal kind of way. The next summer, I went on another F**k It Retreat in Italy. This time, in Roxy my Porsche. I still have Roxy. I get joy from her every day. I occasionally double-take at the garage bills. But it's been worth every minute. And I've gone from saying 'F**k It, I'll buy a Porsche,' to 'F**k, I've got a Porsche.'

Mark Seabright, *UK*

Just one of 100 F**k It stories in the new e-book I Said F**k It, available at www.thefuckitlife.com/extras.

---

* British colloquialism meaning exhausting; also knackered (derived from 'knackers yard,' slang for an abattoir).

= THE
F**K
IT
STATE

On F**k It Retreats, we often ask people to write down what's going on in their heads. We ask them to write rapidly, and without thinking too much or censoring. We call this a 'brain-drain.'

And what they write is fascinating, though it's usually pretty grim and negative.

But it still probably isn't a true look at what goes on in their heads on a normal day. You see, even when they 'brain-drain' without censoring a word, they are, after all, away from home in a beautiful place with very little to do, a thousand or more miles away from the source of their problems.

And, anyway, who does get a clear, unadulterated look at what goes on in their heads? Unless you meditate regularly, and are used to that 'watching' quality you get after a while in meditation, you're unlikely to be fully aware of what's actually going on in there. It's hard to be in a thought and outside, looking at it, at exactly the same time.

So, to save you the effort of this mental contortion, let me have a guess at what's going on in your brain much of the time. I do this from years of being told what's going on in other people's brains (from such exercises) and from listening to my own.

'Everything was so important, even the things that clearly weren't.'

'I was lost in my thoughts.'

'I know I was always looking at what was wrong with my situation and my life.'

'I was completely in my head and my thoughts; I wasn't really aware what was going on around me.'

'I spent most of the time thinking about the past or the future.'

'My thoughts were racing, thinking about what I had to do and when I had to do it.'

'I felt uptight – so much so my shoulders and neck were hurting.'

'I wasn't really aware of anything going on in my body, I was entirely in my head.'

'I know I was judging everyone and everything… that the situation wasn't good, or that what so and so had done was awful.'

'I could tell there was a moment when a sad thought came up, but I pushed it away and got on with the day.'

'I was really pissed off, I could have screamed.'

'I could see all the hate and negativity that there is in the world.'

'I planned a lot… how to focus and get what I wanted.'

'I was taking everything so seriously.'

'I was feeling anxious and afraid.'

'Most of my thoughts were very dull, planning things and the like.'

'I felt alone, as if no one understands me.'

Whoa. Heavy stuff.

On F**k It Retreats we then take everyone through a deep relaxation process. Everyone gets very chilled. Some people go to sleep. And next we ask them to write down what they felt like and experienced during the relaxation. You can do this yourself very easily (that way you'll believe this).

These are the kinds of things that people say (taken from what people have actually said):

'It felt like things didn't matter so much.'

'I was very aware of any thoughts that were popping up in my head, but almost as if I was distant from them.'

'I felt very "grateful" for being here, and being me.'

'I felt very present to everything that was going on in my head and my body and everything around me, too, to the point where I could hear all the details of the smallest sounds.'

'I was entirely present.'

'My mind just went kind of blank. There was actually NOTHING going on in there. It was just blank.'

'I felt more relaxed than I've ever felt in my life.'

'I felt a tingling and a warm sense all over my body.'

'I had this sense of being neutral, that everything is just the same, not good, or bad, just that it kind of "is."'

'I felt very sad actually.'

'I just started crying, for no obvious reason. I just felt the tears coming, so I let them.'

'I felt this amazing sense of LOVE, for everyone and everything.'

'I felt this strong sense of trust… that everything I need will come to me.'

'I felt very light and playful.'

'I felt completely safe.'

'I was having some weird thoughts and ideas.'

'I felt very connected, to other people, but also to everything on the planet, as I'm just part of it all.'

Now, if you've been switched on (and that's probably more the first list than the second, so don't worry if you weren't 'switched on'), you may have noticed that the qualities identified in the second list were pretty much the opposite of those on the first list.

In fact, if you were super switched on, you'd have noticed that they were also in the same order.

If you were super, super switched on, you could probably have related some of those qualities identified with preceding chapters. So, from these observations and responses at least, it seems that we're in a pretty much opposite state when we're very relaxed, than we are in our normal, busy, everyday life. Remember, these responses haven't been made up, they've been taken from real responses we've noted in exercises we've done over the years to explore the qualities of these two 'states.'

> **When you're in this state, you are naturally very F**k It: things matter less and you're completely relaxed.**

And 'states' is not a bad word to use here. In Qigong, the state you get into when you relax deeply is called 'The Qigong State.' In hypnotherapy, the hypnotherapist aims to 'induce' a client into this more relaxed state using a 'script' of calming suggestions and visualizations, and calls this state 'the light trance state.' On F**k It Retreats we call this state –

'The F**k It State.'

When you're in this state, you are naturally very F**k It: things matter less, you're not so bothered, and you're completely relaxed.

I have always been very interested in this state. For two reasons:

1 I could tell this state was very healing for me. And I was sick, so that was important.

2 I could tell this state was very creative. And I was a professional creative, so that was important.

In fact, probably without realizing this coincidence at first, I explored the areas of Qigong (primarily for the healing side of this state) and hypnotherapy (primarily for the creative side of this state) very deeply over the years.

And…

1 I knew if I could get into this state at will, and get into it more often and for longer, I would most likely heal.

2 I knew that if I could get into this state at will, and get into it more often and for longer, I would be able to generate many more ideas.

This fascinated me, too. I was in an industry (advertising) where the people who came up with the ideas actually had coined a noun ('a creative') from what was normally only an adjective ('creative'). And we were paid a good amount of money to be creative(s). Yet very few people investigated the act of creativity or the state that best fostered creativity. In fact, it's just the opposite. I think many creative people are afraid to investigate their creativity too deeply in case they kill the magic. I took the risk and found that there was a reason many of us creatives would sit around reading the paper, or play pool, or find it difficult to sit in an office and head off to cafés and bars instead. I saw there was a reason that I seemed to get most of my best ideas in the shower, or while I was walking home from the train, or during the night, or when I wasn't actively thinking about the problem…

The reason was that the best ideas were only popping up once I was in a special relaxed state. And I got into that state when I was doing all those things listed above, but rarely when I was sitting at a desk looking at a brief on a piece of paper and trying to 'crack it.' And rarely in meetings. All the ideas came outside that space: the space particularly designed for creative people to sit in (an office).

Once I'd explored hypnotherapy, I understood, scientifically, how this state was working. I knew the simple things I could do to get myself in that state quickly and, crucially, ANYWHERE. Ironically, I found a way to become very creative in exactly the place where people were supposed to be creative in the first place (but were not): in an office.

And I can sense a very big metaphysical point there in that last paragraph, which I'll try to convey before it disappears, never to be sensed again: when you do get into the F**k It state you realize that there's actually nowhere to go and nothing to do. You can stay in your office and be fine. You can stay in your job and be fine. You can stay in your relationship and be fine. You can stay in your life and be fine. The Zen saying goes 'Before enlightenment, chopping wood, carrying water. After enlightenment, chopping wood, carrying water' – which has lost some of its impact for those of us who spend zilch time either chopping wood or carrying water. So this is the F**k It Zen update: 'Before enlightenment, browsing Facebook and fiddling with your iThing. After enlightenment, browsing Facebook and fiddling with your iThing.'

Now, this difference in state has been interpreted and explained in many ways over the years, but let me take one explanation that I think you'll find attractive and helpful – that of the brain. It also allows me to draw on the amazing story of Jill Bolte Taylor, which I can allow to help illustrate the astonishing qualities and power of this F**k It state, and, indeed, to remind you why it's fundamentally important for you to be able to access this state.

JBT, as I'll call her (though I admit it makes her sound like a whiskey, or a construction company, or even a disease), is a neuroanatomist. She has always been fascinated by how the brain works. And, of course, she has had more of an idea than most of us of how the brain worked, which turned out to be very fortunate indeed.

One day she woke up with a sharp pain behind her left eye. Over the following few minutes, as she did some exercise then made her way to the bathroom, she experienced a peculiar sensation of dissociation, seeing her own movements as if in a movie; she began to have problems moving fluidly and balancing; and, on running her bath, the water sounded like a deafening roar. She began to realize that she was probably having a stroke. And when her right arm dropped, paralyzed, to her side, she knew it.

She knew that blood was flooding into, and slowly incapacitating, the left side of her brain. She knew that she needed to get help, but her ability to get help was rapidly deteriorating (she was losing memories, including the memory of a neighbor living close by and the ability to recall numbers to make a phone call).

Throughout this rapid deterioration, though, she felt calm. In fact, she felt a remarkable sense of peace and 'oneness' with everything, a sense of liberation, tranquility, and safety (although she was objectively in the most dangerous position of her life).

She knew that the flooding of her left brain was allowing her consciousness to shift into her right brain, as she puts it:

'In the absence of my left hemisphere's analytical judgment, I was completely entranced by the feelings of tranquility, safety, blessedness, euphoria, and omniscience.'

Her stroke, in other words, was giving her a remarkable 'spiritual' experience: an experience of enlightenment or 'nirvana.'

She managed, by the way, to summon help (by laboriously piecing together the phone number of a colleague at work). And she made a remarkable recovery (through her own efforts). In fact, the story of her recovery is doubly interesting… because she had to make the decision as to whether to remain in the blissful state that her incapacitated left brain had left her, but have trouble operating in the world, or to rehabilitate that side of her brain, and be able to operate successfully in the world, but lose that state of bliss.

She now teaches people how to create more of a balance between the two sides of the brain, and to effectively temper the bully-like dominance of the left brain. Her greatest insight has been that, based on losing her left brain, she knows that a deep sense of peace is located in the neurological circuitry of the right brain. The sense of peace is always there, it's something that we simply have to tap into (by quieting the left brain).

Wow. Please read her book *My Stroke of Insight*. It's awesome. And it saves you having to suffer a stroke yourself to gain this level of insight.

And here's the point… (I'm going to prematurely go off-page now, because I don't want this massive point, and revealing information, to be so easy to find again that you have a page number to find it with)…

This is how we got to the idea of F**k It in the first place. After years (and years) of exploring this 'state,' in all its aspects (creative, healing, spiritual, etc.,); of trying to find easy ways to access that state and stay in it for longer, we found a very simple 'password' that could unlock this state very quickly – F**K IT.

Of all the ways in all the world to access this magical, healing, blissful, peaceful, enlightened state, we'd found a way that contained a swear word and that seemed to work more quickly and more powerfully than any other way. Wow!

We've spent the years since saying a very long 'WWOOOWWWWWW,' in fact. We've spent a long time (and many words) trying to understand and articulate why it does work so well. And along the way, hundreds of thousands of people have joined with us in saying 'WOW.' In just about every language, people have said, 'Wow, that profane expression actually works in making me feel more free, wow.'

So, yes, there are many ways to help you make the jump from the left brain to the right brain (including flooding the left brain with blood), but there is none quicker or more powerful than saying F**k It.

That's because F**k It is unique in our language in summing up the essence you feel (and think) in the right-brain state; that things don't matter so much.

*F**k It is unique in our language in summing up the essence you feel (and think) in the right-brain state; that things don't matter so much.*

If you were to imagine a F**k It person, you'd end up with a person who was operating from the right brain much of the time (though clearly, not all of the time, read your Jill Bolte Taylor).

And it's possible to live like that. Live It. No, not running around with your eyes closed, finding horses in steep fields. But it's possible to apply what you experience in something like Free Qigong and spread it out into your real life. It wouldn't be called 'practice' otherwise, would it?

SECRET SECTION

THE
MAGIC
TECHNIQUES
DISTILLED
INTO
'THE
MAGIC
SIX'

THE
MAGIC
SIX

We set out in this book partly to reveal the therapeutic process we take people through on a F**k It Week. We've elaborated and deeply investigated that process here. And on our weeks we tend to work around a Six-part Magic F**k It process. In fact, we elaborated it so much that we realized it would be nice to sum it up and distill it again for you as a new F**kiteer. And we've done so in the 'secret section' – i.e., it's not visible on the Contents pages. We've even taken off the page numbers; which will make it a bugger* to refer back to. It also makes it a bugger for us when we sign books, because we normally turn randomly to a page, like taking a Tarot card, and offer that as our gift to the person. It's often spot on.

(Digressing for a moment about the books we write. If you mention a particular section or story to me and I look confused, it's because I don't remember writing it, sometimes because I wrote it a while back, other times because I'm just plain forgetful. I had two people in the last week say to me, 'I loved F**k It, the only bit I struggled with was when you suggest that it's fine to smoke.' Fine to smoke? What? I said that. Why would I say that? I don't smoke. It's clearly dangerous to smoke – for me and for others around me. Why would I say it's fine to smoke? Is there someone on the editorial team who's secretly funded by a tobacco giant, who slips in positive references to smoking on the sly? Did she think 'Aha, F**k It is the perfect medium for my pro-smoking message. It's been so tough with all these spiritual and healing books getting in a mention, but Parkin will love it, yeah, say F**k It and smoke yourself to death, they'll love it.'

Well, I just looked it up. I wrote, under the chapter *Say F**k It to Illness and Disease:*

> 'Some people get so tired and bored of trying everything and spending lots of money and investing so much energy that they simply give up. They say one big F**k It and finally give up wanting to be whole and well and perfect. They're still feeling pain and discomfort like they always did and they just say F**k It and give in to it. Nothing makes any difference anyway, so why should they go through the added pain of hoping it's going to go away?

> They give in fully to their condition. They surrender completely to their pain. They give up wanting to be any different to how they are, just as they are, now. They probably start eating things they haven't eaten for a while, they may start drinking and smoking again. What they certainly do is RELAX. The one thing you'll always do when you really say F**k It is relax.'

Blast. And what I meant, of course, was that the relaxing and giving up has surprising effects, because you don't care so much, even in ways that look so unhealthy.

I didn't mean smoking is good. It's probably better if you don't smoke, don't do drugs, don't consciously harm other people, don't fart in lifts, don't say you don't like food that's been cooked for you by other people, and don't do a garlic burp in someone's face.

Now, if you come to me in five years' time and say, 'John, I loved *F**k It Therapy*, the only bit I struggled with was when you say it's wrong to fart in lifts, because I'm chronically flatulent and it's not a voluntary thing, it just happens, like, all the time, and, rather than sticking an orthopedic cork up my bottom, I prefer to say F**k It and let it go, and relax around it,' I'll do a garlic burp in your face. In fact, I'll carry some garlic in my pocket especially for signings. And if you do mention something that hasn't quite worked for you, I'll pause, reach for the garlic, chew on a bit, gargle some sparkling water, then burp on you.)

This is the Bermuda Triangle of F**k It Therapy. Enter this magic, focused, and distilled area at your peril. The distilled magic techniques are so powerful that you certainly won't exit the section the same person. You might not exit at all. Or if you do, you'll come back in the pristine uniform of a World War II bomber pilot.

This may well become the most thumbed bit of the book for you.

And, talking of thumbs, the Magic Six is so easy to remember you can almost count it on one hand. In fact, we had one guest who was so keen to be able to count off the Magic Six on one hand that she had surgery in which one finger was taken off her left hand and then sewn on to her right hand. Where did she

This is the Bermuda Triangle of F**k It Therapy.

put it, you're wondering, aren't you? Good question. She had it sewn right in-between her index and ring fingers. To be honest, as well as the pain and the expense, I don't personally think it was worth it. It now plays havoc with her ability to identify which one is her 'ring' finger. Is it the finger that was previously her ring finger? Or is it this additional finger, which now sits there next to the index finger? I don't know whether she'll ever figure it out.

* Tricky or difficult to pin down.

1. OPEN

Open to new possibilities. Open to things
changing. Open to life panning out in a
way you would never have expected.

2. RELAX

Relax your body. Relax your mind. Take some deep breaths and feel the tension dissolving as you breathe out very slowly. Consciously relax every part of your body.

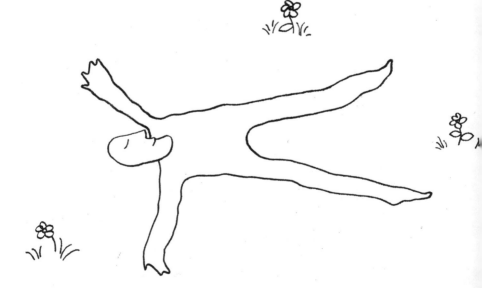

3. SHIFT PERSPECTIVE

Just getting perspective is a shift in perspective. See that things you worry about don't matter so much in the grand scheme of things.

4. TUNE IN

Become conscious of what's going on for you at every level and really feel it, without judging it and without ignoring it.

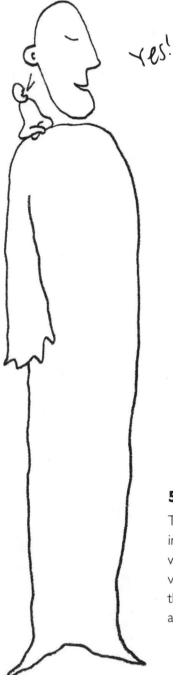

5. TRUST

Trust what you feel when you tune
in, or that the messages you get
when you tune in (e.g., 'I'm tired') are
valuable and true. Pay attention to
them like you would to the words of
a legendary guru.

6. FOLLOW

Follow whatever it is that feels right
once you've tuned in. If you trust that
movement or feeling enough, you will
feel it and express it fully in your life.

THE MAGIC SIX DAILY PRACTICE

Start by using the Magic Six in your daily practice. You can use the guide to Qigong in Energize It on pages 152–163 to get into how the qi feels. Then really start to play with Spontaneous Qigong.

Using the **Magic Six**, it goes something like this. Put some music on and stand still.

Open to the possibility that amazing things might happen in the next 20 minutes, possibly something that could make a dramatic difference to your life.

Relax your whole body, using your breath if need be.

Shift perspective when you realize that you're tapping into something that you don't fully understand here, that life and healing might well not work in the ways that you thought or believed.

Tune in to what's going on for you. Do so by asking, 'What do I feel like doing?'

Trust that the messages you get back (e.g., 'Shake your arm about') are valuable.

Follow that message – go ahead and do what it tells you (e.g., shake your arm about).

Go through that process until you don't have to think about it anymore in your practice: you'll just be standing, then following the qi in the end.

You'll see soon enough the magic of this practice.

And, if you do continue to practice like this, watch as the magic spreads out into your life. Use the Magic Six steps consciously if you wish. But it will soon start to happen naturally (though there's likely to be the Magic Six process present in everything that you do, underneath).

We explore how to live like this in *Life On the Outside – Being Free* (*Living the F**k It Life*) in Part VIII, pages 242–303.

PART VII

GETTING SHOT AT AND SURVIVING IT

SAYING
F**K
IT
TO
WHAT
OTHERS
THINK

WHO
WILL
BE
SHOOTING
AT
YOU?

Well, it would be nice to think that, given you've been in your prison of sorts, and that it's clearly not been pleasant for you, and now you're trying to find freedom in your life, escape from that prison, use the power and magic of F**k It to bring freedom, freshness, and happiness into your life… it would be nice to think that people around you would support, nay, applaud you, for your noble pursuit of freedom.

It would be nice to think that people would only be inspired by the new life they see in you, and maybe that they, too, would be so inspired that they'd ask you what had happened and what you'd done, and that they'd then start to make similar changes in their lives.

It would be nice to think that you'd become a local role model in your community, whom people point at and whisper reverently, 'They managed to escape this prison we're all in, they had the courage to say F**k It and make a break for freedom.' People would start to follow you around, hoping that, just by being near you, some of the delicious sense of freedom that you carry might somehow rub off on them. You'd be a like a F**k It Pied Piper.

It would be nice.

And it does happen. Many people who come on F**k It Retreats do so because they have a friend who came once and they couldn't believe the change in them after just one week… they had to have whatever it was that the friend had had, so they booked a week for themselves. Those who have been on F**k It Retreats do e-mail us to say that people have been amazed by the changes – that they look different, that they're calmer, seem to have more time for them, etc., etc.

But it's not always like that.

You see, when you make your break for freedom, you tend to remind everyone else around you that they're not free. And people who are in prison, but tend not to think about it too much, people who don't actually want to make their break for freedom at this moment, don't particularly like being reminded that they're not free.

> *Many people who come on F**k It Retreats do so because they have a friend who came once and they couldn't believe the change in them after just one week…*

Let's look at an example. You work, even though you don't like your job, because you have a mortgage to pay. You have a mortgage to pay because you need somewhere to live, and you didn't want to throw money down the drain on rent. You need somewhere to live that's pleasant, too, and in this town/city, somewhere pleasant has its price, and its price means that your mortgage is high. So you don't even have the chance to shift jobs, because any cut in pay would be critical to your mortgage-paying capacity. And that situation is similar for your work colleagues. Many of them are even more obliged to stay where they are, even if they don't like it, because they have families to support, too. And that situation, or something close to it, is present across every office, every store, every factory, every hospital, and every brothel in the town/city where you live. And everyone has kind of accepted that's the way it is.

Except you, who's decided that doing a job that you don't like is killing you. Life is short and precious, and you're pissing it away spending 43 hours a week doing something that's not you. You had dreams once. You wanted to be a singer or an actor. But you were put off by your first rejection letter from the drama college you applied to, aged 18. Now you're 38, living out the uneventful drama of an unfulfilled life, an actor without an audience living someone else's life.

Enough.

You start researching drama colleges on the internet. It gives you a thrill just to look at the sites. The thought of spending three years learning how to act, acting, and hanging out with amazing people, gives you a rush. You say F**k It and apply to three colleges, including the best in London, in the UK, probably the world, where many illustrious actors have learned their trade. You use the tricks you've learned about F**k It manifestation (Attract It), and you focus on what you want, but you don't hold on to it too tightly. And you know that if this route doesn't work, another route will pop up for you magically.

Six weeks later, after interviews and auditions, you get a place at the best drama college in the world, to start in September, which is three months off.

You say F**k It, resign, giving a month's notice, and start to plan a mammoth trip for your free two months.

So you'd think everyone would be pleased for you, wouldn't you? And some are.

Subject: WOW!!!!!

Sarah,

Wow! Jenny told me you've got into RADA, and you're off around the world. F**k Me, Wow! Big congrats. Am so jealous. You got room in your bag for just one little one? LOL.

Annie xx

And…

Subject: Jammy Sod

S,

WTF! Where did that come from? Don't do this to me. Don't leave me on my own with Lechy Lenny in the stationery cupboard. That's just vicious. You're a hero… Go For It.

Love and envy,

Tx

But there are others.

Subject: Your News

Hey Sarah,

Bro here. Mom told me your news. Wow, that's some change you're making. You know me, I'm personally all for following your dreams (why else would I be working here at Goldman Sachs otherwise?), but is this not a little extreme?

Mom and Dad are worried, too. You've done so well to get on the housing ladder, so why burn it now? Do you know how many actors there are out there vying for every job? And you already had a job!

Don't get it myself, but your life is yours to lead as you fancy.

Please, though, give Mom and Dad a call, they're worried.

xDavid

And…

Subject: Your Decision

Sarah,

Phil here. I've talked to the other directors about your decision to leave and go back to college, and we're all very disappointed. You've been a valuable member of the team and you'll be missed.

We're secretly hoping that you'll see the error of your ways and change your mind. If so, there's always a desk here for you. In fact, Cliff reminded me of another promising manager, Isabelle, who went off to become an artist. She went back to college too, with the hope of doing what she loved and making it big in the art world… and Cliff heard recently that she's temping at some city firm. Ouch!

Of course, we wish you all the best, and hope that it all works out for you in the acting world.

Phil

And there are always some very honest mates.

Subject: Nutter on the Loose

Sarah,

*Now you know I love you to bits, always have, but WHAT THE F**K ARE YOU DOING?*

I've got friends who would kill for your job and that money. And your apartment is so LOVELY.

Why are you throwing it all away? For the chance of a bit part in a TV cop drama?

You been taking the bonkers pills? Sorry, I know this sounds harsh, but someone's got to talk a bit of sense into you. Call me. Text me. Change your mind and reassure me.

Yikes,

Tanny x

HOW
TO
AVOID
GETTING
HIT

A key part of F**k It Therapy is learning to care less what others think.

Whenever we do our F**k It Retreats, one of the most significant things holding people back from doing what they want, being who they want to be, is fear of what others will think and say.

It's a key part of the F**k It Therapy process because the steps you're taking to become free involve learning to listen more carefully to what you want, deep down inside. Much of the process revolves around this: opening, relaxing, tuning in, being more conscious of how you feel, really listening to the messages you receive, trusting those messages, and eventually following (your heart). It's all about another perspective shift: from orienting your life around what's expected of you by family, friends, school, work, society and doing what you believe you should and ought to do… to going inside yourself and listening to what you'd like to do and who you'd like to be.

Given that you've listened to what others think for so long, it's clearly going to be hard when you come to some conclusions about what you want that are different from the things that others would want for you. It's going to be hard. But there is most likely going to be that dissonance (otherwise how did you end up in the prison that you were in, anyway?). What you're doing in the F**k It Therapy process is reducing the value you place on the messages you get from outside yourself (parents, friends, teachers, leaders, politicians, celebrities, etc.), and placing more value on the messages you get from inside yourself.

Picture this. You're in a crowded room of adults – a cocktail party, maybe. It's very noisy. Everyone, it seems, is talking. Everyone has their opinion, and they love giving it. Everyone has a story to tell, and they love telling it. Unnoticed by everyone except you, a young girl, maybe five years old, has entered the room. She's so small that no one sees her, except you. She's so quiet that, when she speaks, no one hears her, not even you. It really is so noisy in there. You try to get closer to her. And she continues to speak. She clearly has something to say. Soon, you're right next to her. And you lean down to hear her. You hear a few words – 'I just wanted to say that…' But the noise in the room is just too much to catch any more. You ask her to wait a second. You stand up to your full height and say to the adults in this crowded room, at the top of your normal voice, but without shouting:

'Excuse me, excuse me… Sorry… quiet please for a moment. Please be quiet, just for a moment.' It does quiet down after a while. 'Sorry, but there's a little girl here, and she has something to say to us all… please go ahead.'

And the girl speaks. And what she says is for you. Or you think it's for you. And it touches you deeply. And it makes you realize that you've got it all wrong. That even being in this crowded room is all wrong. And you feel sad and happy at the same time. And you thank the girl from your heart. And you say that, whenever she wants to speak, you'll not only listen, but you'll quiet everyone else down so you can hear exactly what she's saying. But you leave the room anyway, because it's just too noisy and you don't know why you were there in the first place: all those self-important, opinionated people.

That's F**k It Therapy. You have to quiet down the noise in order to hear what's being said by the little voice inside you. You have to listen carefully to that voice and give it value. You then have to act on that voice, and that usually means either keeping the other noisy adult voices in the room quiet or getting out of there.

You have to say a big F**k It to what others think of you.

You have to, in other words, say a big F**k It to what others think of you, and say, about you.

Of course, this doesn't mean that you'll ignore everything anyone says to you, like a rebellious teenager who says 'bollocks' every time someone speaks. We're talking about re-balancing here. Once you're more attuned to what's going on inside you and what you really want in life, then you can hear what's being said out there from a different place. In fact, there are infinite wonderful things being said out there that can help you to continue to be free. And, when they align with what you want, those external voices can assist you along the whole way. We're talking about a shift of emphasis or perspective, and a dramatic one, from placing most worth on messages that come to you from the outside to messages that you get from the inside (when you listen hard enough). This, if you want, is the 'inner journey' that spiritual people talk about. This, if you prefer, is listening to your inner voice or your higher self. It's your instinct. Or it's God. Or it's the intelligent field of energy that pervades everything. Whatever it is, you have to care less about what's going on 'out there' in order to tune in and give value to what's being said 'in here.'

And the simple words F**k It become like a magic shield in this respect. Whenever you hear the messages that try to put you back in your box, back in your prison – the fear-mongering, risk-avoiding, follow-the-crowd voices – and it doesn't feel right for you, then just say F**k It and keep listening and trusting and following your own way. You can imagine, if you want, a F**k It magic shield surrounding you, deflecting all the arrows of fear that are shot toward you when you make your break for freedom.

GAIA'S MAGIC WORDS
'I don't want to'

How does it feel to read that line?

'I don't want to.'

When did you last dare to say that?

A lovely woman in one of my groups found herself saying it in the middle of a session. And it sounded like a little girl's forgotten voice.

How many things there are that we don't want to do or be!

As children, we said it. We made ourselves heard as much as we could. Whenever things didn't fit with our rhythm and our world... 'I don't want to.'

You see, that magical child has got their own rhythm, their own amazing wisdom, their knowing that isn't based on knowledge, and doesn't need much prodding, just love and security. Instead the adults think that their role is to teach the child and dictate how to be. So eventually the magical child shuts up, and we end up with a thousand 'I don't want to's' that remain unsaid.

And yet if you talk to anyone, there are so many things they don't want, but don't dare to talk about, or even to feel.

This is because of our culture of 'grin and bear it.' People say 'we need to be adults; enough of the child,' so we need to grow up; we need to face the world, our responsibilities; we need to make this adult thing work. We can't be children; we can't say 'I don't want to.'

But we have forgotten that the child is an integral part of us. Growing up doesn't mean discarding the child. It can mean having it all: the magical child AND the able adult.

But the magical child comes also with their dose of pain and needs, so we give up the magic in the hope of giving up the pain and needs. It doesn't really work like that. We end up feeling rather cut off.

It is time we let ourselves say 'I don't want to' and make some space for that Magical Child. Their pain is only there because people haven't listened to them. So, are you going to do the same? Not listen? They are you. And when you stop ignoring them, you realize that there's a whole world of self-love, self-respect, wonder and magic, intuition and introspection, which you'd forgotten because you believed you couldn't say 'I don't want to.'

WHEN
YOU
GET
HIT

There are going to be times, of course, when what other people are thinking and saying gets to you (you might wonder how you'd know what people are thinking if they're not saying it, but you do, you know you do), especially, if you love them and value their opinion. Just like getting hit in your figurative prison escape, there's a variety of things you can do:

RETREAT OR TAKE COVER

You understand what's not working for you, you've made your escape plan, and you've started to enact it. And everyone around you thinks you're potty. And that bothers you. Well, pause for a while. Don't jump yet. Give it some time. Think things through some more. You've got all the time in the world and there may well be more than one way of skinning a cat, not putting all your eggs in the same basket, not burning bridges, etc., etc. After all, a bird in the hand is worth two in the bush, the early bird catches the worm, and you can't teach an old dog new tricks (those last three were randomly included when I realized all those tasked with translating this new book will recoil in horror when they see I've used some idiosyncratic idioms that have little relevance to the original point). Google them!

The process of pushing out and then retreating back a little is very natural. So use it. It's how we make progress in most areas of our lives. It's what TV and delivery pizzas were made for. You need the yin of retreat to balance the yang of the breakout.

GET MEDICAL ATTENTION

Your break for freedom can often feel very lonely. So get some help. Find a guide – someone who understands what you're going through and what you're trying to do, and can help you from an objective standpoint (i.e., someone who's not invested in you staying exactly where and who you are). There are also many 'guides' available on the bookshelves and internet – teachers (like us) who can help you in a variety of ways at different stages of your journey to freedom. And what you need from a teacher and guide may well change as you progress. Open to the idea that the help you need will appear when you need it. Just remembering that you could do with some help (the medical attention) at times is usually enough to attract that help into your life.

PERSEVERE AND HOPE YOU DON'T BLEED TO DEATH

Keep at it. No one said it was going to be easy. Keep trusting yourself. This is the road less travelled, and because of that it's not perfectly surfaced and maintained. It can be bumpy, rutted, and difficult to keep to. At times you can't even see which way the road goes. You even forget why you took this road in the first place. But it's hard to go back. In fact, going back is just as bumpy and rutted. Take a rest occasionally, but if you're using your heart and your gut as your compass, keep sticking to your chosen direction and, in the end, you can't go wrong.

LIE DOWN AND PRETEND TO BE DEAD

Do you know anyone who does this: you ask them to do something that would help you and improve the relationship, and they reply that of course they will and they completely understand, and they're sorry if their behavior has caused difficulty... then they go away and don't change a thing. You talk to them again. And they reply in exactly the same positive way. But they go away and, again, nothing changes. It's confusing to deal with.

And it's the equivalent of playing dead. When you talk to the person, there's no resistance, just complete agreement. But when you walk away, they carry on as they were. Just like when you approach the prone body, there's no movement, no breathing, but when you turn your back and walk away, they start dancing a jig – until you turn and look at them and they drop to the floor, 'dead' again.

It's confusing, but it can be very effective. So this is what you could try. When anyone comes to you expressing their concern or disagreement, you sit there calmly and agree with everything they're saying, and you completely understand what they're saying. But you don't add the 'but' that normally comes next. You offer no resistance. You make it look as if they've helped you to see the error of your ways, and you'll walk away from that helpful conversation and change everything (back).

But you change nothing. You carry on as you were. When they come to you again, somewhat baffled that you haven't changed a thing, use the same tactic and agree with them entirely but do nothing.

After a few rounds of this, they'll leave you alone. It hasn't been unpleasant for you or them. But you've achieved what you wanted (which was to be left alone). In fact, ironically enough, what you'll most likely elicit in them is a gentle 'Oh, F**k It.' They'll feel they tried, that they did their duty, but it's just not worth it. They'll leave you alone, but then be happy for you when it all works out. In fact, peculiarly enough, they might well feel part of it. Nice.

PART VIII

LIFE ON THE OUTSIDE – BEING FREE

LIVING
THE
F**K
IT
LIFE

BEING
FREE
AND
ARRIVING
IN A
TOWN
WHERE
YOU
FORGET
WHAT
YOU
CAME
FOR

An abiding memory from my childhood is of my mother arriving in a room with a sense of purpose, then stopping and saying, 'Now what did I come in here for?' It happens to us all, especially as we get older. I was about to write 'sadly' after 'it happens to us all' there. But then forgot what I'd come to write. No. No. Actually I don't find it that sad. It just means a little more walking around the house, and that's not a bad thing. I sometimes descend the two staircases between my office and the ground floor to pick up something I need, then get back to my desk and realize I've returned with something I didn't go for (usually food) and entirely forgotten what I intended to go for (something non-food). It just means I have to get a bit more exercise (which helps burn the calories off the unintended food pickups).

It's not sad either because it reminds me of a beautiful universal truth: we all arrive in this thing called life and, at some point, we say, 'Now what did I come in here for?' We assume, you see, that we've all come here for something, but just can't remember what it is. We then wander, slowly, but still desperately, around the room, trying to work out what the f**k it was. Some of us persuade ourselves that we've remembered ('ah, yes, I came in for the scissors, yes, that was it, I definitely came in here to pick up the scissors, because, yes, I have to cut some paper downstairs, that's it'). Some of us think we've remembered, but then are unsure, and keep wandering and looking ('Ah, but was it really the scissors I came for?... I know I need to cut some paper downstairs, but that can't have been the only reason I came up here, there must be something else, something more important, surely'). Some of us have no idea what we came in for, and don't really care anyway, it's cool just to be in the room, and we'll see what turns up in the room.

Contrary to Pascal, I'd prefer to take the risk – not live a lie for the sake of a 'possible' future salvation.

Now, of course, it could well be that you did come in for something, but have simply forgotten it. In that case, if it was actually the scissors, well done. Well, well done for remembering the scissors, but maybe there were plenty of other things in the room you missed by grabbing the scissors and rushing off back downstairs. If you did definitely come in for something, but really don't know what it is, and you're constantly wondering, and you're not really going to be happy in the room until you've worked out what it is, even though you've got those scissors in your hands, then your life is probably quite tiring. But you could argue that, given that you did come in for something, you could never be happy anyway until you've worked out what it was.

Contrary to Pascal, though, who asserted that, logically speaking, it's better to believe in God because if you believe in God and it turns out there is a God, then you're saved, rather than not believing and risking the chance that, if there is a God, you'd be damned. It's a kind of cosmic hedging of bets. Contrary to Pascal, I'd prefer to take the risk – not live a lie for the sake of a 'possible' future salvation, but open to the possibility that, just because I've forgotten what I came in for, I might not have actually come in for anything in the first place and I'm curious as to what's in here anyway, maybe I will realize that I came in for something specific, maybe not; or maybe I'll realize that, but then change my mind, then realize I was wrong all along, but nevertheless enjoy the whole process of not knowing, of wondering, of being there. Of being here.

So here's the happy ending. Mom used to arrive in that room with a sense of purpose, then stop, and say, 'Now what did I come in here for?' Then she'd pause and say, 'Oh, I don't know. Oh, hello, John, why don't we play a game?' And we did. And I carried on playing, forever and ever. Amen.

BEING
FREE
IN
WORK
TOWN

What do you imagine when you read those words 'Work Town'? Do you see an industrial town, all factories, grime, and smoke, with exhausted waif-like people shuffling to grinding dirty jobs that pay little but take too much? Do you see a town full of offices, with commuters squeezed together at the same time each morning to arrive for a 9 a.m. start to a day that will consist of tapping away at a keyboard or yapping away in meetings? Do you see a town full of home-workers, flexi-workers, sitting over laptops in Starbucks, having Skype meetings over their smart phones with other teleworkers in different time zones, fitting work around their lives, not the other way round, dropping in and out of work clubs, private clubs, health clubs, club lounges, creating passive incomes from e-businesses and smart investments?

Do you see work as something unpleasant, which you have to do and tolerate so that you can earn money to pay for your life? Do you long for clocking off and the weekend and payday and vacations?

Or do you love your work? Does your work give you so much satisfaction, so much meaning, that you're happy to work into the evening, through the weekends, and skip the vacations?

Do you want me to stop asking so many questions, given I can't hear what you're replying? Yes? Oh, go on, just a couple more…

Do you need to continue to earn money to live?

Do you need to earn as much as you do to live?

There are some people who can answer 'no' to the first question; the lucky few who can sustain their lifestyles (higher or lower) without ever earning another dime. There are not many of you, but you're out there, and working out what you want to do with your time and your life is as potent a question for you as it will be for the other 99 percent.

And of the 99 percent, I'm pretty sure that many of you could downsize if you really wanted to, or had to.

So this is where we start with work: examine your approach to work, your assumptions about work, and all your ideas about money and lifestyle. Just a small task.

Or you could start here:

What do you LOVE doing?

If you didn't have to earn any money to live, what would you do? How would you spend your time?

If you won the jackpot, say enough money to keep you going at your current lifestyle level for two years, what would you do with your time?

Write the answers down. You could even buy a little notebook, or open a page on your smartphone notebook app and call it 'WHAT I LOVE DOING.' Don't censor yourself. You're not trying to work out if you can make any money from this. Not yet. You're just writing everything down.

I do it all the time. And I'll do it now. I will make some notes LIVE, publicly, of WHAT I LOVE DOING:

- I love listening to music on my own in the car, really loud.

- I love waking our boys up in the morning with the same line 'Good morning, beautiful boys!' to hear them moaning in complaint (at being woken up and my repetitive line).

- I love having ideas for new projects.

- I love Qigong.

- I love having meals out in Urbino with Gaia.

- I love making music then playing it to people in groups without them knowing it's mine.

- I love walking.

- I love it when I work something out about myself or life or how things are.

- I love writing stuff down for people to read.

- I love making people laugh.

- I love making people think.

- I love swimming in a warm sea.

- I love the winter and always mourn its passing.

- I love the summer and always mourn its passing.

- I love eating Chinese food with my sister and our folks.

- I love my trips to London, staying in hotels and absorbing the buzz.

- I love you.

- I love me.

- I love being well, feeling fully alive.

- I love feeling tired and climbing into bed.

- I love to see the meaning of things become clear over time.

- I love to fall back into the randomness of it all.

- I love playing football with the boys.

- I love doing radio interviews.

- I love to be paid for doing what I love.

Okay, I haven't censored or edited it.

Don't censor or edit your list (even if 'I love masturbating' is up there at the top). Don't get upset that you didn't put apparently worthwhile stuff (or people) closest to the top. If you spent some time dreaming up all the ways you'd love to spend your time in *Breaking Through the Wall of Lack of Imagination*, now is the time to just write down what comes to mind as it comes to mind. Do it quickly.

You can spend a couple of weeks doing this if you fancy. Carry your notebook/smartphone around with you so that you can add things as you go. I've done this many times. I end up adding lots of stuff. Because I realize, in the course of actually living, that I've forgotten some important things that I really love.

And by doing this you create a comprehensive idea of what you love doing in life. You'll probably, too, remember things that you used to love doing that you don't do anymore. I did this exercise a few years ago and realized that what I used to REALLY love doing when I was younger was making music (on a guitar). I realized in that moment that I could make music again, not on the guitar this time, but digitally – I could create the music I love to listen to (electronica) myself. Awesome. It took me a while to learn the required bits of software. But I figured it out. I loved it. I love it. And I'll soon be earning some moolah* from doing it, too†.

And thus we move on to the next question: can you earn any money from any of the things you love doing? If you reply that you don't want to earn money from what you love doing because it would ruin the thing you so love doing then please go back to the beginning of this chapter and examine your relationship with work and money.

The idea here, in case you haven't spotted it, is to make money (small or large amounts depending on the desired lifestyle) from doing what you love.

And it takes some F**k It. It takes some 'F**k It, I don't want to do this for the rest of my life.' And it takes some 'F**k It, yes I can make this work.' And it takes some 'F**k It, I don't care what you lot say, I'm going to do this.'

Yes, I know, you're looking at your list thinking 'how can I make money from 'arranging flowers in a Zen way?' or 'making models of watering cans out of matchsticks?'

But it's possible to make money out of just about anything, especially if you love doing it.

The second point first: when you love doing something, you put everything you have into it; you're happy to be doing it, and people pick up on that. You make money when other people want what you've got to give. And they're more likely to want what you've got to give when they feel that it comes from your heart and your passion.

Simple example: you go into a hardware store to buy fork handles. There's a slovenly youth behind the counter listening to some dub-hop on his iThing. You ask him 'Excuse me, do you have fork handles for me to purchase, perchance?'

He suddenly realizes you're there. He pulls out his earphones and asks you, 'What?' So you repeat your question. He replies, 'Dunno, probably not, try the candle store, mate.' You don't understand, but are too irritated, especially by his overfamiliar use of the word 'mate,' and leave.

Compare that to the experience you would have had with the chap who worked in a factory most of his adult life, but always dreamed of owning a hardware store. He just loved hardware stores – oh, to have one store that could stock so many useful items for people! He just loved the idea of rows and rows of tools, screws, tapes, key copies, handles, etc. So when he was made redundant from the factory, he used the money to open his own hardware store.

And there he is behind the counter, polishing his old-fashioned cash till when you come in:

'Excuse me, do you have fork handles for me to purchase, perchance?'

'Of course, sir. Can I ask you what size you're thinking of?'

'Why, I'm imagining just a usual size, I suppose.'

'What, tall and thin, or short and stubby, white or a color, we have so many, sir. Would you like me to show you some, and you can take your pick?'

'Why, thank you, that would be marvelous.'

You are delighted with this chap and his open, friendly manner. You will, of course, buy the fork handles he brings out for you to view.

When he brings out a range of candles, you are confused. But the confusion is soon cleared up. You said 'fork handles;' he thought you said 'four candles.' You both have a laugh. And you pay for four fork handles that combine as novelty candles so that, on birthdays, you can both tuck into the birthday cake with your fork, and light the fork at the same time to blow out and celebrate your birthday.

Now the first point, second: it's possible to make money out of just about anything – especially with a variety of modern technologies (zippy ways to make and produce things, and zippy ways to spread the word about things and get your zippy things to zippy people all over the world). Combine the zippy technologies with some imagination and you could end up doing what you love and earning money from it very quickly. When you've earned enough money from it to know that you don't have to continue

'F**k It, I can and will make a living out of doing what I love.'

doing the thing that you don't love so much but have done because you had to earn money, you can stop doing the thing(s) you don't love in favor of the thing(s) you do love. And that's a good thing.

This is the formula:

1 Work out what you love.

2 Use your imagination to find ways to make money out of what you love.

3 Use zippy technology to make it all happen.

If you can't work out ways to make money, have a lie down and dream a bit more, talk to friends… there is an answer in there… you just need to let it come to you.

You can do it. Come on. Say after me:

'F**k It, I can and will make a living out of doing what I love.' And in the process I'll be showing everyone I know that it's possible to make a living of the things that they love, too. Until the whole world is doing what it loves and making a living out of it.

I make a living out of doing what I love. Gaia makes a living out of doing what she loves. Part of that happens to be teaching other people to say 'F**k It' and make a living out of doing what they love. Lovely jubbly‡.

---

* Money (origin unknown) but often described as such in the UK.

† Listen to F**k It Music at www.thefuckitlife.com

‡A jocular expression meaning loveliness itself (and you really need to rub your hands together while saying it in a jolly sort of way). The inimitable Del Boy Trotter, in the smashing British sitcom of the '80s and '90s *Only Fools and Horses*, made this phrase famous.

BEING FREE IN MONEY TOWN

It's not easy to be free in Money Town. It's a dazzling place in which all the riches you could imagine allow you to live a life you could only dream about.

In Money Town, those who don't have much are constantly reminded by those who do (have enough, and more) that it's the money that matters: the making of the money, the accumulating of the money, the spending of the money. It's the money that gives you value in Money Town. Given that money is the currency for everything (including self-esteem), people who are out of the currency loop feel terrible. They're always looking at those who have the money with envy. Of course, there are older people who remember the times, long ago now, before the money took over, when people were happy without it and happy to be out of the loop. In fact, they even saw being in the loop as a little vulgar. But the whole system in Money Town is there to reinforce the idea that money matters. It's in the name of the town, after all. So money does matter. It has to. If it didn't matter, then less of it would go around. And then where would the citizens of Money Town be?

But it's not all easy for people who are in the loop either, for those who have the money and access to all the wonders of Money Town that only money can buy. Sure, they have a great lifestyle. But they see people without money lurking in the shadows of the town: dirty, desperate, hopeless souls. And they spend every moment in fear that they could lose their money and end up in the shadows, too. They also fear that they don't have enough, that there are always new people coming into the town grabbing their share of the money, and that there are older people hanging on to their money and not letting it flow around the loop. Both are threats. Surely there's not enough money to go round with so much new grabbing and old hoarding.

Is anyone happy in Money Town, then? Is it the money that's to blame? Or does Money Town just attract unhappy people who then blame the money for their unhappiness?

Well, sure, quite a few of the happy people on the planet simply moved out of Money Town. They decided it wasn't worth worrying about, so they moved to places where they weren't reminded every day of how important money is. Or they gave up their highly paid jobs and decided that they could live on less, and moved out of town to enjoy living, not just making a living.

But the surprise news is that there are many people in Money Town who *are* happy. There are those who don't have much, who still enjoy what they have, and celebrate the success of others, even when the others have a lot more than they do. There are those who have an awful lot, and enjoy every cent to the fullest, but they don't hang on to it. They know that the money doesn't matter SO much, and they'd probably be okay without so much of it anyway. They actually see the making of the money as a bit of a game.

WHERE DO YOU LIVE?

It's not easy to be free in Money Town, but it is possible.

Within our circle of friends and acquaintances, I know people from all sides of Money Town, and many people who have moved out of town, too.

Our interest, given that much of our society is dominated by money, is not to avoid it, or opt out, but to see how it's possible to be free with money. How is it possible to say F**k It around money?

How is it possible to enjoy money and all that it brings without getting attached to it and becoming its slave?

I don't know. So let's move on to the next chapter, *How to Clean Out a Hamster Cage*.

Actually I do. Don't worry.

What's my money story? Well, both my parents came from modest backgrounds. They worked hard and succeeded in creating a 'very comfortable' (as my mother would say when I asked, as a kid, 'Mom, are we rich?') home and life for us. We knew we were lucky. And we all liked what that money bought: a lovely home, a big Bang & Olufsen TV, vacations, meals out, etc. (I know that sounds peculiar now, but this was back when having a meal out was a real treat.) But there was some guilt there, too. Mine was a Christian family. And though it was satisfying to drive up to the local church in a nice car with leather seats, the dissonance was also felt.

So I grew up, went off to university, and then went into a job. I had what I thought was a very healthy attitude to money: I believed that if I did what I loved, then money would follow. I judged those who worked just for the money, and those who displayed their wealth ostentatiously. But I still, I know, wanted to be 'very comfortable.' I decided not to continue along an academic path because I wanted to try my hand in the real world (and that included earning some real cash). I did relatively well, relatively early on. I had a great job doing what I loved, which was writing and coming up with ideas, and it paid well.

But I was in conflict and, at times, I knew it. I wanted the bigger paycheck and all that it bought (a bigger apartment, a better car, some security, maybe even 'freedom'). But I also regarded money as somehow vulgar. I only worked on projects I believed in, and even persuaded myself that I was making a difference in some of the things I did. Like the environment I grew up in, I had an ongoing, ever-present dissonance, the desire for something, but then the accompanying guilt with it.

Fast-forward a few years. Gaia and I decided to leave the well-paid jobs and all their security behind to set up a retreat in Italy. We wanted to live a simpler life, in the countryside, and do what we loved – practice and teach holistic disciplines. We packed up our belongings into a campervan (including our one-year-old twin boys) and headed off to Italy to find a location for the retreat. And we found the perfect spot remarkably quickly: a hill near Urbino with two abandoned farmhouses on it. So we began to plan how to purchase, renovate, and establish the retreat business.

A few months later we returned to London to earn a bit of cash. We lived in a one-bedroom apartment in Balham. Gaia would do one-to-one breathwork sessions with clients in one room, and I would escape to the local park with the boys in their buggy.

And during that time we had to start filling in the details of how the whole project would work. I had to create a business plan (I'd never done one before) and we had to raise money (I'd never had to raise so much money before). I got nervous. We needed what felt like a huge amount of money. And I realized, with a jolt, at that moment, I had issues around money. I realized that, though I needed lots of money to make our 'simpler living' plan work, I was suspicious of money. It became very clear to me that, at the same time, I wanted it and didn't want it. I wanted it, but it was vulgar. I wanted it on my terms. I would judge other people with money entirely on the terms that I had created around money: it's okay to have it as long as you don't flash it around too much, and you use your money to 'put something back.' I could feel, all of a sudden, all the contradictions and blockages and issues I personally had around money.

So I decided it was time to clear them. I wrote dozens of positive sentences about money: sentences that I knew full well were different from my money beliefs, sentences that went against any moral logic. I had (you'll see), sentences that contradicted any economic laws I'd learned (specifically that we live on a planet of finite resources).

This was the kind of thing:

- Money is coming at us from all directions.

- There is plenty of money to go around.

- I love money and money loves me.

- We are attracting more than enough money for our retreat project and for our personal needs.

- I celebrate all those with money as abundant souls.

And so on.

Don't judge.

Okay, so I tapped this out on my laptop in that tiny apartment. I printed them up and stuck them all over the walls of the living room. I started reading them out repeatedly and relentlessly. I encouraged Gaia to do the same. I didn't force our 18-month-old boys to do so (someone might have called in the social services – 'those Parkins are indoctrinating their babies with positive money psychology, it's DISGUSTING').

The next day I took the boys, as usual, while Gaia helped someone else overcome anxiety, or whatever, and I had to call in at the post office on an errand. As I stopped to grab the door and negotiate the boys' vehicle through the gap, I looked down and saw a £20 note on the ground. I picked it up. I didn't pocket it straight away. I looked around. I waited to see if anyone came out of the post office looking for a lost note. But they didn't. So I kept it. It was working ALREADY. Money was coming at me from all directions. Wow. I had never found more than 10p on the ground before, and here I was, the very day after reciting all those positive sentences, finding money on the ground.

The next day we got a call from Gaia's mum. She'd just come into some money, and wanted to share some of it with us. It was a significant amount, enough to get us over the first financial hurdle. And we were off.

I was stunned. This shit worked. It didn't just surprise me that it worked, but that it worked so damned quickly.

We went on to set up the retreat, calling it 'The Hill That Breathes.' And the retreat did well. We lived (and still live) in a fantastic place, and were (and still are) earning enough money to lead a comfortable life.

And I have had, since then, what feels like a very healthy relationship with money. We are very abundant, in that we're happy to spend money on ourselves, on other people, and invest in new and exciting projects, knowing that the money returns eventually, usually multiplied. We don't judge or resent others who have money, whoever they are, however they spend it. We don't think there is too little to go around, so we have to hold on to money or things. Yet we don't think that there's an infinite supply of money or things so that we can make waste.

I personally have just about everything I could want. But I sometimes fantasize about having more (like a nice car with leather seats) and enjoy those thoughts. I personally enjoy owning stuff, quite a bit of stuff. But I don't hang on to it too tightly, knowing that if it all went, we'd probably still be okay. I know I'm saying this from a fortunate position.

This is how to say F**k It to money, and many other things in life: Get conscious, clear issues and blockages, judge less, and recognize you'd be okay without it.

So let's go back to that original question: how is it possible to say F**k It around money?

How is it possible to enjoy money and all that it brings without getting attached to it and becoming its slave?

It is possible when you become conscious about your relationship with money; it is possible when you clear any issues around money; it is possible when you lose any judgment of money or those who have it (or don't have it); it is possible when you realize you'd probably be okay without it.

That is how to say F**k It to money, and many other things in life: get conscious, clear issues and blockages, judge less, and recognize you'd be okay without it.

Mundane example to make the point that this isn't just about money...

You realize you're having problems with close friends. First, get conscious: what really happens for you around friends? Next, clear issues and blockages: do you fear being abandoned because your best friend at school went off with someone else? Next, judge less: don't be jealous of those with loads of friends, or dismissive of those with none. Then, recognize you'd be okay without them: know that you'd be fine if you did lose some of your friends.

And that little process creates some veritable F**k It Magic. Not just for your dollars and cents... but for everything. It makes a lot of sense.

BEING
FREE
IN
RELATIONSHIPS
TOWN

Now I had this idea of waiting until Gaia and I had a vicious argument before writing this chapter. Why? Because from the outside we seem to have the ideal relationship. We've been together for 15 years; we share so much good stuff. We have two amazing kids. We even manage to spend a lot more time together than most couples because we work together. Many of the lovely folk who come on our F**k It Retreats comment how good we are as a couple. Some people have said that we have restored their faith in relationships, that it's possible to find your soul mate, and make it work with them on a day-to-day basis.

So I write this, as promised, after a humdinger of an argument – a dirty, stinky, insult-throwing, 'I-don't-even-like-you' round of blows to the head, heart, and belly. There were even illegal, below-the-belt blows.

Saying F**k It and being free in Relationships Town is a difficult one. Saying F**k It and being free in any town can be difficult, but relationships always, it seems to us, present their challenges. Even, or maybe, especially, when you're getting into a F**k It frame of mind.

The statistics are not good when you look at long-term relationships. Between 40 and 50 percent of first marriages end in divorce. And who's to say how many of the remaining percent are happy marriages? How many of them are staying put because of the kids, or because of a religious belief, or because of fear (of what would happen to them outside the marriage)? How would you define 'happy marriage' anyway? Is there anyone out there who has a consistently happy marriage, even a generally happy marriage with the odd hiccup? Yes, I think there probably is. But not many.

Given the stats and given the facts of your experience of relationships, what's the point in even trying? Is the very idea of a long-term relationship some culturally imposed pipe dream, anyway? Ah, you say, but it's very natural to be in long-term relationships, it's part of our fabric of being, the idea of meeting a life partner with whom you have offspring, and then rear said offspring. But have long-term relationships ever been the norm? Has the number of couples who stay together long-term ever gotten over that halfway mark? If we look back, we assume that divorce rates used to be lower, that people stayed together longer. But we live in an age when people live longer than they ever have (on average, of course). You don't have to go back that far to find that many people were dying in what we now refer to as 'middle age.' It's not that long ago that many women would die in childbirth. And that's to say nothing of the mass elimination of young men (mainly) in the two World Wars.

When you look at it like this, the idea that you meet someone when you're relatively young, and you stay with him or her until you're relatively old, has probably always been as unlikely as it is now. Before it was probably because one of you would get knocked out early involuntarily. Now it's because one of you has had enough and knocks off early voluntarily.

So while we're into the knocking, why don't we knock on the head the idea that a sign of a successful life, and a successful relationship, is its longevity?

Ah, that feels better.

So, your relationship working or not working isn't a reflection of how you're doing, or have done, in life, okay?

If you're five times divorced, it doesn't mean you've done any worse or better than Mr. and Mrs. Bloggins over there who are still bickering over who should make the tea for their 50th wedding anniversary.

SO, WHAT ARE YOU AFTER IN RELATIONSHIPS TOWN?

It's worth asking yourself that. In fact, it's worth going through a whole F**k It process around your approach to relationships.

If we take those six F**k It steps we looked at in the *Secret Section* (see page… ah, they aren't numbered are they?)… Okay, I'll summarize:

Open, first, to more possibilities in the life of your relationship (and we're talking here about a relationship with a significant other, though you can clearly spread these ideas out to other relationships in your life). Open, clearly, if you haven't already, to the possibility of it becoming more or less close (i.e., that you commit more, or you commit less and leave).

Relax around the relationship. It's not the be all and end all. Your life isn't going to be judged on the success of this one. Your life probably won't fall apart if it doesn't work. Ease up a bit on yourself, and your expectations of the relationship. Ease up a bit on your partner. Ease up on the pictures you have in your head of where this relationship could go (and you probably have opposing pictures of an idyllic future and one where you leave this person, too).

Shift your perspective. Just realizing that the very idea of long-long-term relationships is, practically speaking, quite a new one, and the reality is, statistically speaking, pretty grim, shifts your perspective. Shift your perspective, too, from backward or forward looking (either looking back at your dodgy past relationship experiences or creating weighty expectations of future relationships) to present looking, just seeing how things are now, and working with that.

Tune in and listen to yourself and the reality of relationships. What are you really feeling about this relationship and your role in it? Tune into your partner, too. Start (if you don't already) talking to them about how you and they feel, but generally and about your relationship. If you really, consciously, gently, tune in, you'll get a huge amount of information about what's going on.

Trust the messages you get. If when you finally slow down and tune in to how you feel about your relationship, every part of you screams with fury about how hopeless and miserable you are in this place, then trust the irrefutable truth of this. It's time to stop ignoring it. And the opposite holds, too. If you spend your days bickering with each other, but when you tune in (to yourself and each other), you find you really still love your partner deeply, then listen to that, trust that, and work out ways to sort out that bickering.

Follow wherever these messages take you. And this takes a lot of F**k It courage. Following might well take you right out of a dysfunctional, miserable relationship. Doing so might well mean you saying F**k It to what others might think of you, or what will happen to your partner, or what will happen to you outside of the relationship. But sometimes it needs to be done. If kids are involved, it clearly becomes even more difficult and painful. But we know many people who have left families, or been left with the kids, who are doing fine, and often better in the new situation than they were in the old. The kids, too; it's always difficult to judge, but we all know how difficult it must be to grow up with warring parents. And following (what you're trusting is the strong message you get when you tune in) might also lead you deeper into the present relationship, bringing freshness, and new ideas, acceptance, and renewal.

There are no rules. There's just a process.

Us? We certainly don't have an idyllic relationship, as some people might believe. They see the best of us, usually. But we do love each other very much. We do live with the underlying assumption that we're together for better or for worse. We do, even in the crappy bits, know that we'll come through it together.

But none of this means it's easy.

Yesterday we pretty much despised each other. Neither of us could really imagine how it could work. Everything we do drives the other one barmy. Whatever we talk about bores the other one silly. Gaia lives in a different world from me. She has different priorities. She's heart; I'm head. She's late; I'm punctual. She's spontaneous; I plan. She is sad when I'm happy. And she's happy when I'm sad. Her yin resents my yang. My yang tramples on her yin. Her yang ignores my yin. My yin is drowned out by her yang. It's all gone to shit. There's no hope.

And today we realize that we love each other deeply. And all that stuff from yesterday seems like a distant bad dream, as if someone else was saying and feeling it. How could I have felt something so deeply, so painfully, yesterday, but don't feel any of it today? It feels now like that was surface disturbance on a pool that is deep and lovely and fine.

We realized, as we talked about it this morning, that we both, at times, get into our own particular deepest fears, and then see the fear manifesting before us in the form of the other person. So, not only are we presented with our deepest fears manifest, but also they're manifested in the form of our partner, to whom we're practically inextricably bound. And as I wrote that I had a peculiar image. It's like being allergic to feathers and worrying all the time that somehow you'll come into contact with feathers, then realizing that you're married to a duck. Or, in the image that I had in my head (which is not unpleasant, I have to say), of my partner covered in feathers. 'Ach-oo,' but 'he-llo.'

So Gaia was playing out the behavior that I most fear in someone. And I was playing out hers. As we look back on it, we realize that the very fear of it amplified the behavior in the other that was triggering the fear. A vicious circle of fear of feathers, feathers sprouting, and sneezing.

Nice ending? Who knows? It feels great today, but tomorrow? F**k It, that's all part of the game. Who knows?

BEING FREE IN WELLBEING TOWN

Bloody hell, I'm starting to write this chapter while stuffing my face with a bar of chocolate. Bad boy, John. At least grab a salad leaf if you're going to be writing about wellbeing. But I don't have any at hand. All I have is the rest of this choccie bar. And I can't have it lying around. It'll melt, or something dangerous like that.

Wellbeing. That a funny construction, isn't it? I wonder how that came about? (I'm not Wi-Fi'd up at the moment, so I can't Google it, sorry). Someone sitting there thinking *there's really no word for the whole wide area of wellness, feeling well… something that denotes a state of mind as well as body… of really being well… aha, I know WELLBEING.* And why has no one else picked up on this snappy construction? Sexybeing, coolbeing, hotbeing… ah, that's why.

I'm sitting here writing this right next to a 'Wellbeing Center' – a spa, really. Though when I'm in there I do feel really well. You can't help it while lolling around in hot water or steam, or being massaged, or sitting on a strong jet in the hot tub.

Now, I'm going to do something I haven't (intentionally) done much of in this book: refer back to the original *F**k It* book. I've avoided references because a) I wanted those of you who hadn't read the first one to be able to read this one happily without thinking you had to buy and read the first one in a kind of subtle sales pitch (I don't do subtle: **That First *F**k It* Book is Totally Excellent and Makes the Perfect Companion to This One.** After all, 250,000 PEOPLE CAN'T BE WRONG! SMILEY. LOL. EXCLAMATION MARK. SMILEY.)

And b) because I didn't want those of you who had read the first book (available in all good bookstores and, of course, on Amazon) to think we were going over the same ground.

The thing is, what I wrote in the first one about food, health, and wellbeing was pretty good, but I've since had seven years' experience with how it all works in reality. And I'm going to share that now.

So, in a nutshell, I basically said that the best thing to do is to lose your tension around the whole wellbeing thing (and, thanks to the guy who invented that phrase, we can roll into this heading: exercise, food, health issues, etc.). With food, for example, it's the tension around the thought that we're too heavy (or too light, but usually too heavy) that makes us do the silly things we all do; namely, subject ourselves to difficult-to-keep eating regimes, then break them and eat the cupboards and refrigerator bare. We yo-yo because we're so-so tense about our weight.

Say no-no to yo-yo.

The idea was that, if we could only relax around food, our weight might stabilize. Sure, we probably wouldn't lose a huge amount of weight (though we might lose some), but we wouldn't put on any more weight either. This was the F**k It Diet. It didn't mean saying F**k It and eating the contents of the house until you're fat as a house. It meant chilling out about food, chilled and heated.

And the same went for exercise. It's the tension around exercise – the thought that we feel we really OUGHT to do more exercise (or do some exercise) – that creates the same start–stop mentality. We don't exercise because we like exercising, we do so because we think we have to. Just like a diet, we do it for a while, because we have the best intentions. But the pain is too hard to bear over a long period, so we stop altogether. Look at the business models of gyms if you want confirmation of how most people approach exercise. Gyms make the most of people's good intentions (by getting them to sign up with hefty join-up fees and binding monthly payments) and still milk it when the enthusiasm has long gone (because stopping your membership shows you've given up). It's a beautiful business model based on the triumph of hope over reality. They cash in on your wonderful, positive hope that, this time, it will be different.

So, I invited the readers to relax around this feeling of obligation to exercise… to give up on the idea that you *have* to do it, and to see instead when you *want* to do it. To see if, when you do only the exercise you really fancy doing, you might actually exercise more than you do than when you commit yourself to a get-fit regime.

And when it came to health issues, I told my story: I desperately wanted to be well for years, had tried everything, I'd even moved countries in order to fix my health. But that this very desire to be well (or 'whole,' as the holistic nomenclature would have it) created a tension in me that, very likely, helped keep me in tension. The moment (and it was a specific moment) that I said F**k It to the idea of being completely well in my life, when I realized that my life was pretty good anyway, that I had a lot to be grateful for, and should stop putting off happiness until something rather unlikely had happened…then something rather unlikely happened – I got better. Dramatically better. Within six months I was better than I had been in 20 years. I wrote F**k It that summer, sitting in the relief and loveliness of being fully well for the first time since I was a teenager.

That's what I wrote. And here's what I've learned since.

FOOD

Eating what I wanted, when I wanted, meant that my diet became pretty balanced. I moved from yo-yo nutrition (periods of very healthy to periods of snack rubbish) to balanced nutrition. I would eat snacks occasionally, burgers occasionally, a can of cola occasionally, but generally maintained a very balanced diet. My weight moved up slightly and remained pretty much consistent when I was eating the F**k It Diet. Whenever I did any kind of diet, it would drop down then shoot up higher than where I'd started. I found that F**k It Eating was a great maintenance diet actually (contrary to what you might think of it, as a sure-fire way to weight gain).

Here's the thing, though. I decided that I did want to be thinner, permanently. So I decided to apply F**k It ideas to dieting. I decided to say F**k It and really go for it with diets. If a diet didn't work for me, I'd dump it and try another one. And I've found that most diets don't really work for me, smiley, LOL, that my weight always shoots up. The most effective thing I found was Alternate Day Fasting, where you do what it says on the label (i.e., The can says Eat Me one day, but Don't Eat Me the next). It's apparently very, very good for your body (and if you're a mouse or rat it means you live a lot longer than you otherwise would). But it's BLOODY difficult to do. I thought it was easier at the beginning – the idea is that you squeeze your diet pain into a limited period, then relax on the other day. But that one day of fasting is very hard. Break it and, given that you're eating more calories on the eating day, it all goes askew again. Anyway, I liked that one, but I just couldn't stick to it for more than a couple of weeks. And my weight would then drift up again immediately.

So I consciously gave up again. And put out the message for a new way of eating to land on my doorstep (preferably next to a steaming pizza delivery box). And one did. It involves food combining (i.e., not combining proteins and carbs) and a host of other stuff. It involves eating as much as you want, as long at you stick to certain principles. And any diet that involves the same words as you'd find on the window of a downtown, downmarket Chinese buffet restaurant –

EAT AS MUCH AS YOU WANT – has my vote. And it works. It really does. I lost weight, slacked off, put a bit back on, but my weight has now leveled out at a lower level. But I like this one. It's something I can do, isn't too painful (it's not super-easy either), and works. Next time I write a book I'll tell you how it went in the long-term.

So, we now have two F**k It approaches to food:

1. The F**k It eating regime, which may not make you any lighter but will probably help you to maintain your weight and get you out of that nasty yo-yo merry-go-round (a mixing of metaphors there that could make for quite an interesting evening out – using long-stringed yo-yos on fast-moving merry-go-rounds)...

2. The F**k It, I WILL find a way that works for me to lose some of these extra pounds (the F**k It quality there, as well as in the determination, is to refuse to be a victim and settle for repeated defeats – 'Oh, diets just don't work for me, it has to be my genes' – but to keep at it until you find something that's perfect for you).

EXERCISE

It works. Since doing what I wanted, exercise-wise, I've done more. Sometimes I exercise very inconsistently, but I've certainly done more. I got into running. I loved it. But didn't feel like it in the winter, so I stopped. But I really felt like it again the next spring. I didn't go out again because I felt I had to, or because I'd decided I was now a runner (even if just a fair-weather one), but because I just wanted to... I couldn't really stop myself, actually; I just wanted to run. Like I now really fancy going for a walk for an hour, so I will.

I'm back. Try it. This is F**k It in action (literally, in action and inaction). This is putting the six principles into action: you open to a new way of exercising; you relax around the obligation to exercise; you shift your perspective and realize it could work just as well; you tune in and only exercise when you fancy and how you fancy; you trust that that message has value, and you follow it up by getting off your arse when the whim takes you; and staying on your arse when that whim takes you.

AND HEALTH

Well, that was tough. I'll tell you what happened. I loved being well. Even though I seemed to have gotten to the point of being well by accepting the state I was in, it was obviously so much better being well. So, of course, I got scared that I'd get sick again. I knew there was this lingering tension and fear that I'd get sick. I got through another winter and summer feeling great… but then the next winter, I got really sick again. Crikey, what a shock. It hit me hard. I wondered if that was it, if the spell was broken, if I'd now return to being chronically sick again. But, come spring, I got better again and was clear all summer. So now I was thinking, *Ah, this is a winter thing then, oh well*, and I got tense again as we went into September. But I was fine, completely fine. In fact, since then I've been pretty well. During the winter, if I work too hard, I might relapse a little. But generally things are okay. And after seven years I suppose that the fear of returning to the bad old days has dissipated, too. And, of course, because I'm more relaxed about it, I'm more likely to stay well.

One thing I did notice – and I've talked to other people with similar healing experiences who say the same thing – is that I've constantly tried to reconstruct why I got better so dramatically in the first place. Was it really just because I'd let go? Or was it a combination of that and the diet I was on at the time? Or was it the place we were staying? I'd wrack my brain trying to piece together the exact circumstances so that I could reproduce them if required. And when the need arose, i.e., when I got sick again, I did try to re-create some of those circumstances again. But nothing seemed to work in the same way. I realized – though it took me a while – that you couldn't re-create anything in the same way ever again. My body was different by the time it got sick again, my mind was different, and my environment was subtly different. I had changed and the world had changed. And though the sickness was similar (it was never, in truth, exactly the same), the ways to alleviate the sickness would always have to be different.

As I think about it now, I suppose the learning for me has been that – yes, the 'letting go' was very important – probably critical at that time – but the ongoing lesson is that nothing specific is the answer. It's a combination of just 'being there' to what's going on in the moment, and then listening to any strong messages that arise in that moment.

And, funnily enough, this book represents that shift, too: from the idea that F**k It is about letting go and relaxing (which it is, of course) to a wider idea that F**k It is an all-embracing presence in the face of whatever's happening (tension, relaxation, good, bad, wellness, and sickness).

I said 'F**k It' – and lost weight

Diets do not work. I have tried all of them. Been there, done that: tons of cabbage soup, Atkins, metabolic balance... In fact, I was on my first diet at six months old – my family already thought I was too big. And this ran like a thread through my adolescence, puberty, and up to my 30s. A beautiful girl BUT with too much gold on her hips and her belly... I have never felt beautiful, just miserable about my weight and not being strong enough to slim down... misery!

*Then the book F**k It. The Ultimate Spiritual Way came to me by chance. When I read 'say F**k It to dieting,' my first thought was that this would never work... but I was so tired of trying hard that I gave the idea of just letting go and eating what I wanted a chance.*

*I started to just say F**k It and swore to myself never ever to go on a f**king diet again in my life. It was not easy at the beginning – my fear was I'd grow fat until I looked like a stranded whale... but the relief of never dieting again was bigger and my fear slowly turned into confidence... And I also started to tell myself how beautiful, lovable, adorable, wonderful, and sexy I am... that actually I AM gorgeous and perfect the way I am!*

*So... at first I gained some more kilos (no panic), but then, slowly, step-by-step, my body started to change. And the kilos started to come off... And in total I have lost 7kg just by saying F**k it!*

*Now, I have an easy relationship with food: if I want a piece of chocolate or cake, I say F**k It and enjoy it. If I do not want to eat what I am served, I say F**k It and leave it on the plate. If I am keen to do some sport, I say F**k It and go for it... If I feel lazy lying in bed and do not want to move even my little toe, guess what? I say F**k It and stay and enjoy.*

*I will continue with my 'F**k it Diet,' because it is the only way my life seems to work ... and if I lose some more weight it is okay, and if I stay just the way I am now, feeling happy, well then I simply say F**k It, that's just fine.*

Lydia Plankensteiner, *Austria*

*Just one of 100 F**k It stories in the new e-book I Said F**k It, available at www.thefuckitlife.com/extras.*

That, then, is how to be free in Wellbeing Town, how to apply F**k It to wellbeing: don't label it, just tune in and follow it. It works in funny, mysterious ways sometimes, which you can't pick apart and understand, but it works.

BEING
FREE
IN THE
TOWN
WHERE
NOTHING
WORKS

I intended to write this chapter this morning; I was pondering what to write about regarding how to be okay in a Town Where Nothing Works. I started to set up in the place I would be writing for the next few days – the Urbino Estate and Spa – the luxurious venue we use for many of our F**k It Retreats. I found a suitable table near a window for some sunshine and fresh air, and near a power source to plug in this laptop. And I went to insert the plug into the socket and found it wouldn't fit. I tried another socket, but it wouldn't fit there either. Now I know what you're thinking if you're from any organized, sane country on this Earth… 'What, John, you were trying to insert a foreign plug into an Italian socket?' No, friends, I was trying to insert an Italian plug into an Italian socket. And it wouldn't fit because there's more than one type of plug in Italy, and more than one type of socket. Some plugs have three pins; others have two, but not two at the same distance apart… some are wider, some are narrower. Grrrrrr. So we have lots of adapters in a drawer at home that turn one type of plug into another type of plug, and thus allow you to plug whatever you have into whatever someone's decided to put in a wall as a socket. Grrrrrr.

Now I know we Brits have a different kind of plug from everyone else, with its three pins in a triangular shape. But at least we have that and nothing else. If you're foreign (definition of 'foreign' in this case is you don't live in Britain, not just that you speak another language. I realize that there will be some of you who are foreign in this sense, but don't speak foreign at all, like Americans, for example, who, I think, have a different kind of plug from the Brits, but I'm sure have a standardized plug. In fact I remember reading once about an American woman who was driven mad by the different light bulb fittings and bulb types in the UK, she was used in to a standard fitting in the USA)… Okay, if you're foreign, just buy an adapter from your foreign plug to a UK plug and you're sorted for the duration of your stay.

It's the same with our roads. We drive on the other side, but we're consistent in that. You don't cross over the border to Wales, for example, and have to switch to the other side of the road (Wales, by the way, is a small and beautiful country attached to the side of England like a big beer belly, not that the Welsh are famous for drinking beer… they're famous for loving relationships – with sheep – mining, rugby, singing, and lovely, fluffy, attractive sheep).

I'm surprised here in Italy that they've managed to keep it together in deciding which side of the road to drive on. That said, if you're used to driving on the country roads, as we are, you'll know that most of the locals don't seem to know which side of the road to drive on at all, especially on bends.

Back to plugs. Gaia, thankfully, had packed some adapters, which I found after a few minutes of rummaging through bags. So here I am, adapted to the hilt and tapping away happily. But whenever I face such a plug crisis, I do wonder how a country can expect even to start to work things out for its people, and go out there and do well in the world, if it can't even organize a simple, consistent system for its plugs? It's not that bloody difficult, is it?

I think the same thing when I have to go to the post office to pay a variety of things because nobody can be bothered to work out a way for you to pay online, or even at the bank.

And why does the post office have a cashier for every type of task you might want to carry out (e.g., mailing something, or paying something, or withdrawing money), for which you take a different type of ticket and wait for 20 minutes? Now I know it would have seemed like a good idea at the time… so efficient, a leap forward in customer service technology akin to Adam Smith's industry-changing division of labor… but, surely, ten minutes after this bright idea, someone in the office should have said, 'But…' and then continued with a long list of reasons why it wasn't such a bright idea. For example, if I wanted to take some money out, and with that money pay my phone bill, and then send a letter to my mum, this is what I'd have to do: get a ticket to withdraw the money, wait 20 minutes, get my money; get a ticket for paying bills, wait 20 minutes, pay the bill; get a ticket for the postage cashier, wait 30 minutes (usually), and mail said letter.

Madness.

Last week I had to pay a bill and mail a letter. When I asked the woman who was processing my bill payment if she could just slip through my letter, pretty please, she looked at me as if I was the first person ever to ask. I explained that otherwise I'd have to line up again to post the letter and I was, after all, here now, with her, and that I'm sure she'd been trained to put a stamp on a letter as thoroughly as she'd been trained to process bill payments. She tutted and walked across to the lady who looks after postage and explained to her very loudly that I wanted to post a letter, and that lady tutted, then the whole line of people waiting with their letters looked over at me and tutted (though I have to say they all looked rather hungry, I suspect they'd been there for days, joining various queues and waiting patiently). But I got my letter posted. Success.

Hey, crikey, let's stop the list… just the post-office system is enough to write a book about. It's crap.

Italy is a funny place. People push ahead so naturally, so confidently, that I've had to give up telling them to 'Get the F**k in line like everyone else' because they invariably turn to me, looking all hurt, saying sorry, they didn't realize and, of course, they'll join the back of the line that they've, all of a sudden, realized is there.

It's very hard to get anything done here. Everything is so bureaucratic it could drive you mad. And it does drive us mad sometimes. Italy is one big Town That Doesn't Work. The economy is going down the pan. But 'the Powers That Be' still seem intent on raising every tax, making it harder to employ people, and making the red tape even thicker. Bonkers.

Yet we still live here. Why? Because it's beautiful (Tuscan rolling hills, alpine mountains, Sardinian sea, southern olive groves, etc.); it's rich in culture (Urbino is where the renaissance was born and is Raphael's hometown); the people are generally warm, friendly, and hugely expressive (just watch the way they gesticulate when they talk, *mamma mia*); the food is the best on the planet (even in truck stops); and the women and men are nice to look at.

Italy is an AMAZING place.

But it's also unbelievably RUBBISH.

HOW DO WE LIVE IN A TOWN THAT DOESN'T WORK?

First off, we've both lived in enough places to know that no town really works like you'd hope (and by 'town' here we're clearly referring to street, town, city, country, or continent). There's always something, isn't there? I suppose the only exception might be Switzerland, where everything works, everything is clean, there's no crime, and you don't pay much tax. But even the perfection that is Switzerland has its price and that's part of the problem – everything is very expensive. And the rules are astonishing. If you move into a new apartment, for example, you'll be bombarded by a list of rules. The police patrol the streets looking for people who are shaking their rugs over their balconies, or doing the vacuuming at the wrong time, or throwing water down the wrong drain, or putting a glass bottle in the wrong container – eek, give me South London any day.

LATER…

I had to add this extra paragraph, because it's beautiful and astonishing… I wrote earlier about Switzerland being so 'perfect' then went off to lunch and found that one of the guests (and it's a deliberately small group week this week, one of 'Gaia's Magic Six' weeks, where the maximum is six people) is Swiss, and I mentioned my reference to perfect Switzerland and she said that she'd just received a call from her mother who'd told her that there had been a bomb alert in town (think small, perfect, picturesque town) just that morning. Bloody hell. Point made in every conceivable way, thank you very much. Not only does perfect Switzerland have its disadvantages in terms of personal freedom, it ALSO has the bomb alerts and crime like everywhere else. Actually, now I'm not so sure whether I'd still prefer South London. What you mean I can get bomb alerts, crime, tense threatening atmosphere AND the Swiss mountains, trains that run on time, and low taxes? Hold on, I'm packing my bags).

So, we realize that there's no ideal place. We've chosen the place that suits us most, given a whole variety of variables. And then we could descend into a series of clichés to keep us sane, such as 'Take the rough with the smooth,' 'You've made your bed, so lie in it,' 'Better the devil you know…'

But we have a simple approach to the stuff that doesn't work: 1) we either decide to leave (which we don't want to do at the moment), or 2) we find a way of getting around it (we gave up running a retreat center, for example, because it was so difficult to run a business like that); or 3) if there's no getting around it, we try to accept it.

And each way is a different expression of F**k It:

1 F**k It, we're off. It takes guts to make the big moves, but sometimes you have to.

2 F**k It, we'll find a way. When you're determined to find your way around an obstacle, you usually can.

3 F**k It, we need to chill, because there's F**k all we can do about this. Don't sweat the small stuff. It's only a plug after all. To do this, you need to be flexible (okay, in my case, so I won't write like I planned today, I'll have a swim instead). And you need to be able to tap into calm, even when you're feeling totally wound up.

And, of course, there's a deep F**k It approach to the whole Not Working thing, too; that everything is working in its own perfect way (even the things that appear not to be working at all), and that everything placed before me in this unfolding beautiful mystery of life is placed intentionally and with love and for me, and so I will be guided by whatever it is that seems to be doing the guiding, lovingly and safely through things that may appear difficult, through times that might feel challenging, and through places that appear flawed but are actually all just right for me and my journey.

There's a deep F**k It approach to the whole Not Working thing, too; that everything is working in its own perfect way.

Or I can ignore 1, 2, and 3 and the Deep F**k It Approach, and bust a blood vessel getting pissed over the plug. Which, of course, I still will do occasionally. And that's me, John C. Parkin, exercising my free will to be a stupid bugger. And that's just perfect, too.

BEING
FREE
IN A
TOWN
WHERE
SHIT
HAPPENS

As seems to be happening on most days at the moment, when I start to think about writing a chapter, something happens in the real world, which dramatically informs that chapter.

This is what happened this morning. I'd dropped off the boys at school and had just turned onto the long track that comes down to our house. There are two other houses toward the top of the track. In the first house lives an elderly couple in their 80s and their son. The guy is coming out of his driveway as I pass their house. I stop to say hello. Now this man isn't a pure-living Zen master (that's our other neighbor). He smokes like a chimney and grumbles a lot. That said, he's got a good heart, well, in the figurative sense, in the literal sense I think that not having such a good heart anymore is one of the problems. So he's coming out of his driveway and I stop. And he tells me that his wife isn't well again, and that they've called the ambulance, and he's going up to the top of the track to make sure the ambulance doesn't go sailing past our track (it's easy to miss). He was clearly a little shaky and upset. It wasn't an emergency, but it was a sign of how things were becoming very difficult.

And he said to me:

'Ma dobbiamo abbracciare quello che arriva, non e vero?'

Isn't that amazing? In such circumstances to say something like that. It blew me away. Especially coming from such an unexpected source. What's that? What does it mean? Oh, sorry, yes. It means 'We should embrace whatever happens, shouldn't we?'

Easier said than done, of course. But that he was there in the middle of it, saying it, was enough for me. He was clearly trying to be at peace with the circumstances of his life in that moment: that – his wife is become sicker by the day and may not be on this Earth for long, and that he also might not be around for long either.

It's a funny expression, but Shit Happens. And, sadly, Shit Happens in every town. If only we could immunize ourselves against Shit. But we can't. Bad things happen to all of us. Bad things happen every day, in every part of the world. You're just thinking that life is pretty sweet, then something awful happens. You're just thinking that things couldn't get any worse, then they do.

I haven't been looking forward to writing this chapter because I don't have a magic F**k It pill that can make the pain go away. In fact, quite a few people will ask me, 'But surely there are some things you can't say F**k It to in life?' And I answer, 'It depends how you define F**k It, but of course there are some things that are going to hurt like hell however much you want them not to matter so much.' You can't say F**k It to the sickly, wrenching pain of the grief of losing someone close to you, and stop feeling it.

I don't have a definitive spiritual answer to deal with shit when it happens: i.e., 'They're happy up There, at peace now,' or 'This is God's Plan,' or 'Everything happens for a reason.' These sincerely held beliefs and sincerely meant reassurances, though, just feel to me like platitudes in the real time of need.

I don't have the definitive therapeutic answer either: a six-step process to work through grief, or a positive-thinking philosophy to pull yourself out of a rut that's beset you because of shit happening.

What I have is my experience of Shit Happening in my life, and of what I did and what helped.

First, it's fine to be distraught when shit happens. You don't have to put on a brave face, or bottle it up, or get on with things. It's fine to howl at the wind, and curse the gods, and feel thoroughly sorry for yourself. We're so keen to praise those who are brave in the face of adversity, those who are so positive in the face of the terminal diagnosis, but such praise then makes the opposite reaction wrong. And it's probably best to feel something fully, whatever it is, before you put on that brave face (if you feel you have to at all). It seems that emotions felt fully move through us more quickly than emotions that are only half-felt, half-allowed, or suppressed entirely.

You don't have to be brave. You don't have to face it full on. Feel your pain and your upset. Scream and shout and sob if need be. There will probably come a time when you want to be brave, but that might not be now. So allow yourself that.

When the time comes to move a little out of the pain, there are, of course, things you can do that will make you feel better. When shit has happened to me, it has always helped me to think of what I have, rather than what I've lost. It's the 'at least' list: *Well, at least I have this, or that.* So being grateful for what you have can help. If that just feels wrong and stupid, then it's not your time. It also depends how the shit has happened. I was about to argue that if you're in a concentration camp, with little hope for survival, having lost your family, and starving to death, then doing a gratitude list isn't going to help you. But there are those who have endured such awful experiences who teach that the only way to survive such an experience (psychologically at least) is to find something to appreciate and to find something that has meaning for you. In fact, there's a whole branch of therapy, Logotherapy, based on this idea.

It does help to remember that there are (usually) people worse off that you. There are people who've experienced more tragedy, been even unluckier, been sicker, experienced more pain. I always feel slightly guilty when I do end up thinking about those who are worse off, because it feels like we're using them for our comfort (or, at least, reduced discomfort). But the world would be a much poorer, sicker, more painful place to be without the efforts of those who have experienced their share of awfulness, then gone out and helped people in more difficult positions than themselves.

Don't punish yourself with constant what-ifs and questions: 'If only I'd done this, things would be different,' or 'Why did this happen to me, what have I done to deserve this?' In terms of the 'what if,' if you apply it the other way around, you'll find many shit things that you've avoided simply because you left home at a different time, or you happened to be somewhere else at that time, etc., etc. As for deserving something or not: I know too many good people, leading positive, contributing lives, who have been beset by shit from all angles and for no obvious reason, to know that you don't need to deserve anything to get it ('bad' or 'good'). Sometimes you just get it.

*I've often described F**k It as giving you the perspective that you get when bad things happen to you.*

And surely this is something you can't say F**k It to: when really bad things happen. Again, it depends on the definition. You can use these words in many ways when facing pain and difficulty in life. 'F**k It, I don't care how I "should" behave, I feel terrible and I'm just going to stay in bed and wail,' 'F**k It, this has all made me realize that I'm living a lie, I'm off'; 'F**k It, I might as well do what I fancy now, it can't get any worse than this,' etc.

In fact, I've often described F**k It as giving you the perspective that you get when bad things happen to you. When shit happens – when you get sick, or someone close to you dies, or you lose everything, or you're made redundant, or your child disowns you, or the economy collapses, or your country goes to war – your world shifts in a moment. You realize instantly that what you worry about every day doesn't matter so much. All your compass points change. What you wanted and what you aimed for no longer seems to matter.

And this shift in perspective can be very positive. It's just a bummer that it generally seems to happen when bad things happen. If I had a dollar for every time someone has said to me, 'I thought it was the worst thing that could happen to me, but it turns out that...' and they explain how many amazing things have happened to them because of the shit and the perspective-transforming effect that that shit had.

Shit things give us perspective. And that can turn out to be a good thing, even though you won't appreciate that in the middle of the shit. The point about F**k It is that it can help you get perspective (i.e., it doesn't matter so much after all) before perspective gets you (i.e., the shit things make you realize that it doesn't matter so much after all).

So in a Town Where Shit Happens, which is every town, F**k It can help in a variety of ways when the shit is happening, but it can also help you live from the true perspective of someone who knows that shit happens, but doesn't have to experience perpetual shit in order to live more freely.

Stop the presses: since writing that, shit made an unexpected visit to my town. And I've recalled another couple of things that I do in the presence of such shit:

1   I try to remember that things usually get better. And, indeed, they have already.

2   I endeavour to take one step at a time when times are tough. This is a knack I've always tried to employ: even at school when I was dreading (and I mean DREADING) a day of lessons ahead, I learned that simply trying to cope with the idea of the first lesson, would usually get me through. Now, when the shit is heavier than a math lesson, I still try simply to think of what I need to do next, and nothing more. 'Just keep swimming,' as Dory says in *Finding Nemo*.

GAIA'S MAGIC WORDS
Don't be brave

I think in our culture there is an underlying belief that to be a grown-up man or woman, you have to brave, as if being an adult is something you graduate to; as if it is about feeling the responsibility and fighting to prove that you can take it, whatever it takes.

But don't you think that if we were all allowed to feel supported and accepted in being in whatever state we are in, we would naturally find our feet, we would naturally become comfortable with whatever feelings we have, and we would be able to function in society in our highs and lows with more softness and naturalness, making space for all the shades of being human?

We are a mix of things. All life is; it's normal. Sometimes we are naturally brave and strong and outgoing. Sometimes action is what comes naturally. And we can do it because it is in us. But sometimes we're vulnerable and uncertain and scared and incapable of action.

So ask yourself, what's so terrible about that?

When you were a small child you weren't ashamed of your feelings. Children feel fully and then they're able to move on fully. Who said this couldn't work for adults?

Certainly all this hiding of our fears isn't working so well for adults or for our society.

So it is well worth trying the alternative. Don't lie; don't be brave when you're not, no matter what others will make of it.

You may just find that being vulnerable when you feel that way makes you stronger.

Gaia's Magic Weeks, held in Italy, are part of the F**k It Retreats program. Find out more at www.thefuckitlife.com

BEING
FREE
AND
LIVING
THE
BETA
LIFE

I've mainly used Yahoo for e-mail for the last decade. And for much of that time I've been working on a 'beta' version. Beta is a test version. Software developers used to put the beta version out to a select group in order to iron out any bugs (though I'm sure software developers don't 'iron out' bugs, but please don't write in with what they actually do with their bugs) before releasing onto the mass market. It's a fine and simple idea to test something before you release it fully. You'd like to think that the new headache drug you buy at the drugstore has been thoroughly tested before you take it. Same with your software, as software bugs can be lethal.

Well, I remember being a little surprised whenever it was, years ago, when Yahoo suggested that I try their beta version. They told me how much better the beta version was than the 'original' version that I was using, and that I could switch back any time. I was somewhat hesitant. Why would I want to use an unfinished system, especially for something as essential as e-mails? Why can't they be bothered to finish it before they release it to me? But they kept asking me, pleading with me even, to try it... they kept telling me about all the new features that their beta version boasted. So I went for it. And I liked it. In fact, I pretty soon forgot that it was a beta version. And so did they, it seems, because they never asked me if I'd found any bugs they could iron out. Clearly there were Yahoo worker ants somewhere in the world rapidly ironing out any bugs that people were telling them about (or rather shouting at them about, which is more likely the case).

I was happy, anyway. But what I noticed is that they continued to refer to this version as the 'beta' version. It never seemed to become the real version (whatever that would have been: Yahoo 7.8 or something). It stuck stubbornly to beta. And this was interesting to me.

Then, a couple of years later, when I logged into my account, I received a new invitation to upgrade to their new 'beta' version. This puzzled me. I was under the impression that they were still testing the old version and here they were trying to get me to use yet another version, and 'beta' at that. But I went for it – more easily this time. And it was good. But I wasn't asked what I thought. They continued to call it beta... yes... you guessed it... until the next beta version came along.

And I realized that it must all be a game, that Yahoo had somehow shifted the idea of 'beta' for all of us. They'd clearly seen, in the early days of beta versions, that many people wanted to have the beta version, even if it contained some bugs, because it meant you had the very latest version. You were an early adopter, living in the frontier land of software design. A beta version implied – yes, something that wasn't quite finished, or polished, or perfected – but also something that was edgy, pushing the boundaries. Its rougher, edgier, unfinished quality became its benefit. And Yahoo (and I should think many others) saw that and offered it to the mass market. Who knows how 'beta' those versions really were.

And I've seen this beta version mentality everywhere on the web. Everything is faster, shoot-from-the-hip, suck-it-and-see. It's easier to try something out and then change it if it doesn't work. Brands don't spend a whole year planning and developing ad campaigns anymore – you can knock up a viral bit of video in a day and put it out there and see if it sticks. If not, do another one. Try something; it doesn't have to be perfect, in fact it's even better if it feels a bit rough and edgy. If it doesn't work, dump it, and try something else. Do this so frequently that, after a while, the aim ceases to become finding the perfect answer, or software, or piece of communication, but just the act of putting stuff out there and keeping the conversation going.

And what a way that would be to live! Look how most of us live. We like to get things right, deliberate big time before making any decisions, worry about putting a foot wrong, plan ahead in detail… we even see ourselves as a project that we'll improve and develop to the point where we smooth off the rough edges and become calmer, kinder, more generous, more educated, more efficient, etc., etc. We tend to have a 'perfect' version of ourselves in mind that we then work toward.

F**k It.

*The Beta Life requires that you're not so bothered, the essential F**k It quality.*

How would it be to live a Beta Life? To live in perpetual test mode; to try things out and if they work, great, if not, to dump them; to not have a fixed idea of where you're heading, (you're certainly not heading toward some far-off perfect version of yourself), you're just happy trying things out on a daily basis. The pressure is off. It's time to play. And that's what beta is about: living by your wits. The Beta Life requires that you're not so bothered, the essential F**k It quality. After all, because you're trying new things out all the time, you're more likely to fail (just as you're more likely to hit gold, in whatever realm you're operating).

F**k It Living is Beta Living. Open to a new way of living. Relax and take your foot off the pedal. Shift your perspective – things don't have to be perfect; you don't have to be perfect. Tune in to see what you feel like doing. Trust the value of that message. Follow and do it – test it, and find out if it works for you; if not, move on. Quickly. It's an organic, living process, this life thing, by definition. It's us that try to fix it, hold it, remodel it, perfect it. But life isn't like that. Life is ever-changing, totally dynamic, rough, imperfect, unpredictable. 'Life' isn't just calm, peaceful, consistent, sorted, predictable, perfect, reliable. It's everything else, too.

And so are you. If you tune in, fully, to your instinct, it is all of everything, too. Because your instinct is your fastest way to that 'life' energy. So practice Beta Living and you'll very soon be living your F**k It Life.

BEING
FREE
AND
UPGRADING
YOUR
LIFE

I write this from the suite of a five-star hotel in central London. Gaia is about to have a swim. Later we'll walk into Soho for a Chinese meal. Tomorrow morning, we'll sit in the spa here and prepare for the F**k It Days we're doing here over the weekend.

And you may well have noticed that I've referred to a few hotels during the course of this book. And they are all lovely hotels, too. It's not that we're loaded and money is no object, it's that I've learned how to upgrade.

Let's start with this one. It's the week before Easter, and London is busier than ever in the year of the Olympics. And yet we're sitting and swimming and sleeping and eating in the very lap of luxury in the heart of it all for… well, the room I booked cost 40 percent of the usual room-rate price. And when we arrived at reception just now, the receptionist happened to be Italian and, without us even asking, upgraded us to a suite. And I've just looked up the price of a suite. So we're now paying a measly 25 percent of the 'advertised' room-rate price.

We live an Upgraded Life, and I'm about to teach you how. It takes a lot of F**k It. First, let's look at the actual upgrade (which is usually the last part of the process).

I've been upgraded in every single one of the last ten hotels I've stayed in. I'm not a business user. I'm scruffy as hell. So how do I do it? First, be incredibly polite to the receptionist. Take a real interest in them – not because you're about to ask for an upgrade, but because you're actually interested in them (there's a difference and it's felt). Now, if you've booked your room through a discount bookings agency, there's a chance you've been given the smallest room in the hotel, and the receptionist will know that. But, unless they take a real shine to you (as just happened here), they'll still go ahead and install you in that room (many four-star hotels nowadays, for example, have utilized very small spaces then decked them out wonderfully, so that they can still make money when they discount online). So you take your key-card, grab your luggage, and head to the elevators, knowing that you'll be down again in three minutes. Go to the room; put your bag in the hall. Don't touch anything. Don't sit on the bed. Just check it's not the suite already and you got lucky. Then leave your bag there and go back down to reception. Be really polite, and say that you've just been to the room, that you actually want to spend a lot of time in the room over your stay as you have a lot of work to do, and would it be possible to have a bigger room, please… and that you'd be so grateful if s/he could help you out. Then add that you haven't touched anything in the room, you haven't even sat down. And, rooms permitting (which they usually are), s/he'll upgrade you.

That's the actual upgrade. What about the room you booked into at a fraction of the cost? Just 20 minutes of hard work on the web. You need two or three great discount booking sites. And you occasionally need to take a risk. Lastminute.com, for example, have something called 'Secret Hotels,' which offer incredible discounts, but you don't know exactly where they are, or what they're called, or what they're like. You try your best to establish where they are, etc., from the details they give. One thing I've noticed is that once you've found out the details of a 'Secret Hotel' (which you do by booking and staying there once), they always use the same code on the site. So I now know the 'code' of five or six hotels in London. The deals are usually 50 percent or less. So you can stay in a four- or five-star hotel for the price of a two-star, or less – a hostel. You can sleep rough in the best hotels in town. That's how you live this part of the Upgraded Life.

Clearly your best chance of upgrading across the board is to travel, stay, rent, eat, view, out of season during periods or times that other people wouldn't think to travel, stay, rent, eat, or view. You can have the lifestyle of a celebrity if you're able to pick and choose when you move around (unless, of course, you are a celebrity, in which case you're probably being followed around by someone with a camera, you're already booked into the best rooms in town, and you're not particularly bothered about the idea of literal upgrading). But you're hanging on for what you know is the bigger point here, which is… how to upgrade your life above and beyond upgrading your hotel rooms and flights.

I said that the hotel upgrading takes a little 'F**k It'… F**k It, I can do this. It takes some chutzpah. What it also takes is the belief that you DESERVE it. Yes, I may have only paid a few bucks for a space in this hotel, but I know they've got a lovely suite up there that no one's booked for tonight, and I DESERVE that luxury.

And to feel we deserve something, we have to have a positive view of ourselves. Back in the hotel I could elaborate the auto-conversation thus: 'You John, are a wonderful man; you support your family; you bring something interesting and helpful to the world in the form of F**k It – my God, the least you deserve is a luxurious room to rest your head tonight.' Don't get me wrong; this isn't a process of self-justification, this is self-worth. Self-justification comes from low self-worth: 'I know I don't deserve this, but I should really have it because, after all, no one else is staying there, and if I don't then it's just a waste anyway, and why would you want to waste when there are people out there sleeping on the streets, blah, blah excuse, excuse, blah.'

So start by appreciating yourself big time. Pat yourself on the back (it's also good for the qi anyway) and say, 'Well done, you... you really are doing SO well in life... you deserve the very best that life has to offer.'

You really do deserve the very best that life has to offer. So start to expect it. Develop a sense of entitlement (in the best sense of that word, not the spoiled brat, trust-funded, silver-spoon type sense of entitlement) that you deserve the very best in life. And not just in terms of the material things (and the literal upgrades), but in every aspect of life: you deserve the best opportunities, the best relationships, the best health, the best chance to follow your dreams, the best sex, the best wine, the best friends.

Feel you deserve the best... go say F**k It and Upgrade Your Life.

So, yes, go say F**k It and upgrade your hotel. But say F**k It, too, to your self-doubts, your limited beliefs, your sense of being a victim of life's vicissitudes, and feel you deserve the best... go say F**k It and Upgrade Your Life.

BEING
FREE
AND
JUST
TURNING
UP IN
A TOWN

We watched *Cowboys and Aliens* two nights ago, when hunky Daniel Craig wakes up in the Wild West, not remembering anything, but with a futuristic bangle on his wrist. What a lucky cowboy! Not only does he wake up with a perfect but rugged countenance, he has a futuristic machine gun strapped to his arm. So he just turns up at the nearest town and establishes his cowboy credentials immediately by putting the local bully in his place.

We're currently teaching at a F**k It Retreat for 24 people. The theme of the week seems to be the idea of 'turning up.' (I say 'seems to be' because a week can go in any direction, depending on the group and what, well, 'turns up' during the week.) We all know about the idea of living in the now: the possibility that we could think less about the past and future, and be present to what is going on, now. Each moment, in theory, is entirely new and fresh, full of limitless possibilities.

Yet most of us approach the moment with so many prejudices, ideas, and judgments that it's hard to see what's really there. There's the expression that we see everything through 'rose-tinted glasses,' when we see the best in everything (and the implication of the idiom is that we are overly idealistic, too). What we actually wear as we approach the moment (okay, okay, please don't pick me up on that, I know we're never really 'approaching a moment,' that there is only ever the 'moment,' the 'now,' and nothing else exists, blah, blah, blah, but bear with me a second, please) are glasses that focus on very specific areas to the exclusion of others; glasses that wildly distort some parts of the image, color other parts of the image either with 'rose' or with darkness, that completely block out much of the image. And this is very natural. And I don't say that lightly. It's not just natural, it's also probably necessary to a certain extent.

As I alluded to earlier in *Why Do Prisons Exist?* we do have to do some degree of filtering. In each moment there are billions of bits of information being fed into our brains in different ways from the apparent reality outside. Not only are we seeing, hearing, smelling, and feeling, we're sensing at other levels, too. Even if you just take the seeing bit, we've evolved to 'see' only a fraction of the full frequency range. If we couldn't and didn't filter, our brains would be overwhelmed. If we could take in all the information of just one moment, and absorb it, we could probably live a lifetime in a moment. But we don't. And can't. We spread out the experience of apparent reality over several human decades, so it seems fine to filter the ongoing experience down to a manageable frequency range in every respect.

As I say, it's 'natural.' That's how our brains work. We tend to recognize and process in the outside reality only what we already know. The other bits are ignored.

So far, so interesting. What am I suggesting? That we try to widen the range of frequencies we're able to see by sitting in a low-lit room, staring at our cat, trying to see other colors? No. Unless you really want to. I'm suggesting that we become conscious of the extreme way we drag previous perceptions, judgments, opinions, and prejudices into the present moment. Think for a moment how you react when you're introduced to new people. You prejudge them based on how they look, or talk, or act, very quickly (when I talk about 'prejudice' in this sense I'm not talking about race or gender prejudice, but the universal prejudgment of anyone or anything based on previous experience). For the sake of convenience, we rapidly 'label' everyone and everything we come across. I'm suggesting, too, that we become more conscious of the extreme way we drag an agenda into the present moment. We always approach the moment wanting something. We work out what we want in life, then we make our plan, set some goals, and we follow that plan, trying to achieve those goals. It seems like a very healthy process, but it means that we hit each moment with an idea of how it *should* be, of how it *could* serve us. And this, of course, is another form of judgment based on our ideas. We judge and filter based on what is 'good' and 'bad' out there, what is helpful or unhelpful, what serves our purpose or not.

Imagine it's possible to live in the moment, to operate very effectively in the moment, in fact, without recourse to all previous behaviors, reactions, and ideas.

By becoming more conscious of how we load each moment with judgment, prejudiced selection, and an agenda, we're likely to see the ways in which we can become more open. And this expression of 'just turning up' to the moment can really help. It implies that we put aside all those ideas about how things should be, and what we want out of something, and how it could turn out, and 'just turn up.' We see that there are limitless possibilities in every moment and we open more to those. We simply become curious about what could be there. There's a delicious sense of freedom in the idea that we just turn up to each moment, unburdened by all the other stuff.

Daniel Craig in *Cowboys and Aliens* had the turning-up thing forced upon him. Without any memory, he found himself in the Wild West. Without any idea of how he should react, he reacted to new situations, new input simply in a way that felt natural, or instinctive. You don't have to knock yourself on the head to try this. Imagine it's possible to live in the moment, to operate very effectively in the moment, in fact, without recourse to all previous behaviors, reactions, and ideas. Faced with exactly the same circumstances (which is, of course, impossible, but still…), one day you might react in one way, the next day you might react in a completely different way. That is 'just turning up.' And it's a surefire step to freedom.

BREAKING FREE, BEING FREE, STAYING FREE, UNDERSTANDING 'FREE'

THE 'REAL NATURE' OF F**K IT THERAPY

So we've taken you through a thorough process in this book of F**k It Therapy. How to use those powerful two words – 'F**k' and 'It' together in the unbeatable, almost holy union of F**k It' – to create freedom in your life.

We've investigated why most of us need to say F**k It (because we're in prison, in one way or another).

And we've looked at what the 'Its' are that most of us need to 'F**k' in order to be free.

We've explored magic techniques, which arise directly and naturally from the 'F**k It State' – the care-free state we reach when we're deeply relaxed. And we've seen that the magic words 'F**k It' can take us back to that state, or at least remind us of it.

We've equipped ourselves for the moment people criticize us, and learned to say 'F**k It' to what people think.

Then we've played with how to Live the F**k It Life in day-to-day situations.

So we've looked at how to use F**k It when we're not free, in order to break free and then stay free.

But what does being 'free' really mean?

As we've alluded to many times in this book (including toward the beginning, when we suggested that we might be giving away the ending), true freedom embraces all the apparent states we experience. This means you can be free while you're still in 'prison' (whatever that means to you). This means that you were free all along anyway, after all. And this is the real nature of F**k It Therapy.

This is a higher level of understanding freedom, just as it's a higher level of understanding F**k It. In the dualistic, wrong and right, trapped and free, tense and relaxed, sick and ill, material and spiritual etc., world, we constantly crave movement between these states. And that's fine. It's not just fine, it's beautiful. We want to move from bad to good, from prison to freedom, from stressed to chilled, from materialistic to spiritual and peaceful.

*It's a higher level of understanding of F**k It.*

The desire for movement is natural and beautiful, and the movement itself can be natural and beautiful. That is life, it seems. At least a life lived positively, consciously and beneficially (a life lived negatively and unconsciously can lead everything in the opposite direction).

But.

But.

Don't we just love the word 'but.' It indicates that there's always another way to look at things. Yes, that's true, but… And if what follows is also true, you turn a 'but' into an 'and.'

Let's have a go.

But… we are most free when we realize that it's all the same: all states are natural and are part of the overall flow; the apparent prison we're in is fine for now and is where we're meant to be; the tension and anxiety we feel are necessary for the blossoming of what follows next; materialism is as valid as spiritualism because it's all, in the end, the same thing.

One thing can be true, and its opposite can be true, too. We are solid, separate individuals governed by Newtonian physical laws, fighting for survival in a harsh and alien environment AND we're non-solid, energetic beings, all connected (or just 'one'), bathing in one energetic field, which is probably all love.

And we probably won't get 'it' fully, ever. But by realizing that we won't get it, everything about us relaxes and loosens, so we become more like 'it' anyway, which is always soft and loose and moving.

And F**k It helps us with all of that. Sure, F**k the Its in the dualistic world keeping you trapped and causing you pain. F**k the Its who criticize you and are holding you back from feeling free. F**k It and break free, no matter what anyone else thinks.

But say F**k It, too, to the idea that you're trapped in the first place, that there's anywhere to go from and to; that there's anything you have to do or anywhere you have to go.

Can you hold those two ideas at the same time? That takes some F**k It. Some clever clogs, and I don't think it was Einstein this time, said that genius was 'the ability to hold two opposing ideas in mind at the same time.' *

Can you throw yourself into a F**k It Life? Where you're living with more clarity, consciousness, openness, and freedom; where you recognize the things that aren't working, and the tensions and anxieties in your life, and you find your F**k It ways to become free...

AND

You see that it's all the same anyway. There's nothing to be done and nowhere to go. F**k It to the search, you're there already. Even when you think you're not, you are.

F**k It was about relaxation, and the wonderful space (the F**k It State) and the life that such F**k It relaxation can create.

F**k It Therapy recognizes the value of all the stuff you thought you were moving away from, because the true F**k It State is one where everything is embraced.

The true therapy (i.e., the healing) is to realize not what you can do to heal, but that you're already healed. That's F**k It Therapy.

And if you don't get it, that's fine. It takes time. How can understanding two paradoxical ideas be easy? To the getting of it, say 'F**k It.' And that, my friends, is the beginning of your journey. And the end.

The End.

*The true therapy (i.e., the healing) is to realize not what you can do to heal, but that you're already healed. That's F**k It Therapy.*

* And Google informs me that the genius in question was F. Scott Fitzgerald.

AFTERWORD

From now on, I am non-teaching.

There is something that bothers me majorly about any form of communication: as soon as you say one thing, you exclude all the others.

That is the nature of words – they define.

If I tell you that relaxation is good for you, I immediately create a judgment of all that is not relaxation. Then whenever you feel stressed, as well as feeling stressed, you now think that you are doing badly.

If I tell you that living in the moment is a great thing, then not living in the moment starts to become a bad thing, to be avoided.

If I tell you that being in qi energy is very healing and, even worse, I show you what that it is like so you learn all the lovely sensations and ways to connect to it, then when you are not there, you feel like you are in some way failing.

It is practically impossible to mention an idea without creating a tension in people.

If I talk about the beauty of not trying, then everyone sets off trying not to try.

That is beautiful and also totally unavoidable.

So from now on, I am non-teaching.

This could look like me simply cleaning my house instead of talking to you. Yes, that is a pretty successful form of non-teaching. But as I love being with people in this non-telling-them-what-to-do-to-become-a-better-person-kind-of-way (as I know that all is okay and doesn't need fixing), then I will non-teach.

And after that I'll offer you some non-dinner.

Easy.

Gaia

ACKNOWLEDGMENTS

Gaia. I'm glad we have your words in here, too, not just your thoughts behind my words. None of this would be this without you.

Boys. You inspire me in every single moment.

Mum and Dad. For everything. This house is built on rock.

Rach, sis. You're a perfect sister. And loving this new chapter, too.

Barefoot Stephen. Friend, brother in spirit. Thanks for existing.

Hay House. Michelle and Reid, for your vision, support, and ability to move mountains. Julie, Sandy, Steve, Jessica, Cameron, Amy, and the rest of the Hay House team for everything you've done and are doing for this book.

And all our friends, family, colleagues, guests, the people who e-mail us with their F**k It stories, the people who never get in touch but wish us well all the same, thanks to you all out there for allowing us to live the F**k It Life by doing what we love.

APPENDIX I

WHAT IT IS AND WHY YOU NEED IT

The appendix (or vermiform appendix) is a blind-ended, worm-like pouch connected to the cecum and attached to the large intestine, near the junction of the small intestine and the large intestine. The appendix varies in length, but usually measures about 4 inches long in most humans.

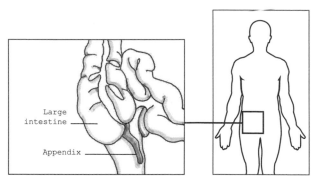

The role of the human appendix has changed over the millennia, probably in response to changes in the human diet, as most humans have exchanged a diet rich in cellulose-dense plants (e.g., tree bark) for one that favors more easily digestible foods (e.g., a Big Mac and fries).

Although the appendix houses friendly bacteria and may still play a role in the immune system in modern humans, it is generally described as a vestigial structure (meaning that it has lost all or most of its original function through the process of evolution), and can be removed (by a procedure called an appendectomy) without any ill effects. As a result, some scientists believe that one day it will just disappear.*

* This introduction to the appendix was compiled with a little help from Wikipedia.

APPENDIX II

OUR TOP FIVE STUFF

BOOKS

BEDSIDE

1 *When You're Falling, Dive,* Mark Matousek

2 *Complete Prose,* Woody Allen

3 *You Can Create an Exceptional Life,* Louise L. Hay and Cheryl Richardson

4 *Revolution in the Head,* Ian MacDonald

5 *Mystery Experience,* Timothy Freke

THERAPY

1 *Unstuck,* Dr. James S. Gordon

2 *The Essential Jung: Selected Writings,* Anthony Storr

3 *Liberation,* Barefoot Doctor

4 *Man's Search for Meaning,* Viktor E. Frankl

5 *Flow: The Psychology of Happiness,* Mihaly Csikszentmihalyi

SPIRITUALITY MEETS SCIENCE

1 *The Field,* Lynn McTaggart

2 *How Your Mind Can Heal Your Body,* Dr. David Hamilton

3 *The Divine Matrix,* Gregg Braden

4 *The Biology of Belief,* Bruce Lipton

5 *The Tao of Physics,* Fritjof Capra

QIGONG

1 *The Healing Promise of Qi,* Roger Jahnke

2 *The Way of Energy,* Master Lam Kam Chuen

3 *Chi Kung for Health and Vitality,* Wong Kiew Kit

4 *Listen to Your Body,* Master Bisong Guo and Andrew Powell

5 Anything written by Mantak Chia

READ AGAIN AND AGAIN

1 *Sum: Forty Tales from the Afterlives,* David Eagleman

2 *Be Here Now,* Ram Dass

3 *Barefoot Doctor's Handbook for the Urban Warrior,* Barefoot Doctor

4 *You Can Heal Your Life,* Louise L. Hay

5 *The Open Secret,* Tony Parsons

PLACES

1 Home, Urbino, Italy

2 London, UK

3 Stromboli Volcano, Italy

4 New York, USA

5 Wuyi Mountains, China

FOODS

GAIA

1 Pizza from Trianon, Naples

2 Lobster with ginger and spring onion on crispy fried noodles

3 Mozzarella from Puglia

4 Grandmother's homemade gnocchi

5 Tiramisu

JOHN

1 Tagliatelle al ragu

2 Crispy duck with pancakes

3 Formaggio di Fossa con Miele

4 Pizza from Trianon, Naples

5 Crème brûlée

PRISON MOVIES

1 *The Shawshank Redemption* (1994)

2 *Escape from Alcatraz* (1979)

3 *Escape to Victory* (1981)

4 *The Green Mile* (1999)

5 *The Colditz Story* (1955)

APPENDIX III

THE F**K IT STATE QUIZ SCORING SYSTEM

Remember, we've also created an online version of this quiz that calculates your score automatically, at www.thefuckitlife.com/extras.

For questions 1, 3, 4, 9, 10, score as follows:

10 for A. Not at all

8 for B. A bit

6 for C. Yes and no

4 for D. Mostly

2 for E. Completely

For questions 2, 5, 6, 7, 8, score as follows:

2 for A. Not at all

4 for B. A bit

6 for C. Yes and no

8 for D. Mostly

10 for E. Completely

There are ten questions, and each question receives a score out of ten, so you will end up with a total score out of 100*.

So you will know your F**k It State as a percentage. For example, you might be 78 percent F**k It. If you're 100 percent F**k It, you probably won't care anyway.

If you do care, here's a quick guide to what those percentages could mean:

0–20%: Please continue to read this book until your score improves. This is an urgent matter and MUST NOT BE IGNORED.

20–40%: Well, to look on the bright side: you're going to notice some amazing changes in your life if you start to say F**k It. Enjoy the ride.

40–60%: We're getting there: this all rings a bell doesn't it, but you're still feeling stuck. Keep reading and keep saying the magic words until your score improves.

60–80%: Well done, you're pretty close. Just some tweaking required: caring less a little here, going for it a little more there, and the F**k It jackpot will soon be yours.

80–100%: You've been on a F**k It Retreat, haven't you? Continuing to read this book will give you a lovely smug feeling as you realize that you're already there.

---

* This quiz was developed by John C. Parkin and Mark Seabright of In The Moment Consultancy.

APPENDIX IV

THE ENDING OF *THE SHAWSHANK REDEMPTION*

The protagonist, Andy Dufresne (Tim Robbins) escapes from Shawshank prison. He withdraws the money he made through corrupt schemes he ran on behalf of Norton, the prison governor. He sends evidence of the corruption and murders at the prison to a local newspaper. The police go to apprehend Norton, who shoots himself to avoid arrest. Red, Andy's friend, gains parole, after serving 40 years inside, but violates it by crossing the border into Mexico. On the beach of Zihuatanejo, the two friends are reunited. Happy ending.

GAIA'S FINAL MAGIC WORDS
The problem with words (even 'Magic' ones)

I was doing a one-to-one session, where the person was exploring the energy of openness.

As we stepped outside, she looked around. On the left, in the distance, there was lots of smoke coming from a farm on the hills. After a while the woman said to me that she had seen the smoke. But she was just curious, like a child, about the smoke. As if she had no word for fire, she made no 'assumptions' or connections in her head about there being a fire. She was just looking at the smoke.

You see, even having a vocabulary stops the experiences. It is as if we know too much all the time, so we can't really experience what's happening. Because of our knowledge, immediate connections are made and everything is boxed into a known realm pretty quickly.

This invites us to think about the fact that everything we refer to in everyday speech is an agreement of meaning and form between people. My friends Michael and Petra, who are shamans, were talking to me about this: that the moment we give a name to something it becomes a supposed known thing, and it loses its magic. But the name is not the thing.

The woman in my session then looked at the grass and the daisies, and she said she felt the same curiosity; it was like looking at them for the first time, with inquiry, rather than with 'knowledge.' She was just exploring, as if there was a whole world there in that grass (why do you think a kid can spend an hour looking at an ant?).

So in a culture where we want to know it all, the real fun is perhaps in knowing less.

In that way, we could see the world immediately next to us (a chair, a paving stone, smoke) and notice that it is very beautiful indeed.

Gaia's Magic Weeks, held in Italy, are part of the F**k It Retreats program. Find out more at www.thefuckitlife.com

ABOUT THE AUTHOR

John C. Parkin is the UK's bestselling wisdom teacher. *F**k It: The Ultimate Spiritual Way* has sold more than 250,000 copies around the world and is available in 22 languages.

The son of Anglican preachers, John realized that saying F**k It was as good as all the Eastern spiritual practices he'd been studying for 20 years.

Having said F**k It to a top job in London, he escaped to Italy with his wife, Gaia, and their twin boys, where they now teach their famous F**k It Retreats in various spectacular locations (such as the volcano of Stromboli).

John has been featured on *The Graham Norton Show* and on the radio, and in magazines and newspapers around the world, including *The Times, The Guardian, The Observer, Psychologies*, and *Cosmopolitan*.

He spends his days spreading the F**k It message, with words (that often make people laugh) and music (that often makes people dance and whoop), then saying F**k It and lying by the pool or napping.

www.thefuckitlife.com

YOU'VE READ THE BOOK — NOW GO ON A F**K IT RETREAT IN ITALY

This is where it all started: John and Gaia ran their first F**k It Retreat in 2005. They're now running these famous retreats in spectacular locations around Italy, including an estate and spa in Urbino, and on the volcano of Stromboli.
Say F**k It and treat yourself to a F**k It Retreat.

'Anything that helps you let go is okay on a F**k It Retreat.' THE OBSERVER
'I witnessed some remarkable transformations during my F**k It Retreat.' KINDRED SPIRIT

F**K IT THERAPY IS NOW ALSO AVAILABLE AS AN ONLINE COURSE,
so you can explore the teaching in this book in depth with John & Gaia from anywhere.

We hope you enjoyed this Hay House book. If you'd like to receive our online catalog featuring additional information on Hay House books and products, or if you'd like to find out more about the Hay Foundation, please contact:

Hay House, Inc., P.O. Box 5100, Carlsbad, CA 92018-5100
(760) 431-7695 or (800) 654-5126
(760) 431-6948 (fax) or (800) 650-5115 (fax)
www.hayhouse.com® • www.hayfoundation.org

***

Published and distributed in Australia by: Hay House Australia Pty. Ltd.,
18/36 Ralph St., Alexandria NSW 2015
Phone: 612-9669-4299 • *Fax:* 612-9669-4144 • www.hayhouse.com.au

Published and distributed in the United Kingdom by: Hay House UK, Ltd.,
Astley House, 33 Notting Hill Gate, London W11 3JQ
Phone: 44-20-3675-2450 • *Fax:* 44-20-3675-2451 • www.hayhouse.co.uk

Published and distributed in the Republic of South Africa by:
Hay House SA (Pty), Ltd., P.O. Box 990, Witkoppen 2068
Phone/Fax: 27-11-467-8904 • www.hayhouse.co.za

Published in India by: Hay House Publishers India,
Muskaan Complex, Plot No. 3, B-2, Vasant Kunj, New Delhi 110 070
Phone: 91-11-4176-1620 • *Fax:* 91-11-4176-1630 • www.hayhouse.co.in

Distributed in Canada by: Raincoast Books,
2440 Viking Way, Richmond, B.C. V6V 1N2
Phone: 1-800-663-5714 • *Fax:* 1-800-565-3770 • www.raincoast.com

***

Take Your Soul on a Vacation

Visit www.HealYourLife.com® to regroup, recharge,
and reconnect with your own magnificence.
Featuring blogs, mind-body-spirit news,
nd life-changing wisdom from Louise Hay and friends.

Visit www.HealYourLife.com today!